the fusion manager

Robert Heller is one of the best-known authorities on management. He was the founding editor of *Managing Today* and took it rapidly to the position of Britain's leading management magazine. His first book, *The Naked Manager* was a bestseller and has been followed by many others, including *The Supermanagers, The Age of the Common Millionaire, Culture Shock – the Office Revolution, The Essential Manager's Manual* and *Roads to Success*, which have sold all over the world. He writes a monthly *Letter to Thinking Managers* with Edward de Bono, and has spoken on management to companies and conferences worldwide. He lives in North London.

the fusion manager

Robert Heller

PROFILE BOOKS

First published in Great Britain in 2003 by
PROFILE BOOKS LTD
58A Hatton Garden
London EC1N 8LX
www.profilebooks.co.uk

1 3 5 7 9 8 6 4 2

Printed and bound in Great Britain by
Clays Ltd, St Ives plc

A CIP catalogue record for this book is available from the British Library.

ISBN 1 86197 646 1

contents

ACKNOWLEDGEMENTS   vii

INTRODUCTION   ix

PART I: THE NEW DYNAMISM   1

How new technology has spurred new forms of rapid growth and new techniques of management to match

1	The Perpetual Revolution	3
2	Secrets of Silicon Management	10
3	The Digital Nerve	17
4	Evolution by Revolution	26
5	Adding Management Value	34

PART II: WINNING POLE POSITION   43

How to lead the competition on the only criteria that matter – those which the customers value most

1	Protecting the Future	45
2	Virtual Virtuality	52
3	Captivating the Customer	60
4	Urging the Entrepreneurs	68
5	Emulating the E-Economy	76

PART III: THE NEW IMPERATIVES   85

What must be done in order to seize the new and endless opportunities – and to defend the base

| 1 | Creating the E-Corporation | 87 |

2 The Thinking Manager   95
3 The Age of Innovation   102
4 Empowering the Business   110
5 Meeting the Threats   117

PART IV: ACQUIRING REAL GROWTH   125

*Why organic growth demands senior management
reform – and better ideas*

1 Trouble with Takeovers   127
2 Exploiting the Slowdowns   135
3 Transforming the Theories   143
4 Curing Power Complexes   151
5 Doom at the Top   159

PART V: THE NEW OLD ORDER   167

*How to perform management's traditional and essential
tasks in new and much more effective ways*

1 Managing the Managers   169
2 Totally Productive Management   176
3 Revolutionising the Strategy   184
4 Breaking the Bonds   192
5 New Century Management   199

PART VI: SHATTERING THE SHIBBOLETHS   207

*How to break free from the old constraints and build
a new and lasting company that will live and learn*

1 Reversing Life-Cycles   209
2 Attract, Motivate and Retain   217
3 The Learning Company   225
4 Image, Reputation and Reality   233
5 Going for Growth   241

acknowledgements

Writing this book would have been impossible without the contribution made by many writers, practitioners and teachers in the fascinating field of management. Their collective wisdom has always impressed me, but has increasingly raised a tricky question. With so much deep knowledge and understanding, constantly refreshed and enlarged, and expressed so lucidly, why was there so much foggy, unwise and uncomprehending management?

Part of the explanation lies in the One Right Way complex – the belief that one course of action and one source of intelligence are the exclusive answer to whatever ails the organization. After living through so many fashions and fads – mostly based on sound and valuable foundations – I felt that managers needed to be freed from their self-inflicted chains and to realize that they inhabit a world in which paradox reigns – and where only Fusion Management can hope to rule.

The thinkers and doers to whom I turned are fully acknowledged in the following pages, and I am deeply grateful to them for my personal enlightenment. Much of what they wrote and spoke has been interpreted and analysed by the admirable journalists who work for publications such as *Fortune, Business Week, The Wall Street Journal* and the *Financial Times*. I must thank them for the quality and depth of the research and observations that I have cited. I also owe a great debt to the excellent *Harvard Business Review* for publishing the several key articles to which I refer in the text.

I am also most grateful for the contributions to my understanding and experience made by colleagues like Psul Spenley of the Leading Change Partnership and my associates at the

Global Future Forum. And I have to thank my secretary Catherine Hill for coping, not only with the workload that this book entailed, but also with its author.

introduction

Why managers have to live with paradox and learn to fuse contradictions

Management is changing. It always is. Nothing stays the same, and the pace of change seems to intensify with each turning of the business cycle. The Digital Revolution is unquestionably the broadest, most significant change that managers of the modern era have seen; a tide so powerful that even executives who try to resist it cannot fail to be swept along. Every aspect of running organisations, for profit or non-profit, is being or will be affected.

And yet . . .

And yet, looking back over three decades, not only of my own writings, but those of many others, you could conclude that management doesn't change at all. This isn't just a case of *plus ça change, plus c'est la même chose*: though that is often only too true. But thought also comes round in cycles. What appears new and revolutionary in the present age often turns out, on closer examination, to be a Golden Oldie – as I discovered when a reader's enquiry sent me back to a book, *The Business of Winning*, which I wrote at the end of 1980.

The book was built around a dozen incontrovertible axioms that formed the acronym IT BECAME FAST:

Improve basic efficiency – all the time
Think as simply and directly as possible about what you're
  doing and why

Behave towards others as you wish them to behave towards you
Evaluate each business and business opportunity with all the
  objective facts and logic you can muster

Concentrate on what you do well
Ask questions ceaselessly about your performance, your
　markets, your objectives
Make money; if you don't you can't do anything else
Economise, because doing the most with the least is the
　name of the game

Flatten the company, so authority is spread over many people
Admit to your failings and shortcomings, because only then
　will you be able to improve on them
Share the benefits of success widely among those who helped
　to achieve it
Tighten up the organisation wherever and whenever you can
　– because success tends to breed slackness

Inspired by my reader's remarkable business success, which he
attributed to following the dozen rules, I used the anecdote to
introduce a recent book on entrepreneurship. But what strikes
me now most forcibly is the similarity between the 1980 precepts and the management nostrums, fads and fashions that
swirled around in the 1990s – and which, in one form or
another, still swirl today.

　Total Quality Management, Business Process Reengineering,
Economic Value Added, the cult of Shareholder Value, even
non-technological aspects of the Digital Revolution itself: all
these money-spinning ideas (spinning for their protagonists,
that is) are only the latest versions of eternal principles. As the
1990s ended, I could only find three additions to the original
dozen, and they proved to be no less immutable, but just as
suitable for new fashions:

Enable everybody in the business to use their individual
　powers to the fullest possible extent.
Serve your customers with all their requirements and desires
　to standards of perceived excellence in quality.
Transform performance by constantly innovating in products
　and processes – including the ways in which the business is
　managed.

To my pleasure, the additions turned the acronym into IT BECAME FASTEST, thus injecting a necessary note of urgency and ambition. You might interpret all this as a cry of Back to Basics. There are quite plainly eternal principles, founded on human nature, common-sense logic and the laws of business economics, that successful managers can exploit to their great profit.

And yet . . .

And yet, if business success is that simple, why is it so evanescent? The IT BECAME FAST acronym was derived from the sensational business success of a British conglomerate, BTR, that failed as abruptly as its star had arisen. The departure of its founding genius, Sir Owen Green, was like the opening of Pandora's Box: troubles flew out in uncontrollable profusion. The same thing happened to another British star, General Electric, after Lord Weinstock departed; in a few short years, the stage was set for a 90% decline in the value of the renamed Marconi.

Look through any list of corporate heroes at any time in the past three decades, and every shining survivor will be matched by a temporarily or permanently fallen idol: European giants like Marks & Spencer, Club Med, Siemens, Fiat, or British Steel (now Corus): Americans like Motorola, Boeing, General Motors, Xerox, Polaroid, or Hewlett-Packard. The bursting of the high-tech bubble rubbed in the same lesson: superstars like Cisco, Lucent, Ericsson and many others plunged from the firmament to the earth – Enron to the depths.

Fate is apparently waiting to strike down high-tech and low-tech companies alike. Yet their very success enabled these companies to buy the brightest and best talent and to back those brains with virtually limitless resources. What went so disastrously wrong?

The answer lies in the inherent conflict between stasis and change, and between tenets and events. Every organisation builds its own set of basic principles and practices. If success follows, these tenets become embedded into its daily life, year after year, decade after decade. Imperceptibly, the past success generates false perceptions of the present strength. As that happens, the forces of stasis start to win over the forces of change – with fateful or fatal results.

With the best of intentions, management theorists can encourage this rake's progress. By concentrating on their particular cause, they encourage a pernicious tendency among senior managers to flit to and from initiative after initiative (the notorious Flavour of the Month technique) while leaving the static forces undisturbed. In truth, you cannot follow the IT BECAME FASTEST precepts singly, or without disturbing the status quo. Nor can organisations respond fully to external events, which change all the time, without changing internally.

Yet you can only change successfully on a foundation of unchanging basic strengths. That's why single-issue themes that have promised so much, never more than in the recent past, have delivered so little. In the 21st century, you need the very opposite and contradiction of single-theme management. You need Fusion Management.

Fusion cooking combines the best of West and East, of old and new. In a sense, Fusion Management does much the same. It combines the thrust of Western management for certainty and novelty with the Eastern knowledge that nothing in human affairs is sure, and that management is essentially a human, not a scientific activity. Like individuals, companies sometimes act rationally, and always speak as if they do; but, just as often, they behave unreasonably in every sense.

The Fusion Manager must accept this paradox, as he or she accepts all the innumerable contradictions of management. Fusion Management sums up the East's unending quest for a perfection that is always beyond reach, and the Western manager's equally paradoxical urge to sustain unsustainable rates of long-term growth. You cannot escape paradox, no matter where you turn. The manager must in theory optimise profits in the short term: the same theory holds that management must optimise profits in the long term. You cannot do both.

Fusion Management is about blending; about combining short-term, medium-term and long-term; discipline and freedom; commercialism with humanity; globalism with local, national and regional marketing; giving the customers what they want while leading them to want it; strengthening the old while nourishing the new; throwing caution to the wind, yet also avoiding undue risk; growing fast while not overstretching the company by exceeding what Peter Senge, the MIT professor, has called 'the limits to growth'.

Sometimes these limits are immediately obvious, like short-ages of production capacity, or component supply, or unsatu-rated markets. More often, the limits are less specific, comprised of several elements, including competitive actions and reactions, market trends, organisational responsiveness, environmental factors, and so on. For an example, telecommunications groups have been paying more and more for networks and subscribers (sometimes ludicrously more, as in the G3 mobile phone auction in the UK), while the prices paid for services by said subscribers are falling sharply. Profit growth in such circumstances is not so much limited as impossible.

On the other hand, what happens if you go too far with seeking near-term profits, and why, is evident in the happenings at Ford Motor. Back in late 1999, I was very impressed by the way in which the automaker had stolen a long march over the rest of the industry, especially the long-suffering General Motors. 'Every company, to greater or lesser extent, is in the same position as Ford', I noted, 'needing to reshape itself to respond to powerful forces of change.'

The remarkable difference at Ford was the timing of the reshaping. Management was virtuously driving ahead to reshape the company, not in response (as in most such cases) to a profits crisis, but while the financial fruits of an earlier revamp were still pouring in. Ford was earning twice the profit of GM or Toyota. That was attributed to a bold move to central-ise its operations around the globe. The main objective (which had been met) was to cut costs by vast amounts.

And yet . . .

And yet cutting costs is never enough, and as fusion managers know, is dangerously inadequate if imaginative, all-round strategic thought does not accompany and justify the cuts. That deficiency explains why the majority of downsizing operations have failed to achieve the downsizers' objectives. Jac Nasser, the new CEO at Ford, did have a strategy, but one that concentrated on external ends. He saw the balance of power shifting towards the consumer, and wanted to shift the corporation accordingly. But other internal strategic needs existed – and the internal and external are inseparable. It's another crucial demonstration of the need for fusion.

At its simplest, this paradox has been well stated by Hal Rosenbluth, the travel-industry entrepreneur who wrote a book with the provocative title, *The Customer Comes Second*. You give priority to the customer, as all managers are advised by all authorities, by giving priority to the welfare, satisfaction and training of staff. Plainly, Nasser's strategy failed this test at Ford: as *Business Week* reported in June 2001, 'Quality, morale, and market share are down.'

The magazine offered an explanation: 'the rest of the company hasn't always followed' where Nasser sought to lead. Some employees – stigmatised as the Old Guard – were in no position to follow. They had been ousted in favour of people from outside, from Mercedes-Benz, Chrysler, RJR Nabisco and VW. That's another paradox. A great company breeds a more than adequate supply of truly excellent managers from within. But it also requires injections of new blood and minds from without. Again, Fusion Management is needed to resolve the paradox.

But like many chief executives in firms of all shapes and sizes, Nasser appears to have been a single-theme manager. According to *Business Week*, 'As employees at all levels struggle to adapt to the host of sweeping changes Nasser has set in motion, many say Ford has lost sight of its fundamental mission; building quality vehicles as efficiently and profitably as possible.' A recently retired engineer asks a plaintive question: 'When we're working on all these things, who's working on the product?'

And the production. Labour productivity at Ford fell by 7% in 2000, an unforgivable lapse at any time, but especially when that of its competitors rose – as should only be expected. The company sank to the bottom of the US quality league and, not surprisingly, lost 1.7% of its market share. The benevolent fusion cycle has quality, productivity and customer appeal moving forward in step, like a Russian troika. Unfused management sends the cycle into reverse.

The trouble is that managements are apt to defend and exalt their prevailing single-theme wisdom, often heavily influenced by the prevailing wisdom of others, at the expense of any alternative view. Every business writer knows this phenomenon. Probably by no coincidence, both *Fortune* and *Business Week* published long articles in 2001 on the same theme. 'Microsoft: 'The Beast is Back', read *Fortune*'s cover line. 'Microsoft is Stronger than Ever', read *BW*, as (like its competitor) it extolled the company's new strategy for moving above and beyond its operating system monopoly.

At any time in its post-Windows 3 history, Microsoft has been utterly confident in its current strategies, even though one of them, the rejection of the Internet, proved to be disastrously mistaken, and had to be dramatically reversed. The limit to growth at Microsoft is that its business model is inseparably linked to the monopoly, and thus to personal computers with Intel microprocessors. The linkage has proved golden beyond all imaginings. But there are three fault-lines in this electronic Klondyke.

First, the 'Wintel' technology may be overtaken by unforeseen developments (just as IBM's mainframe technology was overtaken by Wintel). Second, the PC market is approaching saturation, as customers discover that they already possess far more than enough computing power and speed. Finally, and a most important paradox, strong monopolies are inherently weak. Every example in history has foundered, usually on the rocks of complacency and abuse of economic power.

The antitrust proceedings which so embarrassed Microsoft, without destroying the monopoly, may prove to be just one battle in a war that Microsoft is destined to lose. It's another paradox. The drive to maximise profits postulates maximising prices – what 'the traffic will bear' becomes irrelevant because the traffic, in a monopoly situation, has nowhere else to go. But Fusion Management behaves otherwise. It restrains prices in the interests of sustainable future growth in profits, as opposed to the highest immediately attainable reward. In other words, to preserve a monopoly, behave as if you don't have one.

Will the received view of Microsoft in 2001 seem wildly mistaken in 2003? The facts produced in the excellent articles mentioned above were very largely favourable. They may even have been very largely correct – *at the time of writing*. Those five words are vital. You would never have expected the nemesis at Ford from the press and analysts' reports of 1999 – only two years before the tide of performance and opinion turned. As every manager knows, 'fact' is a fluid word in management, with verity often lying in the eye of the beholder.

For instance, a later issue of *Business Week* mentioned IBM. It opined that, 'Big Blue is back and stronger than ever . . . but generating strong growth is still its challenge.' How much had IBM actually grown in the previous year? The answer is 4.1% – that is, hardly any growth worth speaking of. Far from being stronger than ever, IBM has lost share in many markets, its relative size in the industry has shrivelled, and its once-mighty margins are down to single figures. If informed and intelligent outsiders can present a disappointing company in so flattering a light, how much easier it must be for insiders to fall for their own rosy-figured publicity.

IBM is among the many cases that prove an easily ignored but crucial point. Companies that fall from grace can stage apparently excellent recoveries. But the recovery is mostly incomplete; they seldom return to the supremacy which they once enjoyed. Turnaround chiefs (like IBM's Lou Gerstner) rarely lead the saved company onwards and upwards to new heights. Even with so strong a brand and such deep resources as IBM's, the loss of momentum that caused relative decline is usually lasting – especially if the management (like turnaround experts in general) has concentrated on the short-term requirements and quick fixes that crisis demands.

In other words, the required skills are incompatible and seldom found in the same manager. The expert at salvation is a sprinter: but any company is running a marathon. That doesn't seem at all relevant when bankruptcy is staring you in the face. But remember Sir Winston Churchill. Even when the bombs were raining down on London, and his country's military position looked hopeless, the great statesman was planning ahead for a victorious Britain's place in the post-war settlement.

That is a phenomenal example of Fusion Management, combining short-term tactics with long-term strategy. Fusion is also the answer to the seductions of self-publicity mentioned above. Managers have to combine enthusiastic optimism with hard-headed realism. They tend to be better at using the latter weapon with subordinates, worse with superiors and the outside world. This reverses the fusion order of things. Fusion Management blends strong, decisive management in the top echelons with full deployment of the critical insights, executive talents and business know-how of all ranks.

In fact, Fusion Management abolishes the concept of ranks. Managers in the new dispensation fill roles, not slots in the hierarchy. The roles are linked directly to functions, objectives and outcomes, and seniority has nothing to do with status, and reduced connection with pay. Hierarchy has long been the enemy of great – even adequate – performance, and the enmity has become greater with the unfolding of modern trends in management. The organisation and those within it still need stability; and discipline can't rest on self-discipline alone. But these authoritarian needs (fusion again) have to be won in an anti-authoritarian context.

Yet the sobering truth is that in an anti-authoritarian age, in which the survival of CEOs has become notably less assured, power still rises to the top. Ford's Nasser is a case in great point. The *Business Week* account reads as if the CEO were in sole command: 'wrenching cultural changes' were mapped out by Nasser 'as part of his bold attempt to transform an Old Economy auto-manufacturer into a nimble, Net-savvy consumer power-house'. Nasser wanted to 'go down in history as the man who brought Ford into the 21st century'. He wanted 'Ford – and himself – to one day be as revered as General Electric and its much admired CEO, Jack Welch.'

This passage does much to explain Ford's setbacks in 2000. Three paradoxes come into play. Yes, it's helpful for managers to have corporate and personal role models and to borrow from them. But no two companies are alike – and the Fusion Manager adapts rather than adopts lessons from elsewhere. Yes, companies need strong, driving people at the top, but the strength becomes weakness unless shared, fused with the individual and collective strengths of others.

Yes, companies have to undergo cultural change to achieve business transformation. But changing culture is not the way to transform a business. This is a difficult paradox to grasp at a time when would-be culture-changers are still highly active. But ask yourself: why would I want to change a culture, anyway? The purpose is invariably to change people's behaviours. But what happens if you change how people behave? You inevitably change the culture. For example, if you want to encourage teamwork, you link rewards partly to team performance. Fusion Managers involve the team members in deciding and distributing the rewards: and team culture will duly strengthen.

At Ford, the same objective was pursued by a Nasser-imposed system that ranked employees against their fellows on a percentage scale: the best 10% got As, the next 80% Bs, and the last 10% Cs – and dismissal if it happened twice. The cut in the last band to 5%, made after vigorous complaints, didn't improve the scheme. The disgraced Enron, likewise emulating Jack Welch's GE, had a similar system. It flew in the face of W. Edwards Deming's crucial point: that somebody must always come last, and axing the bottom contributor doesn't improve the performance of the team. Fusion Managers concentrate on raising the collective contribution of all members.

Optimising collective contribution is the best definition of management. More than ever, the joining together of independent minds is the paradoxical but utterly indispensable route to lasting success. That fusion is natural for human beings. The barriers and behaviour that keep people apart are deeply counter-productive – and counter-intuitive. Freed to achieve what they want for themselves, the company's people will best achieve the company's ends. Another paradox of Fusion Management.

PART I: THE NEW DYNAMISM

*How new technology has spurred new forms of rapid
growth and new techniques of management to match*

CHAPTER ONE

the perpetual revolution

The challenge to innovate

As the Old Millennium ended, the managerial economy certainly put on a magnificent show. Megamergers reshaped entire industries at colossal costs. Brand-new companies catapulted to world-beating stock-market prices when no known basis of valuation, past or present, existed for their infant businesses. Established giants suddenly suffered sharp down-rating, even when their businesses, to all intents and purposes, were as strong as ever.

At the level of the individual manager, new and highly seductive choices appeared. Bright young things from Harvard and other business schools no longer headed automatically for consultancy or finance. The rewards of the latter far outdistanced (and still do) those in straight industry or commerce. But none of the alternatives could compare with the instant payback of an e-business flotation, completed or in prospect. Baby entrepreneurs became overnight millionaires, maybe even billionaires.

For the great majority of managers, who in no way joined the e-game, far more than envy was involved. And far more than *Schadenfreude*, rejoicing in others' disaster, is at stake after the bursting of the e-bubble. All managers have to remember that two worlds co-exist in the electronic revolution. Even though unprofitable companies no longer soar to paper values larger than the output of whole nation states, the stock-market universe still exists on its own illogical, almost irrelevant plane.

The bulging and bursting of the bubble is convincing proof of the market's unreality. There is a connection with the real world, of course. But there was always a disconnect between the stock market billions and true digital business, which, while huge in absolute terms, is still relatively small in turnover and smaller in profits. Size doesn't matter, though. Real changes are affecting the way in which companies are managed, goods bought and sold, and business systems operated – and these changes are not only real, but developing at an unprecedented pace.

True, nearly all managers are continuing to conduct business as usual. Even those closest to the firing line – booksellers and travel agents, say – are still selling books and booking airfares as if Amazon and the proliferating cheap flight websites had never been born. Inside most companies, paper, phone and face-to-face meetings are still the norm of communications. Most transactions between companies, moreover, have yet to depart from the traditional paperwork, like purchase orders, invoices and cheques.

Yet the alternatives exist and are being used in rapidly increasing volume. Sooner or later, the shift must be made between the Old World and the New, preserving the best of the old, but fusing it with the dynamism of the new. Until deep into the 1990s, managers could discuss the future of their industries and their companies without even a glance at the Internet. In the first decade of the 2000s, blind eyes can no longer be safely turned. You have to make a decisive choice. The options are strictly limited:

1 Stay where you are. Leave your *modus operandi* unchanged, internally and externally.
2 Adopt Internet technology where it offers savings and/or convenience (i.e., e-mail), but leave basic operations unchanged.
3 Graft Internet commerce on to the existing business, but seek to preserve the latter as your true *modus operandi*.
4 Set up a separate, new e-operation that will pursue its own destiny without reference to the continuing business – even if that means condemning the latter to 'managed decline'.
5 Completely rethink the business and its management

from first principles to take full advantage of the opportunities created by the New World and to counter its threats.

You can find examples of all five reactions, with the first surprisingly common. Not changing always seems safer than change. That human lust for stasis remains a powerful influence, although it is fundamentally false – especially when a great environmental shift is taking place. Since that is plainly the case now, the risk of doing nothing has become greater than that of taking action. But the 'do-nothings' have some solid-seeming arguments on their side. They can point to . . .

1 The small sales and large losses of Internet businesses, whose astronomical figures for traffic or 'hits' were so dubious that new e-businesses sprang up in the fond hope of providing more reliable measurements.

2 The comparisons of the Internet boom-and-bust with the South Sea Bubble, Dutch tulipmania, and Wall Street before 1929, in which the only basis for rising prices was the rise itself – and where the first crack in the price structure unleashed a flood of liquidation.

3 The sheer proliferation of entrants, of whom only a few, unless the laws of economics have been suspended (which they haven't), will survive to become major and enduring corporations.

4 All manner of mostly trivial objections (like the security of credit-card transactions, or the reliability of the network), which all provide good excuses for that most popular of obsolete strategies, 'wait and see'

Like 'wait and see', all these arguments are irrelevant. Much Internet business is extremely solid, and the solid element is growing hourly. The technical and other minor drawbacks are being overcome. The plethora of shakeouts only increases the need to get in quickly while the opportunities are at their largest. As for the bubble, the only really significant connection between the ludicrous Internet valuations and the real world, tenuous at that, was the use of grotesquely inflated paper money to purchase real assets at equally inflated prices.

Cisco Systems thus cheerfully paid $6.9 billion in stock for Cerent, a money-losing start-up with only $100 million of business in a new technology. Cisco was then the third largest US company by market capitalisation. In the spring of 2001, it still ranked 13th, even after a vertiginous fall in its shares. The $146 billion capitalisation of that spring reflected Cisco's its continued importance in key segments of the equipment market for Internet and telecoms connections – a market that will persist and grow no matter what happens on Wall Street or to Cisco's own 'market cap'.

The real price for that market position is constant vigilance. Though nothing is certain in these fields, the Cerent technology, 'optical transport', may prove essential to Cisco's armoury. Operating in fields with product life-cycles measured in months rather than years, the microelectronic leaders cannot afford lags of any kind. But the governing moral is that lags are potentially fatal in any activity – in public and private sectors alike. Even if the Internet had never been invented, all managers would still have a greater than ever need to take a totally new look at what they are doing and why.

That demands what Peter Drucker calls 'the Business X-Ray', which he discusses in relation to innovation. It's a set of questions which gives you the information needed to define 'how much innovation a given business requires, in what areas and within what time-frame'. Basing the questions on work by consultant Michael J. Kami, Drucker asks:

- How much longer will this product still grow?
- How much longer will it maintain itself in the marketplace?
- How soon can it be expected to age and decline – and how fast?
- When will it become obsolescent?

The same questions, with slight modification, apply to the entire activity of the organisation. Remember that its 'business model', the way in which it obtains and spends its revenues, may be losing validity even while the results still seem fine. Good times are as good a moment as any, and very probably the best, to look at those questions with a completely fresh eye. How much longer will this company still grow?

Look for the worst-case answer. Most failures to adopt successfully with changing times result from mind-sets which are so deeply attached to the status quo, and so deeply averse to change, that their owners cannot envisage obsolescence.

I came across an astonishing example of this mind-set at Compaq Computer at a time when its business model, selling highly engineered top-end products only through dealers at just below IBM prices, was still delivering vast margins. How long, I asked a key executive, would the model retain its strength? They had looked ten years ahead, came the answer, and could see no need to change in all that time.

In reality, the company was just about to plunge into its first quarterly loss as the onrush of the PC clones undercut Compaq's pricing strategy, threatened its market share and made its technological leadership irrelevant. That set the scene for a justly famous turnround, led by Eckhard Pfeiffer, who replaced the former model with a diametrically opposed strategy. From then on, Compaq led prices downwards, operated at half its former margins, competed in all market segments, went for maximum volume and moved from high-cost to low-cost production.

The success was fabulous. Yet in mid-1996, Pfeiffer in effect commissioned a 'Business X-Ray', just as Drucker would have recommended. Writing in *Straight from the CEO*, produced by Price Waterhouse, Pfeiffer laid down eight solid principles for the business radiographer:

1 Attack your own business and financial models before somebody else does.
2 Rethink every (a) product (b) service (c) process (d) activity.
3 Question everything about the business.
4 Give people the authority to challenge sacred cows and provide new strategic models and operating frameworks.
5 Do not focus on market leaders, especially if they are

7

losing share (the mistake Pfeiffer's predecessor made by concentrating on IBM).

6 Research beyond the traditional bounds of your industry and its current products.

7 Stretch the organization.

8 Don't rely on incremental steps.

As Pfeiffer wrote, the increments are 'just an excuse not to change. You want to generate BHAGs – "Big Hairy Audacious Goals".' His own initial ambition to become world market leader, which meant trebling market share, and was accomplished in two years, was a BHAG. Yet the mid-1996 X-Ray failed: in 1999 Compaq plunged into new crisis, which cost Pfeiffer his job.

Intensifying competition from smaller rivals – see (5) above – challenged one of Compaq's most sacred cows, selling through dealers only – see (4). The direct-selling Dell model was superior both in serving the customer and in achieving sensationally lower costs and higher operating efficiencies. Pfeiffer did not adequately obey his own first imperative – see (1) above.

General Electric's Jack Welch tried to root out similar disobedience in his vast corporation. Impressed by the e-surge, he ordered every division to start up 'destroyyourbusiness.com' (later toned down to 'growyourbusiness.com') to attack the business model from within. These subversive operations were each to be headed by somebody with disruptive tendencies and a good knowledge of the Net. Welch's principle is one I have been preaching to all my audiences. If you don't find the 'killer apps' (applications) that will undermine your business model via the Net, somebody else probably will.

Note that this is a radically new strategic perspective, and one which must be devolved. The weakness in Pfeiffer's X-Ray was that nobody (save, eventually, the venture capitalist chairman, Ben Rosen) challenged the boss's total supremacy. The prerequisite of fusion management is the genuine, widespread sharing of power. The toppling of so many chief executives in 1999–2003 saw them paying the price for keeping too much misused authority in their own hands.

This mistake is unacceptable at a time when all significant forces, from the ambitions of the young to the technology, encourage a new, participative democracy in decisions and execution. It should be everybody's job, not just the CEO's, to establish the gap between what already exists and what is required to achieve the corporate ambitions. That means treating the business model as a product and asking the adapted Business X-Ray questions.

- How much longer will this business model still generate growth?
- How much longer will it maintain and enhance the company's position in the marketplace?
- How soon can it be expected to age and decline – and how fast?
- When will the business model become obsolescent – if it isn't already?

You will not fill the gap by using the same business model that has served you so well in the past. And you dare not ignore Drucker's warning that 'the gap has to be filled or the company will soon start to die'. For years the gurus have been preaching innovation in products and processes: for years most managers have paid mere lip-service to the sermons. Now the challenge is to innovate in the greatest process of all – the entire business. The years to 2020 and beyond will be merciless to lip-servers, but marvellously rewarding to Fusion Managers, with 20–20 vision, who obey its clear imperatives with decisive, radical action.

secrets of silicon management

Fusion Managers are going back to basics

New kinds of company require new kinds of manager. At least, that seemed logical when the dot.coms exploded and their founders soared to sudden, incredible wealth. Their prime skill was raising venture capital on the grand scale. Their prime achievement was spending said capital without thought to traditional issues like return on that capital, earnings per share or payback. The traditions, they argued, as they invested for payoffs in the great beyond, were for traditional managers – and the birds.

Jeff Bezos, founder of Amazon and the new management's archetype, even rebuked himself for earning an annual profit too early, instead of ploughing still more millions into building website traffic. All that is now revealed as absurdity. The surviving dot.coms have been forced to sober up. Some have even turned for help to veteran managers, like ASDA-hardened Allan Leighton at lastminute.com, to play the role of 'silverback', the older animal who lords it over the gorilla group. It isn't a case of 'the new management is dead, long live the old'. Rather, it's another proof of the need for fusion.

Unlike Leighton, the veterans tend to come from high-tech backgrounds. Thus George Conrades, chairman and CEO of start-up Akamai, which speeds up content delivery over the Web, spent thirty years with IBM before embarking on a string of Internet-related ventures in 1994. He explained the silverback role very clearly to the *Harvard Business Review*. 'I'm the graybeard here. Most of our employees are young – in their 20s and 30s – so I'm the resident 60-year old. I've got the experience and reputation and contacts . . . and the entire organization can draw on those resources.'

Yet the e-world hasn't felt like radical change to Conrades: Akamai seems like any other business which is 'out on the edge, where the energy is and where the new things are happening'. For all the savage glee with which e-sceptics have mocked the collapse of dot.com start-ups, and for all the deep gloom of their investors, the e-commerce boom was not all illusion. Nor are all its ventures headed for destruction: rather, most are carrying on where IBM and other computer pioneers left off. The sceptics and the investors alike should remember that 90% of all start-ups fail in relatively quick order. In that respect, the crash of the dot.coms (so far, a minority of them) merely runs true to standard business form, and has nothing to do with e-commerce itself.

True, the dot.com phenomenon had certain very considerable differences. First, it produced an awful lot of start-ups: not to mention a lot of awful start-ups. Second, the process of rise and fall has been notably faster. Third, the e-entrepreneurs did not suffer from one of the two main causes of start-up failure, under-capitalisation. On the contrary, the newcomers had venture capital running out of their ears. Far from being a blessing, this lavish financing compounded the second main cause of start-up collapse: management which is so incompetent that (as the silverbacks no doubt enjoy pointing out) it hardly deserves the name.

You can hardly expect computer geeks straight from university to be masters of business administration. Even those many new economy entrepreneurs who had real MBAs from business schools exhibited all the common faults of the start-up breed: wildly unrealistic business plans, running before you can walk, mistaking the hype for the actual – or the sizzle for the steak. Since the sizzle produced the instant millions (sometimes billions) of the dot.com boom, you cannot altogether blame the youngsters for being carried away.

But it wasn't only the youngsters. The venture capitalists included many older but no wiser heads. And so did the dot.com managements. Many experienced managers, mostly from high-tech companies, were attracted by the bright lights and the lavish pay-offs of the sector. These older hands fall into two main groups. Some led start-ups themselves, either collecting round them other managers of similar broad experience, or as partners of the dot.com kids. The other group joined individually, at the start or later, as the hired-gun representatives and exponents of professional management.

The injection of professionals into an entrepreneurial business is nothing new. Indeed, it's the essential second stage in the development of a lasting enterprise. In the dot.com context, though, the entrants from conventional businesses faced two disadvantages. First, rich (even paper-rich) and pushy entrepreneurs (at any age) don't like being disciplined by anybody, especially a hired hand. That's common in all sectors. But the second drawback is specific to e-commerce: the entrepreneurs argued that conventional managers did not understand the radical new necessities of the new economy.

To give one of the earliest radical examples, Netscape advanced at rocket speed from obscurity by its revolutionary approach to marketing its browser. As one newspaper report described the approach chosen by Netscape: 'Chairman Jim Clark has adopted a very competitive price for its first product. It's free.' The strategy was to build the market by flat-out free distribution, establishing a dominating position and then exploiting that dominance – by shifting to a paid basis and generating revenues from other companies wanting to leap on the Netscape bandwagon.

But for the intervention of Microsoft, which linked its own free browser to the omnipresent Windows operating system, Netscape would have remained King of the Internet, instead of disappearing (for a pretty price) into the arms of America OnLine, with a vastly reduced market share. But Clark (a veteran of the successful development of Silicon Graphics) and his cohorts had set the pattern for the dot.coms: give priority to pace over profit, and go for market domination as prime objective. It's a hair-raising strategy, maximising stress as well as risk, and it is light-years away from typical big-company management, even in the electronics sector.

Companies like Intel and Cisco, despite their explosive growth and restless innovation, are run as very tight ships. At Cisco,

CEO John Chambers can close the books, and check the company's financial position in detail, every twenty-four hours. The typical dot.com, though, is a loose vessel. Cash is lavished on non-essentials, essential expenditures are laxly controlled, and the response to an excessive 'cash-burn' is to raise more cash to burn – at least, that was the answer before the venture capitalists and other investors got their fingers (and whole arms) scorched. Only in crisis do the dot.com managers turn their attention to mundane issues of cash flow and control.

By then, it may well be too late, as seen in the over-publicised crash of retailer boo.com. It doesn't follow that experienced managers are free from dangerous temptations, though of a different nature. They may well try to manage their e-company, not as a start-up with no revenues and uncertain prospects, but just like the companies they have left – large, established businesses. The result is bureaucracy, delays in decisions and execution, 'turf wars' between departments, and all the other big company ills – none of which a start-up needs or can afford.

They can afford errors more easily if their 'business models are sound', a mantra which trips easily off every manager's tongue; in other words, how you propose to generate revenues and earn profits as a result. Jim Clark's model at Netscape worked well until torpedoed by the disruptive model deployed by Bill Gates. EBay has a sound model, since the commission revenues earned by its auction site comfortably clear the costs. Many e-commerce venturers, however, have only the fuzziest idea of where, how and when they will find enough paying customers willing to pay enough money.

Often, the business plans revolved round getting sufficient peripheral revenue (for instance, by selling advertising space) to compensate for the thinness of income from the core activity. Professional managers should have seen through the gross over-optimism on this count. They should also have spotted the crippling defects of the idea that the number of eyeballs and hits is success in itself. Eyeballs and hits that don't deliver profitable revenues are not worth having. But conventional managers are no less prone to wishful thinking in conventional businesses.

The difference is that they usually have existing profitable interests to compensate for their follies.

As Joseph Nocera and Tim Carvell wrote succinctly in *Fortune*, 'Mediocre old-economy managers make mediocre new-economy managers' (to which they add a corollary, 'People who left good jobs for speculative options got what they deserved'). If the old-economy managers are good, brilliant Fusion Management is possible – in theory. You can hope to combine the fundamental know-how (business lore leavened by the lessons of experience) of the professional manager with the bold enterprise and creative imagination of the innovator: and to apply the fused combination in the uniquely favourable conditions of greenfield development.

Internet start-ups lack all the management advantages that, paradoxically, act to the disadvantage of the established firms. The latter have inhibiting priorities: existing customers, existing products, existing technologies, and existing markets. Their professional managers are employed and rewarded for seeking and winning the best available returns on capital, another inhibiting condition. The start-up must somehow or other find customers and markets for untried products and/or services that depend, at least in part, on untried technologies.

As for returns on capital, they are pies in the sky for a long time after start-up. Building an Amazon or an eBay in these circumstances demands a different kind of management, with or without professionals on board. The fusion described above, however, applies everywhere. For many years now, established companies have been striving, vainly in nearly all cases, to make their managements more adventurous, more entrepreneurial and more innovative. The advent of e-commerce has made this need still more imperative – so traditional and dot.com managements are being drawn closer together.

A clear illustration of this convergence came from the reaction of Jack Welch, when chairman of General Electric, to the e-challenge. 'We must have a break-the-glass mentality to get on top of this fast-moving subject,' he told his troops. 'You will see fanatical commitment from me on this.' In fact, the fanaticism was toned down by Welch's realisation that e-commerce was not going to sweep all before it, in an electronic equivalent of the rushing hordes of Genghis Khan. The new purpose was to get the best of both worlds, the solidity of existing businesses with the venturesome drive of the new.

That must be the Holy Grail for the Fusion Manager, the much-sought outcome which big companies have pursued with such little result. The ultimate reason for this failure, however, is that, for all their protestations, senior managers have been reasonably satisfied with the status quo. Bolstered by lavish cash flows, large shares of markets and well-known brands (and fat stock options), they have no great incentive to turn the company upside-down. The e-commerce companies, because they lack these massive bulwarks, have no option. Either they develop Fusion Management or they die.

Many of the essential characteristics have already been fore-shadowed by the Silicon Valley superstars. For example, their much shorter planning cycles, eighteen months or so, have come down to only 90 days in an e-company like Akamai. New products are at the centre of Silicon Valley planning. Companies take great care and as much time as necessary over design, but then move very rapidly to get the results into production and out to the market. They experiment continually, trying small-scale projects, correcting plans as they go along, rather than waiting to launch a fully-fledged plan on a national or global basis.

These are 5F managements – Fast, Flexible, Focussed, Friendly and Flat. Speed is a *sine qua non* in a world where PCs have a six-month life-cycle, websites need continual development and speed of customer response is a prime competitive advantage. Flexibility is equally indispensable in a world of sudden change – witness Microsoft's U-turn from anti-Net to Net fanatic, or the several strategic shifts, culminating in the Time Warner merger, with which AOL sought (all too vainly) to stay on top. Focus is another necessity: running e-ventures (or any start-up) under the shadow of the established business is a recipe for failure – as is unrelated diversification.

The last is a lesson that e-entrepreneurs learnt the hard way. With Amazon in the van, the easy, false assumption was that their Web technology, used ad lib to serve a captive, loyal customer base with whatever the business chose to sell, was the enabling asset. In fact, the customers are anything but loyal. Footloose and fancy-free, they shop around: buying books from you doesn't make customers more likely to use your auction site than eBay's or any readier to buy your CDs. Brand awareness must be converted into purchases by the familiar methods of excellence and relevance in product and service.

The next generation of e-companies will be careful, like Cisco, Intel, Microsoft, for example, to build their diversification around the original core business, adding capabilities to widen the product and customer base. They will also take extra care over choosing their friends – the allies who can strengthen the business. Instead of treating bricks-and-mortar companies as doomed dinosaurs, enlightened e-companies have been forming partnerships that will combine old and new channels at lesser expense, and with greater commercial impact, than going it alone: Fusion Management again.

George Conrades describes his three silverback roles at Akamai in 5F terms: 'First is to ensure that we stay focused on our business, that we do not get distracted. Second is coordination – making sure our management and organization stay as flat as possible and that everybody keeps communicating.' The third role is especially interesting: 'to absorb uncertainty – to be the guy who, after thorough, wide-open discussions, drives the group to a decision'.

Focus, flatness and decisiveness, of course, have always been driving features of entrepreneurial success. The new management is going back to basics to move forward confidently amid spectacular uncertainties. Most of the old-economy managers have forgotten (if they ever knew) the entrepreneurial basics. Their need to relearn true management is as urgent as that of the e-kids to learn it, period.

the digital nerve

Bill Gates's Digital Nervous System can truly realize high-speed collaboration and execution

Imagine the competitive benefits reaped by managers in a business where 'information about production systems, product problems, customer crises and opportunities, sales shortfalls and other important business news gets through the organisation in a matter of minutes instead of days' and the 'right people' are 'working on the issues within hours'. These benefits of the 'Digital Nervous System' (DNS) are 'more fundamental than any other change since mass production', according to Bill Gates, chairman and presiding genius of Microsoft.

Gates is the sole candidate for the global title of Chief Digital Manager. Once he had grasped that the Net was a deadly threat to Microsoft's existing business model – the richest the world has ever seen – Gates saw an even greater vision. The Net was the future incarnate, a future that would see and create profound change in business practice and consumer markets.

The change was already well under way by the Millennium. With every advance, moreover, Microsoft seemed to move nearer to Gates's goal: making Microsoft synonymous with the Net, just as with personal computing. In June 2001, *Business Week* was moved to comment that:

> [Gates's] latest offerings bring Microsoft closer to the grand vision he has spun since he awoke to the Web six years ago. Gates sees a day when Microsoft software will run on any device, easily connecting people to the Internet wherever they happen to be ... by weaving Microsoft's PC, server, set-top box, cell-phone and handheld programs

in with its Internet service technologies. Once that happens, Microsoft hopes to deliver software like a steady flow of electricity . . .

By end-2002, that dream was still far from reality. Yet well before that date, PCs (in the workplace and at home), e-mail, personal digital assistants (PDAs) like the Palm Pilot and the Handspring, and websites had become standard equipment for millions of users in every country, industry and market. What Gates, in his book *Business@the Speed of Thought*, calls 'Web workstyle' and 'Web lifestyle' are becoming universal, too. 'Web workstyle' transforms business processes: this is the world of B2B, business to business, of extranets and intranets. The world of B2C, business to consumer, is 'Web lifestyle'. It fuses with the workstyle world to produce the new markets and marketing.

The fusion occurs as business processes are changed to serve on-line customers. For a long time to come, these on-line transactions will be heavily outweighed by conventional buying and selling. But the Mach 2 multiplication of B2B and B2C is only the start of a sea-change that managers dare not miss. They will lose out in spectacular fashion unless they replace paperwork electronically; have teams linked together over the network; get real-time information about sales and customers, and react to the latter with real-time responsiveness; and interconnect with business partners over the Web.

The fact that only a minority of managers, and of their transactions, were truly Net-oriented as 2002 gave way to 2003, is opportunity as well as threat for the uninitiated. The opportunity is that they still have time – but probably not much time – to get into the game. The threat is that this is becoming the only game in town. Even by 2001 more than 60% of US households already had PCs and 85% (i.e., virtually all) had Internet access. Irreversible trends are carrying the digital revolution into the home as more and more people use the infinitely expanding Web to select and obtain goods, information and services.

For some time now, managers and gurus have talked of the need to have 'customer focus' and to be 'customer-centric': the jargon is becoming reality. Gates's 'digital nervous system' is the key to serving customers who, he wrote, 'are demanding faster service, stronger relationships and personalisation'.

Fusing the Web workstyle and lifestyle, however, is not easy for managements brought up in the pre-digital era. Both the organisation and its workings have to change. As it happens, however, the digital changes match and continue half a dozen mega-trends that are already transforming organisations all over the world.

- Outsourcing: the spread of 'virtuality' as companies use outside suppliers for all but core activities.
- Decentralisation: reducing the permanent head office to minimal size and using more freelance contributors.
- Globalism: seeking to buy and sell in all valuable markets, wherever they are.
- Centres of excellence: concentrating tasks in the most effective locations.
- Customer focus: working all processes backwards from and then forwards to the satisfied customer, and constantly striving to improve performance.
- Productivity: aiming for minimum cycle time and maximum process speed.

All six mega-trends are enabled and reinforced by the Web. Freelance employees in outside locations can now communicate as effectively as insiders. Would-be new competitors, thanks to the Web, find that differences of corporate size and geographical spread no longer offer impregnable barriers. Specialised suppliers of 'outsourcing' are becoming important global manufacturers as they concentrate and coalesce. Faster and cheaper processes are helping companies to cope with the lower prices enforced by the transparency of the Web. Gates ably explained this higher productivity:

Almost all the time involved in producing an item is in the coordination of the work, not in the actual production . . . Good information systems can remove most of that waiting

time . . . The speed of delivery and the interaction with the
Internet effectively shift products into services.

The typical corporation pays only lip-service to the speed
of 'research, analysis, collaboration and execution' which
is enabled by a DNS. Even an atypical company – Microsoft
itself, for example – fails to exploit the full opportunities. Thus,
bizarrely enough, Microsoft's UK offshoot doesn't release e-mail
addresses to outsiders, which is analogous to keeping your postal
address secret.

That is a minor glitch compared to the fairly serious catalogue
of Microsoft technological errors down the years. Their effects
have all been drowned in the onrushing flood of cash from the
Windows and associated neo-monopolies (a billion dollars a
month in mid-2001). Most important, though, how could a
wised-up and wired-up company have so nearly and fatally
missed the world-changing implications of the Internet? For
that matter, how could such a company have bungled its recovery from this bad start by employing such dubious commercial
tactics against Netscape that a grave anti-trust action descended
on its head?

The defects in Microsoft's performance – which reflect the
personal attributes of its founder to some high degree – empha-
sise that a DNS is only as good as its users. It is not enough
to hire the brightest and best intellects you can find. Digital
management needs an environment in which the best minds
can produce their best output. The DNS stores, makes available
and transmits all the knowledge shared and generated by the
minds. But the deployment and organisation of those minds are
still as decisive in the new era as they were in the old.

What Gates calls a 'high corporate IQ' transcends the individual intelligences. The more information is shared, and the
more people can 'build on each other's ideas', the more intelligent and effective the organisation becomes. The network of
individual intelligences – each learning more all the time – itself
expands its intellectual power. Quality of collaborative working
exploits the constantly growing quantity of knowledge in the
corporate store. Gates expressed the ideal:

The ultimate goal is to have a team develop the best ideas from throughout an organisation and then act with the same unity of purpose and focus that a single, well-motivated person would bring to bear on a situation.

All this is a very tall order. It isn't surprising that Microsoft falls short of its boss's own prescription. The approved cases which Gates unfolds inadvertently indicate the main problem. Systems and knowledge are not ends in themselves. How are they used? He waxed eloquent about a detailed study that involved masses of 'drilling down' through Microsoft's data, a couple of months' work for several people, even involvement of his own No.2, Steve Ballmer (now CEO) – all to answer one question. Where should the company concentrate its promotion efforts for small-to medium-sized US businesses?

That considerable effort was needed, believe it or not, just to prove that the promotions would be most effective and profitable in cities where Microsoft's previous activity had been zero. The answer is so blindingly obvious that it makes you wonder how much wasteful effort is created, rather than eliminated, by the DNS. Similar thoughts arise when you read Gates's rhapsodies about Marks & Spencer and its use of IT to 'respond immediately to customer preferences and to achieve the kind of personalised service that's impossible to get at a typical supermarket'.

That sounded very unconvincing, read just after a Christmas season in which M&S pitched its demand forecasts far too high. In the company's subsequent hard road to recovery, it was widely criticised on many grounds, but especially, of course, for failing to meet customer preferences. In *Business@the Speed of Thought*, Gates also praises Boeing's use of IT (see page 110). But the company's systems didn't prevent Boeing from taking on far more orders than it could meet with its existing production capacity and methods, with disastrous results.

Gates enthused about how, thereafter, a 'new digital process will . . . drive Boeing's entire production': but that's slamming the stable door after the horse (and the boss of airliner production) had both bolted. What's the answer? It cannot be to reject the digital revolution. Gates is wrong when he says: 'Every company can choose whether to lead or follow the emerging digital trends.' The follower option must have disappeared in an environment of chaotic change.

The wired world is a world in constant flux, in which all markets will be deeply affected by many-sided transformation. Gates is on much stronger ground when he puts the choice differently and succinctly: 'it's evolve rapidly or die'. That would be an intimidating formula even if no technological problems existed. In fact, many difficulties persisted in the new millennium, starting with the slow access to (now readily cured) and unreliable performance of the Internet.

One of the wonders of the digital world, though, is that the problem is also the solution. As soon as a hitch appears, new ambitious entrepreneurs start beavering away to remove the obstacle, creating new technology and new fortunes in the process. Gates is right to claim that 'IT is both forcing companies to react to change and giving them the tools by which to stay ahead of it.'

It's still possible to find major companies that have no internal e-mail, or that are losing money by failing to use this excellent tool: for example, £150,000 wasted by a company on faxing weekly crop reports from Africa. A simple e-mail application was far superior in cost (which was negligible) and performance.

As for the Internet, Unisys in 2001 surveyed 400 of the world's top banks, to discover that only 306 had a website that could be found in a 20-minute search. Of those sites that were located, only 142 allowed users to submit a request (via e-mail) to buy a financial product or service. Among these sites, however, only 78 responded (via e-mail or phone call) to this customer request at all. Still worse, almost half of these responses merely referred prospective customers back to the site or provided some other inappropriate message. In sum, only 58 (15%) of these top 400 banks had a website that met even minimal customer requirements.

The would-be digital manager, shunning the sins of the 85%, should set up specific digital projects which are an integral part of the work itself, and which have an immediate and measurable pay-off. The management of data, documents, and projects themselves can all be readily and effectively improved in any business, and in straightforward fashion, by four applications:

- getting and using better information for planning
- raising standards and levels of customer service
- providing and managing people's training programmes
- achieving collaboration over any distance between people working on the same project.

The ultimate aim is the creation of a collaborative culture which does all these things and more, using the digital technology, to change from the DNS metaphor, as a corporate bloodstream which links all the organs of the enterprise. Once you have achieved the critical mass of what Gates calls 'super-smart' people, you can exploit and augment their combined energies. That's the task of 'knowledge management' (KM), which Gates belittles in his book as mere fancy use of words, but which is in fact crucial for the digital manager.

Knowledge management at one level ensures that whenever internal Microsoft consultants finish an assignment, they send their technology solutions to a central Web location. But KM requires very much more effort, first, to constantly 'evangelise' in the cause of sharing and using knowledge, and then to activate that knowledge to achieve excellence.

For important example, regular review of sales forces information by superiors is regarded by Gates as possibly 'the biggest incentive . . . to keep our customer base up-to-date'. His view of this necessity is echoed by Thomas A. Stewart in his book *Intellectual Capital*; by his definition, customer knowledge (which is 'probably . . . the worst managed of all intangible assets') is part of intellectual capital (IC). But as IC guru Leif Edvinsson explains, the key relationship is between two other parts: human capital (which can't be owned by any organisation) and structural capital (which can).

'The better the combination, the greater the IC.' Structural capital means 'all the codified dimensions that you leave behind when you go home'. That takes in everything from processes to manuals, filing systems to software – much of it digital. As Edvinsson points out, 'you don't start from scratch in the morning': the moment you log on, the computer links you with the IC structure. The work of the knowledge manager is to 'transform thoughts' into this structure; and 'the velocity of the transformation is absolutely critical'.

Gates would unquestionably agree: in his words, the aim of the digital manager 'should be to enhance the way people work together, share ideas, sometimes wrangle, and build on one another's ideas – and then act in concert for a common purpose'. You'll never begin to achieve that managerial Utopia as a non-digital manager, who is unfamiliar with tools like databases, e-mail and workflow applications, electronic files and Web technology. But these tools are simplifying and converging, and as they draw together, the nearer Utopian management will come to realisation. It will remain remote. But that ultimate digital goal is one which all fusion managers will approach sooner and closer.

In the wake of the dot.com crash, it was all too easy for recalcitrant managers and gloating critics to reject what they had never actually accepted the fact that the 'Internet changes everything'. But in May 2003 *Business Week* summed up what Web users and suppliers had been saying before, during and after the bubble burst. It quoted Andrew S. Grove, chairman of Intel and Gates's chief accomplice in the digital revolution; 'Everything we said about the Internet is happening'.

'Everything' included a forecast made in 1999 stating that e-commerce between American businesses would reach $1.3 trillion by 2003. The prediction was hopelessly wrong. According to Forrester Research, as 2003 began, networked business-to-business transactions were vastly higher at $2.4 trillion. Not only has e-commerce boomed, so has the productivity which Gates was so sure would benefit. Web-based productivity gains have poured in from better forecasting, lower inventories and real-time communication with suppliers, etc.

The benefits are expected to reach $450 billion annually by 2005, getting on for double earlier forecasts. Wherever *Business Week* looked, it found Web-based booms, benefits and exploded myths. Spending on e-business, far from falling, has risen every year since the crash and now accounts for 27% of all tech spending. While many business-to-business exchanges did indeed bomb, the remainder boomed to $3.9 trillion of current world-wide business. Nor did the glittering prizes go only to the techies: over four-fifths of Web-era productivity gains post-1995 were won in non-tech industries.

Moreover, new technologies are blossoming all the time (like broadband, with its 56% annual growth in the US); and as they bloom, so the tools are simplifying and converging, and as they draw together, the nearer Utopian management will come to realisation. It will remain remote. But that ultimate digital goal is one which all organisations and all managers must seek.

CHAPTER FOUR

evolution by revolution

How to build on valid strengths to create new brilliance

Senior managers seldom pride themselves on being conservative. On the contrary, in these days of fast-moving technological
and market change, they love to pose as dynamic corporate
reengineers, change agents who are driving their businesses
to new heights of 'shareholder value'. So it was something of
a surprise in 2001 to find one global CEO, Peter Brabeck of
Nestlé, setting his face against radical transformation and,
instead of revolution, expounding the case for evolution: 'You
can have slow and steady change, and that is nothing to be
ashamed of.'

Brabeck is no fuddy-duddy – at least, not according to *Business
Week*, which selected him among 'The Stars of Europe', fifty
leaders who are at 'the forefront of change'. Since change at
large is anything but 'slow and steady', Brabeck's selection as
change-leader looks a trifle odd. But his observations uncover a
profound issue for all managers. Are they involved in perpetual
revolution, or is it business, and evolution, as usual?

Brabeck unquestionably echoes the true feelings of most
managers, including, no doubt, many of the professed revolu-
tionaries. Radical change is disruptive, and thus painful for
many people, whether it comes from outside or inside. Brabeck,
in the *Harvard Business Review*, was scathing about the internal
variety:

> When you run a business, you must be pragmatic. Big
> disruptive change programmes are anything but that. You
> cannot underestimate the traumatic impact of abrupt
> change, the distraction it causes in running the business,

26

the fear it provokes in people, the demands it makes on management's time.

In Brabeck's view, the need for any 'one-time change programme' points to previous management failure. He argued that by 'adapting, improving and restructuring as a continuous process' good managements generate steady progress which rules out any call for radical action. He compared his company to a 'strong and trim 40-year-old woman', who is no spectacular stock-market star ('very sexy, like a 20-year-old girl'), but can outstay the latter: the elder woman 'can easily run 10 miles without being pushed and pulled'.

While 40-year-old women won't thank Brabeck for the absurd suggestion that they can't be 'very sexy', the heart of his argument really lies in the last three words: 'pushed and pulled'. He plainly feels that there is a natural and acceptable rate of growth, built into a company's products, markets and nature, and that efforts to force-feed expansion will eventually prove self-defeating as the business hits its limits to growth.

In *Fortune* magazine, Carol Loomis spelt out the powerful reasons why those limits exist. Her title was 'The 15% Delusion'. This once-common target for annual growth in a company's earnings per share may be acceptable, but it certainly isn't natural. Why 15%? The choice bears all the marks of springing from a compromise between 10%, which takes seven years to double a company's earnings, and thus seems too slow, and 20%, which takes three-and-a-half years to double, and looks too speedy for either comfort or credibility.

Loomis shows that 15%, which needs five years to double, is in no way a safer speed. With the aid of Value Line, she studied three long periods (1960–80, 1970–90 and 1980–1999) and 150 large US companies to arrive at an astonishing result: 'Only a handful of the companies managed a rate of 15% or better, and many flunked at growth entirely.' Of the 13 winners, only Philip Morris beat 15% compound annual growth in all three double decades: Boeing made it in the first two periods (but then lapsed badly in the third): pharmaceutical giant Merck succeeded in the last two.

These were the only three companies in the 13 which would be readily identified as growth stars. So the great majority of companies which fastened on 15% goals or higher failed their own test. Why? Loomis lists five convincing reasons:

1 The initial mistake of setting any public goal at all, when business conditions fluctuate too much to make that realistic.
2 The encouragement of unwise accounting and business tactics to give artificial boosts to reported earnings – which can lead all the way to false reporting.
3 The 'sheer difficulty' of growing at 15% p.a. in an economy in which neither GDP nor profits at large are advancing anything like so fast.
4 The dilution effect when companies pursue their 15% targets by acquisitions in which shares are used as currency.
5 The arithmetical certainty that growth will slow badly once a company reaches a certain magnitude.

To demonstrate that last point, a group with a billion in earnings, growing at 15% annually, needs to add $1 billion of profits in the first five years, $2 billion in the following five, $4 billion in the next. At some point in its progress, the limits to growth will be hit. The company will simply be unable to add large enough organic expansion to sustain its growth. That happened to IBM, whose seemingly modest target, to grow with the computer industry in the 1980s, was awesome: it meant adding the equivalent of eight Digital Equipments, then the second largest competitor.

The impossible size of the task, as much perhaps as the inadequacies of management, explains why IBM fell so badly from grace. If you are attempting the impossible, you are bound to fail; but one man's impossibility may be another man's success. Witness Amazon's lightning rise in the book trade, or the way the Japanese cracked the seemingly impregnable Xerox monopoly in copiers. In such cases the attacker overcomes an entrenched and powerful enemy by going round the side, by adopting new and disruptive technologies or channels (or both). You can't go round the side of arithmetical fact.

You can, however, try, by fair means or foul. Loomis points out that many companies exclude restructuring charges when calculating their double-digit growth feats. Over at Nestlé, Brabeck rightly regards this semi-foul practice with considerable scorn. 'We put on our books restructuring charges of up to $300 million, before operating profit, as operating expenses, year after year. Most of our competitors – most companies, in fact – would account for these as extraordinary charges. Very different philosophies, no?'

Now, there was much to be said, even before the Enron mega-scandal and others, for Nestlé's financial conservatism. In many cases extraordinary charges are the equivalent of sweeping dirt under the carpet. The truly good manager wants numbers that tally with the operating cash flows and give an accurate picture of the company's actual performance – getting as near to reality as possible. The trouble with talking about 15% growth that hasn't truly been achieved is that your own managers will begin to believe your half-truths. That will only increase their temptation to start bending the figures to match the fiction, especially if publicly announced targets are involved.

As a non-executive director of a company that had recently floated, I saw this phenomenon at first hand. Forecasts were obligatory, as usual, for the flotation. In the very first year, however, the last tranche of the promised profits proved elusive. Various adjustments were made, perfectly legally, and with the auditors' approval the forecast was met – just. Yet I felt uneasy. Sure enough, subsequent years followed the same pattern of missed forecasts, usually made good by adjustments.

Like Brabeck's 'one-time change programme', this is often not a good sign: management may be underperforming, for reasons that will run far deeper than poor forecasting. Under-forecasting is a safer path to beating your promises, but again doesn't mean that actual performance is excellent. So how does Nestlé's performance match up? The company doesn't, naturally, publish forecasts for the benefit of the financial world. But Brabeck has tied himself to a goal of 4% internal growth, after inflation. He thinks this 'a very ambitious benchmark for a big organisation like ours'. Is it?

Doubling every 17 years is only ambitious by Nestlé's own past low standards. Its dollar sales rose by a mere 61% between 1990 and 2001, with net profits rising 65%. In other words, there was a negligible rise in net margins, which kept below 4%. Not much sign there of the continuous improvement that Brabeck preaches. Not much sign, either, of great benefit from the very large number of acquisitions that Nestlé has made over the years.

Just as the failures of the 15% mythologists point to hard truths about their management, so do figures showing slow growth. Once upon a time, insurance companies used to aim at 7% returns, which double an investment in a decade. That is still a reasonable conservative target. Remember that going returns in the financial markets are available to anybody with money to invest. Businesses are supposed to offer greater and richer yields than interest-bearing investments. Managers who can't better that 7% figure are either in the wrong business or managing it in the wrong way.

Evolution, bluntly, is not enough. As Masaki Imai showed in his essential book *Kaizen*, continuous improvement can be a dynamic force in a company – provided that it becomes the intensive way of life known as Total Quality Management. TQM is revolutionary evolution, a corporate-wide set of processes which produces discontinuous change through Fusion Management. In a discontinuous environment, it's hard to see any sensible alternative. Optional change, however, offers brighter prospects than forced change – as Brabeck himself has seemed to recognise.

Curiously, the Nestlé boss, in some respects, has practised what he doesn't preach. He ripped out the partition walls in the head office on Lake Geneva, and substituted glass walls and smaller rooms. That left spaces for meeting and talking areas. The purpose was clearly not evolutionary, but radical. 'I wanted the building to reflect our philosophy that people and products come first.' That may have been the philosophy, but before the office restructuring, it certainly wasn't being honoured by the building (or by those inside), on Brabeck's own account.

> ... it was a modern-looking building with an old-style interior. Everyone had closed, individual offices. Walking through the halls, you wouldn't see anything – no people, no products. It was almost like we had something to hide ... We made the whole building transparent.

Brabeck was actually fulfilling one of the commandments of turnrounds (the one-off programmes he thinks should be unnecessary). He was using physical change to symbolise a wish for radical change (*kaikaku* in Japanese), seeking to turn an introverted culture outwards.

But *kaikaku* isn't just knocking down walls. As IBM found, you have to knock down far more. Its target of growing with the industry was very reasonable, for anything less would (and did) spell relative failure. Competition was coming from many sides, and had to be met on its own terms, not IBM's. The problem was that many-sided competition couldn't be met effectively without cracking IBM's monolithic structure and segmenting its businesses to match a fast-segmenting industry.

The British department store chain, John Lewis, has a famous slogan – 'Never Knowingly Undersold'. IBM's slogan should have been 'Never Knowingly Beaten to Market'. That would have demanded the creation of smaller, faster-moving units, like the original PC company. After a brief spell of glorious independence, however, the unique spirit of the PC pioneers was broken, and their lessons were lost. Only break-up could have kept IBM abreast of the developments – in storage, laptops, direct selling, microprocessors, etc., – where it lagged behind so badly.

In that kind of situation 'adapting, improving and restructuring', Nestlé-style, do you little good. They may even bring just the same damage that Brabeck so eloquently describes and decries – personal trauma, distraction, fear, diversion of management time. And at the end of the day, like IBM under John Akers, or Xerox in 2001–02, you may well find that your last state is worse than your first. Better by far to return to first principles and the following programme:

- Put yourself in the shoes of an ambitious outsider and think as they would think.
- Explore radical alternatives.
- Choose your radical strategy.
- Put in place the radical changes required to meet that overall objective.

It will require major change, unremitting effort and good fortune to reach any target worth the name – to judge by the tough findings reported by Carol Loomis. In the first period (1960–80) recorded in *Fortune*, 16 of the 150 companies had negative growth, 22 less than 5% per annum, 64 under 10%. In the second period (1970–90), the numbers were respectively 24, 30 and 46. In the third double decade of 1980–1999, which took in the supposedly fabulous 1990s, 33 of the 150 (that's over one-fifth) went backwards, 38 didn't exceed 5%, and 40 came in between 5% and 10%.

Against that dismal background, mediocrity is something of an achievement. Mediocrity, however, is nowhere near good enough. That's the trouble with Brabeck's conservative, evolutionary philosophy. The mediocre conservative can pride himself on the solidity of his company's results, the strength of its finances, and the depth, breadth and excellence of its technology. But IBM could have done the same.

It's perfectly true that IBM's several abortive change programmes did more harm than good in the 1980s. But they were doomed, anyway, because the skin-deep measures were not linked to planned, profound changes in individual and group behaviour. Time and again, that's why companies run off the growth track. They want faster performance, but won't make the changes in design, drivers and back-up staff that will have a chance of winning the business Grand Prix.

Neither Brabeck's toleration of low growth nor its opposite – force-feeding to hit 15% – is acceptable. Evolution alone leads to stagnation. Revolution driven by ambitious, artificial targets puts the cart before the horse. But evolution and revolution are by no means mutually exclusive. You really can fuse the two, building on past, valid strengths, and using those strengths to create new powers that will sustain a brilliant business into the foreseeable future. That's the fusion secret. On all the evidence, achieving that end is extremely hard. But that doesn't mean for a moment that you shouldn't try.

adding management value

How creating CV (Customer Value) builds AV (Added Value), which in turn enhances IV (Intrinsic Value)

Herewith some weighty words of wisdom from a high-tech CEO: 'Stock price is a by-product; stock price isn't a driver. And every time I've seen any of us lose sight of that, it has always been a painful experience.' The words gain greater force from the speaker's identity. This is Henry Schacht, recalled to the colours at Lucent after his successor had presided over a catastrophic fall in the share price from the end-1999 level of $138.

In early 2001 Lucent's price stood at a piddling $7 as pundits speculated over the very survival of the former manufacturing arm of phone giant AT&T. Under Schacht's earlier ministrations, it was hailed as a supreme American example of the spun-off, liberated, reborn business. The share price responded in such spectacular style that you cannot blame 'any of us' for being carried away. Millions of bucks are highly seductive.

But what should Lucent's management (and those of countless other deflated *wunderkinder*, from Cisco and Amazon to Yahoo! and Dell) have been pursuing? The pat answer for a few years now has been 'shareholder value'. But the volatile behaviour of stock markets in the opening years of the Millennium should have dealt a massive blow to this cult of shareholder value – one of the most pervasive notions ever to sweep over the corporate world.

Company after company solemnly dedicated itself to the pursuit of ' SV', which in effect is a euphemism for a higher share price. But value in the hundreds of billions can be wiped off – and has been – by a few days of trading in the world's stock exchanges. For companies that are not publicly traded, this collapse, both of prices and the cult, may seem irrelevant. But there's a fundamental issue beneath the froth. What is 'value' in a business, and how is it created?

The glib and easy answer, that value rests in the market capitalisation, was never adequate, because the market value is determined by forces outside management's control. The level of stock markets in general, and the valuation of individual shares, are not manageable (not by any honest means, that is). And remember Henry Schacht's point. Concentrating on the stock price puts the cart before the horse, the stock market before the business. In a classic denial of Fusion Management, it pursues the former and neglects the latter.

The business and the market value do have a relationship, but it defies analysis. Clever people have devoted much ingenuity to working out an elaborate theoretical base for SV. But the share price, the be-all and end-all of SV, requires no complex theorising. It is the simple product of two variables – the earnings per share (which management can affect, for better or worse) and the multiple which the market applies to the eps number. This price-earnings or PE ratio is subject to outside wisdom, unwisdom and whim.

To be truly useful, any measurement of management success must be (a) objective (b) directly linked to tactical and strategic efficiency and (c) comparable to similar indices elsewhere. Shareholder value, as exalted in recent years, fails all these tests. That's why some companies have linked bonus payments and share options, not to their out-performance of the stock market as a whole, but in relation to their sector. If the company is performing 'better' than its peers in a deadbeat sector, but SV is still dipping, that raises a tough question. Why has management persevered in a business where higher SV is simply not available?

Escaping a low sectoral SV is much easier said than done. In one famous case, a smoke-stack company named Gould, Inc. switched out of duff heavy engineering into dynamic electronics, only to find the new sector slumping while smoke-stack shares boomed. Monsanto's dynamic switch from other, boring chemicals into exciting agrochemicals, especially genetically modified foods, was a more recent jump out of the frying pan into a blazing fire. So was the self-immolation of Marconi by plunging its all into telecoms.

Another tempting but illusory strategy is an acquisition spree, in which high-flying shares are used as currency because they are supposedly cheap. That leads growth fanatics into the deepest trap. Other companies are only worth buying (and a business is only worth running) if they create Economic Value Added: i.e., their profits exceed the cost of the capital spent on the investment. That cost includes not only interest on debt, but the cost (substantially higher) of equity capital. Put the resulting total against earnings on the capital, and not only acquisitions, but the whole company can easily come up negative.

If an apparently solid and successful business suffers a mysterious decline in share value, there's often no mystery: often, EVA has turned negative. It follows that maintaining a high, positive EVA should be a prime financial objective for corporate management. EVA is a key element in what the sage and great investor Warren Buffett calls the intrinsic value (IV) of a company – meaning what its future stream of earnings is worth, as of today.

To be reasonably certain of that stream, Buffett looks at the strength of a company's customer franchise. He wants a business that has demonstrated consistent earning power. It will have earned good returns on equity and incurred little or no debt. It has good management in place, and is simple and understandable. You can easily understand why Buffett shunned the dot. coms. They had no paying customers, or few; no profits and therefore no returns; huge financial liabilities; unproven and often uninspiring management. The business models were often so complex that nobody, not even the dot.entrepreneurs, could understand them.

People prated about a novel kind of company. The paradox is that more Internet companies would have survived and flourished if they had concentrated on the basics of business and not on their own myths. Unlike Shareholder Value, the vital basic isn't directly financial at all – Customer Value, which is what creates a powerful franchise and makes it worth having.

That builds AV (Added Value), which enhances IV (Intrinsic Value).

CV arises in just the same way as a share price: from the individual buying and selling decisions of innumerable people. Its measures – numbers like gross margins, market share, percentage of customer retention, percentage of customers rating products and services as excellent, customer and product profitability – are not easily available to outsiders. But insiders should know these indicators full well and watch them as sharply as the sales numbers.

The CV metrics may even show that you are well advised to trade revenues for other benefits. If a Pareto analysis shows (as usual) that 80% of your profits come from 20% of your customers or products, you may well increase the value of the business by cutting out the unproductive four-fifths. That is precisely what was done by Nypro, the plastics moulding firm beloved by guru Tom Peters. Nypro retained only those customers spending more than $1 million a year: before long, turnover had trebled. However, neither the analysis nor the action taken to reflect the analysis explain Nypro's success.

That resulted from the value which management added by the devotion expended on its remaining customers – locating plants as near to them as possible, and linking computer systems so that Nypro became an intimate part of the customer's business. That is yet another aspect of true management value: the degree of customers' satisfaction with the company's products and services, expressed above all in the purchasers' readiness to buy from you again.

Do not rely, as most companies do, on statistical, quantitative surveys of workers, customers, other employees, etc., to test satisfaction. Use qualitative interviews of representative samples of the clientele (and others) if you really want to find out whether management is adding genuine value, in the sense of worth. In a neat example of verbal fusion matching management fusion, that 'worth' is intimately linked with values in another sense – the beliefs that the company's people share and actually observe in practice.

Achieving short-term performance is only one side of the

values coin. Other values provide the foundation stones of long-term growth and viability. The values that achieve these ends cannot be measured, but they certainly have measurable effects. Do you personally . . .

- give your subordinates stimulating work?
- respect the needs and values of others?
- give priority to individuals and their needs?
- excel in personal relationships?
- treat colleagues as interesting and valuable people?
- get deeply interested in and excited by your work?
- manage with the full consent of others?
- make all appointments strictly on merit?
- compete primarily to beat your own best standards?

You won't find many people who regard these qualities as anything but highly valuable. On the other hand, you won't find many organisations (maybe any) displaying these features. They come from Charles Handy's description of 'Dionysians' in his stimulating book *Gods of Management*. The followers of Dionysus, the god of food and wine, do not, according to Handy, fit into organisations at all. They are by nature freelance anarchists.

The freelance philosophy, though, permeates every modern book on management, every lecture, every Fusion Manager's wish-list. It doesn't matter whether (using Handy's definitions) you are an autocratic Zeus, an Apollonian 'organisation man', or a task-oriented Athenian. You are still more than likely to want your managers to manage in the Dionysian spirit. But wanting gets you nowhere. How can you make it happen?

Values can be enforced in three ways: the Three Rs – Reward, Repetition and Removal. General Electric's Jack Welch fitted managers into one of four categories or 'Types'. Type I delivers on performance commitments and shares the company's people-based values (which include Dionysian features). Type II does not meet commitments and does not share the values. Type III misses the commitments, but shares the values. Type IV delivers on commitments, makes all the numbers, but does not share the values. Each type requires different treatment:

- Type I. Give this person progress and promotion (Reward).
- Type II. Do not keep in the organisation (Removal).
- Type III. Give them a second chance, preferably in a different environment (Repetition).
- Type IV. The most difficult to deal with. Despite his or her high performance, they must either change their ways (usually very difficult) or go (Repetition or Removal).

The last treatment may sound harsh. But if you start arguing that the end (the result) justifies the means (tyrannical or bullying behaviour), you can forget about people-based or Dionysian values – and about being a Fusion Manager. In any event, those values themselves dictate that any statement of the principles you expect people to work by should pass these tests:

- Has it been drawn up with their participation?
- Does it have their explicit consent?
- Is it operable and practical?
- Is it revised periodically as necessary?
- Does it assume that people will live the values?
- Is it concise and clear?

Only six affirmatives will do. Remember, though, that living the values and being Dionysian won't help at all if the organisation is doing the wrong thing or things. Top management earns its rewards and prestige (or should do) by pointing the company in the correct direction – and, even more important, changing direction when that is required: which means before it becomes a dire necessity.

Handy admirably illustrates this imperative with the concept of the 'Sigmoid Curve'. This looks like an S lying on its side. The bulge in the curve is the result of a natural human process. In *The Empty Raincoat*, Handy gives this description: 'We start slowly, experimentally and falteringly, we wax, and then we wane.' The bulge represents the waxing. Towards the top of the bulge lies a point of maximum danger. Here, the organisation is near the height of its powers and achievement. Critics of its methods and strategies are neither welcome nor plausible.

Handy is absolutely right to utter a loud blast of warning. You have reached the critical point, somewhat below the absolute crest, where you should be thinking ahead, and acting, in a truly radical manner. If you wait until the Sigmoid Curve has begun to decline, it will be too late. Against a background of falling profits, market value and morale, you can find yourself running hard up a down escalator. Even a successful battle against these odds is most unlikely to restore the old power and glory.

To do better, act earlier along the First Curve to generate a second Curve, and follow this Handy-inspired creed:

- Assume that your strategy will need replacing at least every three years, probably two.
- Work on developing new strategies, no matter how well the old ones are performing.
- Continue to develop the existing business fully, but do not let its development impede the new.
- Entrust the Second Curve planning to younger people.
- Accept that leadership will pass to this younger group as the new strategy takes over.

It takes courage for an older management to accept the whole of this philosophy. There is always the risk, discussed earlier, of heading off in a new direction, only to find that the new one is wrong and the old still had plenty of life ahead. You can best avoid that trap by applying the strategic insight of expert innovators. They concentrate on (a) maintaining leadership in their core businesses (b) diversifying only into areas where they have deep knowledge, and which relate directly to the core activities. They don't head off in the opposite direction. And they base their new strategies on operating practices which are also values.

Market strength is regularly monitored, with market-research statistics and customer surveys supported (as recommended above) by qualitative interviews. Better performance by other companies is used deliberately as a spur to greater achievement. Everybody is set to working on 'stretch' programmes – for themselves and the unit. Constructive criticism is encouraged, no matter who is criticised. High standards are set, and everybody knows them. And success is treated as a springboard for further advance.

These managements also remember 'Repetition'. They never miss an opportunity to repeat the values message, both to groups and to individuals. Above all, they know that neither Reward, Repetition nor Removal will work without personal example from the leader. That is the fourth and vital R: Role Model.

PART II: WINNING POLE POSITION

*How to lead the competition on the only criteria that matter
– those which the customers value most*

CHAPTER ONE

protecting the future

Mastering the Ten Commandments – and being prepared to break them

Most managers live in the past. That statement may sound ridiculous. What about all the five-year plans, the spending on research and development, the new initiatives in cyberspace, the ambitious acquisitions, and so on? Despite such activity, managers are inevitably and deeply affected by what they already have, by their 'legacy' business and 'legacy' systems – so deeply affected that they resist even unavoidable change.

At Intel, for example, when the foundation business in memory chips collapsed in the early 1980s, much of the management wanted to fight with might and main to achieve the impossible, to turn back a Japanese invasion which had already driven the business into large and persistent losses (see page 205). Half of its managers were unable to accompany the switch to building the business round microprocessors – a strategic masterstroke that created one of the great growth engines of the late century.

The switch to microprocessors followed the famous prescription of computer guru Alan Kay, one of the founding fathers of the personal computer: the best way to predict the future, he said, is to invent it. In the infant 21st century, many companies sorely need to invent a new future – to invent that future, though, many corporations need to invent a new company: and that is never easy.

To read Intel chairman Andy Grove's account of the above events, in *Only the Paranoid Survive*, is to relive a searing and very difficult experience. Note that this was a company with only a short (and highly successful) history. It must be far harder for older and less dynamic organisations to accept that the world has changed, and that the future demands something entirely different from the past. The old question, 'what are you going to do for an encore?', has acquired a new and urgent significance.

Fusion Managers are required to undertake a delicate and difficult exercise achieving the best balance and combination of past, present and future. The past is no more all bad than the future is likely to be all good. In fact, the organisation's inheritance is liable to include some of its greatest, richest strengths. Consequently, one of the prime duties of management is to protect the past, to sustain and exploit the inherited assets. But it's also incumbent on them to protect the future.

That's not easy, either. Appearing on British television in 2000, Michael Dell, the founder of Dell Computer, was asked about 'the next Dell', and replied that he hoped Dell would be the next Dell. There are a few precedents – Intel is one – for strikes of lightning hitting the same company twice. In the vast majority of cases, though, companies that have triumphed in the past are left behind as newcomers usurp the future. This is rarely because the oldcomers have tried and failed in the new businesses and technologies. Mostly, they have ignored the trends, or kept their response too little, too late.

Part of the problem lies in the very steps that good managers take to protect the existing business and to ensure its sound progress. The well-behaved business, for example, is supposed to obey the following Ten Commandments:

1 Set reasonable targets.
2 Focus on your core business.
3 Defend the corporate values.
4 Lead from the top.
5 Concentrate R&D expenditure.
6 Tightly control capital spending.
7 Seek to retain good employees.
8 Only lay bets big enough to make a difference.
9 Concentrate on profitable activities.
10 Administer rewards conservatively.

These rules and principles are fine as far as they go: but that's not far enough. In fact, according to Gary Hamel, a renowned strategic thinker and consultant, the ten precepts are the exact opposite of the ways in which to get 'billion-dollar business ideas' to 'bubble up from the ranks'. If you want a culture that inspires innovation – that is, looks to the future – you need 'to design context rather than invent content'.

This means that 'management's job isn't to build strategies', but to enable them. At Intel, Grove expresses the same vital point in a different way. He is convinced that strategy is shaped by 'strategic action' rather than by the conventional, top-down plans. In his experience, the latter always turn into 'sterile statements, rarely gaining traction in the real work of the corporation'. The differences between plans and actions, wrote Grove, are critical:

- Strategic plans are statements of intention.
- Strategic actions are already taken or being taken and imply longer-term intent.
- Strategic plans sound like political speeches.
- Strategic actions are concrete steps.
- Strategic plans are abstract and usually have no concrete meaning except to management.
- Strategic actions immediately affect people's lives.
- Strategic plans deal with events far in the future and are thus of little relevance to today.
- Strategic actions take place in the present and thus command immediate attention.

The reversal of roles recommended by Grove, switching from planning to action, has built-in energy. The present is the only time in which anybody can live. Bring the future into the present by forming concrete programmes in which everybody participates – in full knowledge of the long-term goals that you want to achieve as you invent the future. Winston Churchill used to court-martial himself every night, demanding to know what he had done that day towards winning the war. What have you done this day to win the future?

Hamel, writing in *Fortune* magazine, strikes exactly the same action-first note. If you really want to face the future, rather than the past, he says, set unreasonable targets. Any target acts as a ceiling on people's ambitions. Set one that they think impossible, and they may surprise themselves – and you: like Jack Welch's people making GE's tubes for X-rays and CT scans, who were told to quadruple tube life, and multiplied it eight times. Never accept 'average industry growth' or some other mediocre standard as the target. If you are not markedly better than average, you shouldn't be in the job.

Second, take a wide view of what constitutes your market. At General Electric, the famous rule – 'Be first or second in your global market, or else' – had been modified by 2000. Units were told to redefine their markets so that their share would come out under 10%. That leaves 90% of the market at which to aim, and is designed to point the management at opportunities beyond the traditional bounds.

Third, managers will move into these extended markets with more energy and enthusiasm if they are creating, not just a business, but a cause. This means pursuing an overall objective which your people can understand and with which they can identify. Intel came out of its crisis by trumpeting its change from a memory company to 'Intel, the microcomputer company'. While this message actually failed to encompass all Intel's activities, the words said it all. They identified the great cause.

Fourth, if you want to do new things, listen to new voices. Charles Handy recommends companies to turn over next-generation strategy to the next generation (see page 40). As Hamel asks, 'Why exclude the very group with the biggest emotional stake in the future – the young – from the process of strategy creation?' He also recommends talking to people at the periphery of the organisation; and getting hold of newcomers and their new thinking right away, before they get hijacked by the old culture.

Fifth, there's no point in listening to new voices unless you are also open to new ideas. Venture capitalists make plenty of mistakes, but failing to listen to innovative propositions is not among them. Few are chosen, but many are called – and listened to. Give everybody a chance to have their ideas considered. Remember that Intel's life-saving, gigantic microprocessor business sprang from the new idea of one man, Ted Hoff, who saw that you could put several chips on the same piece of silicon.

Sixth, forget those capital budgeting rules. People with path-breaking projects very rarely present convincing figures in their business plans (however much the numbers convince the pro-posers themselves). One venture capitalist says he regards business plans as a story about an opportunity, about 'how a committed, passionate person is going to create and capture value'. The investment may well be relatively small. But you should emulate the credo of venture capitalists. Make many bets, and with lofty aims.

The VCs' objective is a tenfold increase in value over five years. They sometimes win far more and thus easily absorb the many inevitable flops. The seventh lesson, though, is that making many bets is not enough: start up many independent units. The case for subdividing your business is now overwhelm-ing. A former hero at the now rightly reviled Enron told Hamel (then an admirer): 'Big businesses will scratch their itch first.' That means concentrating on what you are already doing and giving a lower priority to the new.

As argued throughout this book, your best hope of winning is to spin off the new into new units, with new and loose guide-lines, and a new business model. There is no other effective way. Spinning off has another virtue – the eighth lesson; it helps in opening up the market to talent. Don't go to elaborate lengths to stop people moving. Encourage mobility, but provide the upwardly mobile with abundant opportunities to succeed inside the organisation.

You will have to reward these people accordingly, of course. But that's the ninth point. Nobody will ever end the absurd pay regime, most marked in the US, but with Britain riding fast on the coattails. As a general rule, the regime gives obscene rewards to the undeserving top executives, but underpays people who accomplish real breakthroughs lower down. Ignore the general rule, and establish your own; throw away the salary scales; fit punishment to the crime, reward to the genuine achievement.

Finally, Fusion Managers must learn to think big while acting small. Hamel writes that 'most companies are torn between the majority of their managers, who believe that it is better to be a fast follower than a foolhardy risk taker – and the minority, who argue that to capture new markets a company must be bold'. Fast following is not a good idea: the person you are following will very probably get there first. But bold does not equate with foolhardy, and caution does not equate with conservatism. Have big ambitions for your innovatory experiments, but keep the initial commitment suitably limited.

This is asking a great deal of senior managers who have been brought up on the Ten Commandments listed above. But top managers cannot expect others and the company to change unless they are prepared to change themselves – and to do whatever that takes. The necessity for this personal transformation cannot be evaded. Top managers can no longer manage their own executive lives as they do the business, living in and on the past, and turning their backs on the future.

Grove stresses that the knowledge, skills and expertise of your best people – including you – are as valuable as material resources. Whenever you shift resources from one task to a new challenge, 'you're putting more attention and energy into something, which is wonderful, positive and encouraging'. But you are also subtracting production and managerial resources, and your own time, from other activities.

The natural urge will always be to stick with the familiar, where the risks are known, and the upside limited, rather than to venture into the unfamiliar, where the risks are unquantifiable, but the potential is huge. In the business to consumer area, according to British Telecom's in-house thinker, James Callaghan, there are seven alternative strategies. They offer a rich variety of choice, but all involve radical departures from established channels:

1 www.storefront or 'direct seller'
2 www.mall
3 Virtual megastore
4 Specification takers

5 Online auctions
6 Buyer aggregation
7 Web currency

Taking these in turn, you can sell direct over a website (like Dell), share space with a few others on a 'mall' site (Excite), open or participate in a massive site (Amazon), take orders which you pass on to a supplier (Autobytel), use auctions to bring buyers and sellers together (eBay), aggregate buyers into larger groups to reduce prices (Mercata), or run a kind of trading-stamp operation, in which buyers accumulate 'currency' that can be exchanged for other goods or services (Beenz).

Both Mercato and Beenz, as it happens, are now defunct. But if you sometimes cannot win full value from an unorthodox route to market within an unorthodox business, you certainly can't inside an orthodox one. You need unorthodox people, unorthodox ideas and unorthodox methods. The only orthodox requirement is that you must be prepared, if your pilot project supports the venture, to commit all the resources needed to create success. If you're going the whole way, moving from stores, say, to selling on-line, that means redeploying all the resources you have in order to accomplish a genuine transformation.

Without full resourcing, says Grove, transformation 'turns out to be nothing but an empty cliché'. He adds that 'the most effective way to transform a company is through a series of incremental changes that are consistent with a clearly articulated end-result'. Make up your mind about that end-result, make that truly ambitious and be prepared to go beyond Grove into abrupt, radical change. Then look back at the Ten Commandments and ask which you are prepared to break for the greater good of protecting your future. Do not agonise about your sunk investment. That belongs to the past. It's your new investment that will count.

CHAPTER TWO

virtual virtuality

*Developments and growth in outsourcing pull strongly
towards virtuality*

Business faces a deceptively easy question in the 2000s: to outsource, or not to outsource? The answer seems so obvious.
Companies have no business (literally) undertaking activities
that are not their direct concern. They should find outside
suppliers who provide customers with such peripheral needs.
By definition these specialists will deliver the required goods
and services at lower cost and with greater efficiency as the
result of intelligent concentration and critical mass.

End of story. So today, everybody outsources. Vertical integration *à la* Henry Ford, whose plants imported iron ore at
one end, exported complete cars at the other, and 'insourced'
everything possible in between, is dead. Horizontalism rules.
Modern car companies include complete sub-assemblies in the
bought-in 70% of their products. Even IBM, once Ford-like in
devotion to in-house manufacture and services, abandoned its
faith in the early 1980s, when the PC's famous one-year launch
programme demanded total outsourcing.

In theory, insourcing is slower, costlier, less efficient, and
takes corporate minds off the real 'core' business. The theory,
like all theories, is arguable. But the modern case for outsourcing is not confined to practical arguments. Powerful management ideas spread as great evangelistic causes, for all that they
sometimes diminish into disappointment and disillusion. That
happened to Total Quality Management and Business Process
Reengineering. And, sure enough, outsourcing started along
the same downhill journey with its apotheosis as the Virtual
Corporation.

Such a business contracts out virtually (*le mot juste*) all its activities, reserving only an irreducible core unto its internal self. Nor is this mere theory. Computer giant Sun Microsystems has long practised what the theory preaches, farming out distribution, chip and component manufacture, and servicing, which leaves the crucial design work to Sun – although that, too, can be outsourced successfully. The mouse marketed by Apple (a company repeatedly saved from failure by design brilliance) was actually devised by IDEO, the famous consultancy behind many Silicon Valley innovations.

The Valley, however, is a special case, distinguished by eccentricity and by virtuality which is less planned than inevitable. Like digital watches, personal computers are a 'Mickey Mouse' business. Customers think that they buy from the company which brands the product: but often all the innards come from the same outside sources. Your PC is almost certain to have an Intel microprocessor, and says so ('Intel Inside'). But the monitor, mother-board, chip-set, mouse and other working goodies may well be outsourced, from suppliers who stretch from the Netherlands to Taiwan, Singapore to Scotland. The box is individual, true: but that, too, is made outside.

While outsourcing has mushroomed far beyond the Valley, virtuality hasn't. Like other business religions, it has more gurus than practitioners. The thinkers see their brainchildren, not in narrow, industry-specific terms, but as brand-new visionary concepts that will radically change the business world. The preachers of *The Virtual Corporation* are William H. Davidow and Michael S. Malone. They were not just hymning the cost-effectiveness of using suppliers who are cheaper than your internal resources. They were forecasting a future in which outsourcing animates a transformed organisation:

> To the outside observer, a virtual corporation will appear almost edgeless, the interface between company, suppliers and customers permeable and continuously changing.

That may sound positively ethereal, but the Valley boasts an inordinately successful super-manager who nears the ideal:

Michael Dell. He built the direct-selling Dell on what he calls 'virtual integration'. His 'supplier-partners' send components, etc., on a daily basis. 'Regardless of how long these relationships last,' he says, 'you're basically stitching together a business with partners that are treated as if they're inside the company.' That isn't how most suppliers are treated by most customers: but benefits similar to Dell's are generally available – in theory. They include:

1 Keeping down the numbers and thus management problems of your own labour force.
2 Increasing capacity to grow (Dell: 'If we had to build our own factories for every component of the system, growing at 57% per year just would not be possible').
3 Sharply reducing inventories (and thus carrying costs) by 'just-in-time' delivery of supplies.
4 Cutting lead-times just as sharply, allowing much faster delivery to customers (and strengthening cash flow).
5 Obtaining lower prices and enhancing competitive potential.

As Dell delicately expresses Benefit Number Five, 'supplier-partners' can be used (or fused) in a way that 'creates a lot of value that can be shared between buyer and supplier'. You can identify and insist upon supplier cost reductions which flow into lower charges from them and lower prices (and higher profits) to the customer – you.

Even when companies stop well short of virtuality, you would expect outsourcing, with all that going for it, to have recorded considerable successes. Yet in 1996 PA Consulting Group reported that over half of outsourcing companies studied had not achieved the expected gains. As for the rest, 39% won (if that's the right word) merely mediocre results. A tiny 5% of PA's companies had matched Dell in achieving truly high payoffs.

This raises two disturbing possibilities. Either outsourcing is not, for most companies, what it's cracked up to be. Or the potential is real, but execution is inept. That second explanation is certainly true of the great majority of firms, which treat out-sourcing as a short-term economy measure and not (like Sun and Dell) as a carefully considered long-term strategy.

The laggards may not even know that strategy is at stake. Simply handing over security, or cleaning, or catering, or vehicle requirements to specialist professionals doesn't seem to raise great problems. A maker of mobile phones (or breakfast cereals for that matter) shouldn't waste its time on developing expert-ise, and piling up overheads, in such areas. Even so, there are industries where maintenance is much more vital than manage-ment realises – Railtrack's disasters, compounded by the Hatfield crash, followed from outsourcing track inspection and repair to contractors.

In practice, even 'safe' areas like cleaning and security can prove decidedly unsafe if contractors fall below required stan-dards. The lesson applies to all procurement. Price is not the ultimate factor: 'VM' is crucial, getting necessary Value for Money. A clean, secure plant is more important than saving half of what, anyway, is a small proportion of total costs. But getting 100% performance from contractors is not easy at the best of times: and the times are worst if the contractor has underbid for the business.

With routine outsourcing, contracts run out soon, or can be terminated with relative ease. But that doesn't apply to today's massive outsourcing agreements in information technology, where many years and hundreds of millions are involved. The outsourcing company is effectively locked into the relationship. If performance is unsatisfactory, or unpredictable technological change obsoletes existing systems, what then? If leading com-puter services firms are so reliable, moreover, why have several of their high-profile public-sector projects come so severely adrift?

True, IT doesn't look like a 'core competence' – save for IT firms. But as Percy Barnevik once observed when CEO of ABB, the engineering conglomerate, 'All companies are in the IT business today.' What was true then, before the World Wide Web opened shop (in 1993), is trebly true today. In addition to core competences, in other words, there are core facilities. While companies are surely wise to outsource Internet design and installation to experienced specialists, they are most unwise to leave e-strategy to outsiders.

As Ronan McIvor notes in *Business Strategy Review*, 'There is a risk that, by losing control of key activities, the company will restrict its capacity to exploit new opportunities in the future.' He adds that, 'In a fast-changing industry, the definition of core business must be revisited on a continuous basis.' Today, most industries are fast-changing, or faster-changing than they were. McIvor, however, was thinking of a specific company, nick-named 'Telequip', which is in the ferociously changeable game of telecoms equipment: McIvor's study of Telequip convinced him that even well-considered strategic outsourcing runs into 'messy reality'.

That includes the threat of losing skills if you transfer problem activities to others. Political considerations are another key fac-tor: the attitude of your own employees stops you from rigidly outsourcing to lower-cost external suppliers – companies dare not risk too much internal opposition. Straight cost compari-sons, anyway, can mislead. Deeper analysis may show that outsourcing increases total costs – goodbye, savings. But the strongest lesson of Telequip is the last: 'Misconceptions of a company's core business and a lack of cooperation between business functions [many outsourced] impede the achievement of a company's core business.'

Witness Sir Clive Sinclair, who can claim to have invented the virtual company. Some marketers thought this innovation even more remarkable than the digital watches, pocket calcu-lators and personal computers which Sinclair invented and out-sourced. But their poor quality became legendary, and all three businesses disappeared. All subsequent experience has only con-firmed that a Dell-type, near-virtual 'core business', which runs a fluctuating network of the very best outside sources, is tough to establish and harder still to run well.

The task is made impossible by failure to tackle obvious issues which arise for all outsourcers. First, never assume that out-sourcing brings automatic benefits. The business case for each outside contract has to be carefully made, with the cons studied as rigorously as the pros. The overwhelming disappointments reported to PA Consulting almost certainly reflect excessive expectations more than incompetent execution – although, as noted, the latter certainly occurs. It is more likely if the outsourcer mismanages the thorny issue of control: the second issue.

The ideal supplier partnership is just that: a partnership. Guru Tom Peters describes how his favourite supplier of plastic mouldings, Nypro, became an integral, integrated part of Johnson & Johnson's contact-lens business. Control was achieved by making the outsourced operation effectively a joint venture. Without such closeness, outsourcers must strike a delicate balance between genuine trust (without which you should never sign on the dotted line) and eternal vigilance. The latter requires a constant flow of accurate information about the fulfilment of your requirements.

The third issue is strategic change. Even if the Virtual Corporation is a retreating dream, the trend is towards still less vertical integration. In mobile phones, even the mighty Ericsson in 2001 went outside (in a futile bid) to rescue its profits. In autos, some suppliers are manufacturing sub-assemblies right next door to the customer's assembly lines. In one South American market, Ford has even outsourced complete assembly. A whole new breed of manufacturing conglomerates is growing rapidly, mostly serving IT customers, and offering expertise, not in specific components, but in the management and delivery of outsourced production for many customers.

Here the major argument for outsourcing rests more on economies of scale than on specialisation itself. In that situation, outsourcing is even more attractive for medium-sized companies than for large ones, whose scale economies are built-in. But outsourcing also has a major hidden disadvantage. It obviously makes the Holy Grail of differentiation more difficult to hunt. How can you be truly different from and better than a competitor who has the same parts assembled by the same contract manufacturer?

The issue is one of supply and supplier relationships. As reported earlier, virtual and near-virtual companies like Dell take their outside suppliers deep inside. They will only be expelled if technological change or inadequate performance force the virtual customer's hand. The essence of this new 'real-time supply system' has been well described by Microsoft's Bill Gates: 'capturing and analyzing data in real time can create an information cycle between a business, its partners and its customers that can reshape a company's entire behaviour'.

The leading-edge customers are putting pressure on suppliers' behaviour: in response to the customer's up-to-the-minute sales information, they must operate a 'just-in-time' system, supplying the goods on demand when and where they are demanded. The advantage for the suppliers is that they need only make what is actually being sold: the gain for the customer is fast response. Both sides benefit from lower costs, while the information passed to the supplier is invaluable for planning future products and production.

When computer speaks direct to computer, this new supply chain can be automated. The intelligent computer at the customer end responds to production schedules and inventory records and arranges for delivery of the required goods. The equally bright computer at the supplier's establishment keeps note of the customer's needs or production schedule and orders the correct mix of supplies in the right sequence, just in time. And all this starts from turning a dumb purchase order into an intelligent one, and building on that change as simply and cogently as possible.

There's a flip side, however. In Shikhar Ghosh's unarguable statement in the *Harvard Business Review*: 'The opportunity for those companies that move first to establish electronic channels is a threat to those that do not.' He cites electronic equipment giant Cisco: ten of its largest customers 'are installing new software in their own computers to tie their inventory and procurement systems to Cisco's systems'. The purchasing linkages give their possessors a serious economic advantage.

That means there is no alternative to joining the game, and not only because giant companies like General Electric are applying pressure on suppliers via their purchasing websites. As Ghosh says, 'Ultimately the risk of Internet commerce for established businesses is not from digital tornadoes but from digital termites'. That's true in the digital business itself, where relatively small PC distributors are using the Web to muscle into the territory of their retailers, who in turn are using electronic ordering to make own-brand computers.

'Value chains' in the affected industries (for which, eventually, read 'all industries') are being remade, pirated, taken apart. The car giants will find Internet direct sellers stealing their end-markets and their margins. The giants in turn will seek greater economies by integrating their purchasing with their suppliers still more: the major car industry have already linked arms to route their purchases through collective websites. From every direction, new forces are at work to turn cyberspace into the world's greatest market. Suppliers will find no hiding place from the still unfolding, gigantic consequences.

The battle for strategic dominance will necessarily take precedence over simplistic considerations of internal costs and convenience. Maybe the fashion pendulum will swing back towards the vertical – which makes it even more important to use outsourcing, not as a knee-jerk reaction, but as the proven (which means that you have to prove it) best course for all terms: long, medium and short.

CHAPTER THREE

captivating the customer

What would a fiery new entrant do to win and retain your customers?

Customer strategy is the only strategy. Product and producer-driven strategies are dead in theory – though they haven't altogether died in practice. Few businesses, even in retail, let alone sectors further removed from customers, have reinvented themselves to achieve a truly customer-centric business system. Such a system (in theory) starts with the customer, reworks all processes back from the customer, and aims them towards achieving excellence in the customer's eyes.

Considerable and very clever technology is required to delight customers so thoroughly. That technology is available to every-body else, in fact. But to make the most of the hardware and software, you have to manage your business differently. The object of such a customer-centric system is to deeply understand the customers. Then you can . . .

- give them what they want . . .
- how, where and when they want it . . .
- at a profitable price that they are happy to pay.

All the rest of marketing won't make up for failures on these key strategic elements. Only Fusion Managers can win the day. Not only must the technology support the service, and the product support the promise, but quality must support the 'customer value proposition', and 'human resources' policies must support the customer focus: i.e., if you want contented customers, first get contented staff. Incremental improvement, moreover, is not enough. Nor are excellent systems. The three strategic elements above must all be served – and not lip-served.

Lip-service, however is what happens. 'The customer is King' is a noble mantra, mouthed by senior managers in every industry. True in theory, it is an ignoble lie in most companies. The customers have moved to stage centre in management thought and talk, but in real life they remain, not monarchs, but second-class citizens – even though a whole new discipline, Customer Relationship Management (CRM), has been born and nourished by heavy corporate spending.

Consultants also plot value chains backwards from the supposedly satisfied customer, and work out those irresistible customer value propositions. That doesn't help when a confusing orgy of direct mail descends on customers, willy-nilly. Or when 'call centres' (or even multimedia 'customer contact centres') mushroom in unlikely locales to serve the customer better – and service simply gets worse.

In the much-trumpeted, new, customer-oriented culture, the Internet is meant to help by providing better, faster access and response. By and large, it doesn't. Companies actually selling over the Net appear, according to an explosive new survey, to be even less responsive in cyberspace than on earth. The PLAUT business and technology consultancy, investigating returns policy and performance, found that only 15% of surveyed e-retailers offered excellent service. The rest provided after-sales treatment that ranged from the mediocre to the abysmal.

Service failure is not skin-deep. Its causes go far into the heart of management performance. The mistakes and mishaps are never isolated, unfortunate examples. They invariably spring from defects of the system and those who design and supervise that system. The great American quality guru, W. Edwards Deming, had it right: 85% of all defects are down to management – not to the workers.

No doubt, airline managements, for example, claim to strain nerve and sinew to serve customers better in the skies. Back on earth, though, you sometimes can't contact their salespeople at all. Everybody has shared this depressing experience. Call centres refer you uselessly around the press-button menus, tell you that 'all our operators are busy' (as if you didn't know) and that your call 'is being held in a queue' – which you also know full and furiously well.

Adding patronising insult to injury, an automated voice may tell you that 'your custom is valuable to us', thank you for your patience (as if you had any alternative), and even (this is a major airline) boast that the endless wait is down to the success of their latest wondrous promotion. All this is laced together, naturally, by hideous music. Try to ring the airline's head office to scream for help, and you find, bizarrely, that nothing is listed, only an 0345 number – which takes you straight back into what has been justly nicknamed Voicemail Hell.

All customer relationships rest on personal contact between the buyer and the seller. There are sound reasons, apart from lower cost, for automating that contact as much as possible. But, badly used, the systems ring down an iron wall between customers and suppliers. This is strange, since the supplier's staff are also human (despite their often inhumane behaviour), and they also shop and buy. Top managements must surely sometimes be infuriated by other people's awful systems. Why do they persist with their own?

The answer runs deep into the realities of management. Executives talk about customers as if they are some strange and separate breed, described with demeaning phrases like 'punters' and 'bums on seats'. The executive bums are similarly insensitive to the most important customers of all – their own staff. These customers depend on top management's service for sensible strategic direction, the effective operation of efficient systems, and proactive treatment as humans, not as 'human resources'.

Hard statistical evidence has established a clear link between three types of satisfaction: employee, customer and shareholder. Satisfy the first, and the customers love you more: investors follow suit as sales and profits duly rise. But many managers, even retailers, whose customers are highly visible, prefer the ivory tower to the store floor. They hatch their absurdities (some of them manifest, like Sainsbury's low-price advertising disaster with John Cleese) behind closed doors.

Impervious to suggestions and criticisms (often powerful)

from lower staff, and to the potential huge contribution of middle managers, the hatchers are hardly likely to listen to the customers who are supposed to be kings (and queens). Yet Andy Grove, chairman of Intel, emphasises that customer complaints, 'both internal and external', are 'a very important source of information'. That's patently true. So how chief executives answer personally addressed complaints (or don't) speaks volumes.

Too many respond like the telecoms boss who received a heartfelt moan beginning, 'The service you provide to customers is awful. I hope that this letter will not prove my point all over again by being entrusted to the customer service people for response.' It was, of course. Properly used, the Internet (like other high-tech systems) genuinely can improve responsiveness. That won't happen with a website (an airline again), which lists a 'dedicated' queue-up helpline, with neither names nor e-mail address for any customer service humans.

The sad experiences suggest that senior managers seldom take the elementary step of anonymously sampling their own service and services. If they are afraid of uncovering a can of worms, that's probably what they will find – and what they should always investigate and eradicate, digging right down to the underlying causes. Incommunicado bosses who delegate customer care to underlings, and never check their miserable performance, are themselves infected by systemic diseases that only they can cure. That vicious circle is everybody's problem.

It can only be broken by truly 'giving them what they want', which means finding out what the customer wants by two means: inspired imagination, which anticipates changing demand for goods and services; and simply 'listening' to the customers. That requires no inspiration. But their perceptions are the essential guide to setting and meeting quality standards and achieving excellent and vital customer retention.

My preferred consultancy work is based on talking to people in unstructured, anonymous interviews to investigate the 'perception gap' between what top managements believe to be true, and what their 'constituents' actually think (customers, employees, managers, suppliers, opinion formers). The perception gap is always great – far too great for any kind of comfort.

The research in this area is convincing, ample and not to be ignored. Customers who rate your service 'excellent' or describe themselves as 'very satisfied' are six times more likely to buy from you again than those who think that service 'good' or who are just 'satisfied'. Those are Xerox figures, but AT&T research is just as cogent. If the customers think your service is excellent, all but 10% of your market share is secure – without any need for promotion. A 'good' rating, however, sees 40% of the share (i.e., the customers) depart. Good is just not good enough in this difficult game.

Of the 26 general retailers listed by *Fortune* magazine in April 2001, ten lost money for their investors in the previous year. There were also ten losers out of the 19 food and drug stores. Two dozen of the 54 speciality retailers also failed this elementary test. Over in Britain, the most respected, sector-leading chains, Marks & Spencer and J. Sainsbury, have been humiliated by the surging rise of Tesco. The perception gap in both cases was huge: management did not understand, or even believe, that their self-congratulation was not matched by customer attitudes.

The effective strategic response to the perception gap is simply stated. Be First, Be Fast, Be Fanatical. The battle, as ever, generally goes to the strong, and the race to the swift. The great change is that in today's and tomorrow's markets swift and strong have become synonymous. Big no longer automatically means best when the small, fanatical, fast pioneer can defeat the largest incumbent in almost any market. Fixed assets have become deadweights for companies faced by opposition that has nothing fixed, but which can still rapidly build and consolidate leading market shares – as with the 'infomediators'.

These are business-to-business exchanges, whose trade forecast for 2003 is a gigantic $1.4 trillion. The exchange websites simply publish details of all supplies available in a given sector (steel, paper, chemicals, transport, etc.,), charging a relatively small commission on the trades. Third-party trade over the Web is only part of the picture. Great businesses are either setting up their own purchasing sites (GE), or combining with competitors (like the world's car firms).

If buying over the Web is appropriate, why would anybody choose the conventional route – dearer, slower and more cumbersome? Conventional suppliers are plainly under great threat from the Net. Middlemen will be cut out (just as companies like Dell have excised them); and the prices and margins of suppliers will come under general pressure. The only escape is to focus on the customer in the ways recommended here: to provide the purchaser with a reason or reasons to buy from you that transcend price. In other words, you need a customer strategy that is different, direct and powerful.

That is where Fanaticism comes in. It demands the exercise of self-challenge. If you don't challenge your customer strategy, somebody else will: very probably, a new competitor. Never stop looking critically at your business, and changing it – radically if need be. Stability is far less important, given that customers are now so volatile. If you don't stay with your customers, they will not stay with you.

Too many companies have yet to enter this new mindset and escape from the old one. They still try to serve the customers who they, the suppliers, want, how, where and when they, the suppliers, want to supply them, and at the prices they, the suppliers, want to charge. In conventional hands, the approach is obviously wrong. Paradoxically, however, that degree of customer control is what results from a successful, innovative, customer-leading, customer-centric strategy. The secret of this exercise for the Fusion Manager lies in the power and speed with which you generate and apply new ideas.

Speed is needed as well as power under the rules of the new innovation game. The new rules mean that you simply haven't got time to take your time. Traditional internal processes, deliberate, thorough and slow, are too deliberate and too slow. If you really are customer-centric, you must be geared to rapid change and experiment. The revolutionary company constantly tries new approaches, develops those which work, and discards those that do not – a simple strategy, but highly effective against conservatives who prefer things as they are.

Fanatics look continually for evidence that they are not selling the right things, nor supplying them in the most effective way. They seek ways of becoming the lowest cost producer, while staying fully aware that they must match or outperform their best competitor, not on price alone, but on every aspect that matters to the customer. They constantly open up wider markets, geographically and in applications. They change the direction of thrust to retain the edge which makes customers buy from them rather than from the competition. Above all, they revise and reform their strategies and tactics to ensure that in the years ahead, they will still be highly effective in all the above, vital ways.

Thus, according to *Business Week*, Dell has a new customer-service plan: 'Use the Internet to automate and customise service, in much the same way that Dell streamlined and customised PC production'. Non-corporate customers were to get personalised Web pages under these plans, which unite 'communications links over speedy private networks and the vast Internet'. The company hopes to answer tricky service questions from customers 'with the lightning speed only the Net can deliver'. Every customer already has an individual file, which could be expanded for 'a new kind of direct-service model', in which company and customer are in continuous contact.

Cyberspace in such ways opens up whole new vistas of innovation. The Internet opportunities, though, are being seized by newcomers, not by large established companies. Is this inevitable? It is, if managements shy away from cannibalisation (which means sacrificing the old to capitalise on the new); and place present profit ahead of future payoffs. Being good, even very good, at serving the customers you already have is not enough. Existing customers will desert if you are not also satisfying the new.

The ultimate answer is zero-based strategy. Zero-based budgeting starts from the assumption that the company doesn't need the activity under scrutiny. Zero-based strategy starts from the assumption that nobody needs you or your business. The question is this: if you were a fiery new entrant in the sector, what would you do to win and retain customers – in effect, what would you do to beat yourself? That is a revolutionary mindset. But it is also the way to win.

CHAPTER FOUR

urging the entrepreneurs

Why Fusion Managers must be both adept innovators and masterful managers

Managers are constantly asked to behave like entrepreneurs. The other way round, entrepreneurs are often asked to behave like managers. The manager is supposed to develop the drive and opportunism of the entrepreneur, and the entrepreneur is expected to learn the methodical disciplines of the manager. The pressures on both have become more intense as the world economy has become more competitive, more entrepreneurial, more demanding.

This is a prime arena for Fusion Management. The manager can no more afford to dispense with entrepreneurial skills and attributes than the entrepreneur can succeed without managerial ability. This fusion has often been achieved in the past by the simple device of partnership. The entrepreneur takes a manager on board to supply the necessary management power, as Bill Gates did Steve Ballmer. But today the Fusion Manager must be both adept innovator and masterful manager.

How real is the difference, anyway? The best study of *Innovation and Entrepreneurship* is by Peter Drucker. He writes that entrepreneurs are not capitalists, nor investors, nor employers, although this is highly arguable – especially the last. Also, part of entrepreneurship is knowing how to raise, deploy and invest capital. Drucker is on sure ground, however, in arguing that 'everyone who can face up to decision-making can learn to be an entrepreneur and to behave entrepreneurially'.

But if that is so, why do managers have so much trouble adopting the required behaviours – even though they are constantly urged to do so? The favoured explanation is that entrepreneurship involves taking risks. While that is true, so does all human activity. The risk run when taking an entrepreneurial decision is no different from the non-entrepreneurial risk of, say, offering somebody a job.

The classic definition of the entrepreneur is somebody who 'shifts economic resources out of an area of lower and into an area of higher productivity and greater yield'. That is hardly a risky proposition: the risk lies in a different definition, offered by Drucker – 'the entrepreneur always searches for change, responds to it, and exploits it as an opportunity'.

The crucial word here is 'change'. Change carries the risk that your second state will be worse than the first. That is, you launch a new, innovative product: if it succeeds, all is well: if it fails, your job may fail, too. The calculation is the same one that tilts the balance of executive decisions towards 'No' rather than 'Go'. Approval commits the approver to a new course of action. 'No' preserves the status quo.

The obvious answer, which is to create an atmosphere that encourages positive behaviour and discourages the negative variety, is also supposed to be very difficult to achieve. That, however, is a matter of perception. Most managers, for example, would believe it risky in the extreme to buy companies in a flash, as many as three in three weeks, without doing any more 'due diligence' than the strictly limited time allows. In fact, that sounds imprudent to the point of irresponsibility – but it didn't in cyberspace.

That kind of shooting from the hip became incumbent on what *Fortune* magazine called 'e-CEOs', the men (and a woman or two) who run the revolutionary Internet companies – businesses like Dell, Amazon, Intuit, Cisco, Double Click, Yahoo! and CNET. Note two things about this list. First, the companies are American – not a European or Asian in sight. Second, the range of activity is vast: from PCs to personal finances, books to Internet routers.

There's a third point. Few readers will be able to identify all seven businesses. Yet these are already significant companies, in many cases after only a short span of life – and that life has continued through and after the stock-market catastrophe. The implications of this phenomenon of high-speed rise to market power can pass business people by: rather like the plane that travels overhead so quickly that you don't notice its passing.

Try this quiz: how long did it take radio to reach 50 million consumers? And TV? And the Internet? The answers are 38 years, 13 years and four years. Small wonder that in five years (1994–99) Internet users expanded from three million to 163 million, and counting – superfast counting. In short, the world has never seen a phenomenon of this size and speed.

Fortune is right to detect that the executives at the epicentre are forced to manage very differently from the conventional pattern. Where the magazine's excellent analysis falls short is that all executives, and not just e-executives, will have to shift lifestyle and workstyle in this same, highly entrepreneurial direction. The article's 'old model' manager is actually a rather flattering picture. To fit this bill, you have to be:

- encouraging
- alert
- cordial
- clearly focused
- fast-moving
- intolerant of ambiguity
- sound in judgment.

Many executives don't fit the description, either in part or whole, however much they would like to. Their weak spots, according to *Fortune*, are that they do not fully understand the new technology of information, and its challenge makes them nervous. The e-CEO, of course, is wised up as well as wired up and responds to technological challenge with fanatical enthusiasm. But it's the non-IT characteristics that define the difference between the old model and the new. Answer yes or no to these questions:

1 Do you 'evangelise' about your company and its products and services – both internally and externally?
2 Are you aroused to the extent of competitive paranoia

by threats and actual challenges from rivals new and old?

3 Are you 'brutally frank' in your views and criticisms?

4 Are you intensely focused on the key business and strategy of the organisation?

5 Do you take decisions and act at a speed that's near to instantaneous?

6 Do you like ambiguity and feel comfortable in unclear situations?

7 Is your judgment good?

Seven Yes answers clearly establish your entrepreneurial credentials. It's only the last question that describes both the old and new model managers. But even here there's a difference. The new variety of executive exercises that sound judgment on the run. This probably makes little difference to the quality of decision. But the slower-moving manager's loss of time, of course, can't be recovered. And the faster events are moving, the less you can afford the loss of time.

'Wait and see' has become an unviable strategy. By the time you have finished waiting to see the future, it may be too late to act: some more entrepreneurial spirit will have seized and cornered the opportunity. Some of the opportunities seized by entrepreneurial e-companies follow below. Note that they include internal initiatives. Managers are accustomed to thinking of entrepreneurs as outer-directed. So they are. But you can often accomplish wonders for the external customer by interior innovations.

1 Dell opens a 'Premier Page' website for individual corporate customers (5000-plus in the US). In return for customised, individual service, these customers give Dell $5 million of business a day.

2 Ford Motor places 500,000 'product design resources, production management tools and strategic information assets' on its intranet, and gives each car and truck model its own site 'to track design, production, quality control and delivery processes'.

3 Pitney-Bowes links up with suppliers over the Web for just-in-time delivery, and reckons that one day it will need no inventory at all.

4 Sun Microsystems uses its intranet to get recruitment referrals from current workers.

5 NextCard has used Net advertising to sign up $30 million of new Visa balances in a single month, cutting the costs of acquiring its balances by 70% in a year, and garnering twice the industry norm per average cardholder balance.

6 Federal Express uses the Web to keep customers informed about their shipments and to take orders, and now handles more calls over the Web than over its phone service.

7 Cisco gets complete reports on revenue, margins, orders, discounts and top ten customers every day the next day – which in theory allows executives of this big corporation to stay in tight control while remaining entrepreneurial.

Preserving and developing that 'entrepreneurial spirit' is what it's all about. How can you get a conventional business to act like the e-corporation? In the first place, note that there's nothing truly revolutionary about any of the seven innovations mentioned above. Every company collects the same numbers as Cisco, keeps a check on shipments, advertises for new customers, recruits employees, liaises with suppliers, coordinates design, engineering and production (or tries to), and pays special attention to its major customers. The seven firms above were simply looking for and finding better ways of carrying out basic functions.

That's the guiding rule of Fusion Management and its arch exponent, the 4S company – Single-minded about its core business, Speedy in its response to all stimuli, Sociable in its maintenance of friendly relations, partnerships and alliances inside and outside the firm, and Shallow or flat in its structure. It minimises layers, bypassing command and control structures to enable all three other S-functions. You need all four: miss out only one, and the whole edifice will tumble down.

You couldn't ask for stronger proof than Dell Computer's thumping defeat of Compaq, which led directly to the latter's merger with Hewlett-Packard in 2002. The consequence of Compaq's inability to match either Dell's direct marketing model or the management technology that underpinned those direct sales was decisive. Dell was Speedier, more Sociable (with IT-enabled special relationships with suppliers and, as noted above, with customers), Shallower in structure and more Single-Minded – especially after Compaq's acquisition of Digital Equipment.

This deal was hailed as a strategic masterstroke. But it lumbered Compaq with a monumental task for which it had neither aptitude nor experience: the management of a mammoth merger, complicated in this instance by the fact that Digital was a tired company that had defied three major internal efforts to reform its culture and revive its once splendid success.

I've often cited with great approval General Gus Pagonis, the largely unsung hero of the Desert War whose logistics achievements enabled the left-hook through the sands that shattered Iraqi resistance. Pagonis opined in a *Harvard Business Review* interview that the worst thing a company can do is to reorganise. The costs of disruption often outweigh any benefits. Three reorganisations multiply the costs and the risks – and, anyway, demonstrate that reorganisation isn't working.

Nobody in management practises what Pagonis preaches, though. 'When in doubt, reorganise' has been a sacred governing principle of management down the ages. In this age, it's adopted by Old Economy and New Economy companies alike. Thus Bill Gates and his president, Steve Ballmer, genuinely saw the need to shift the company from product focus to customer focus. That's why in 1999 they launched 'Vision Version 2', a massive reorganisation which involved stepping back and letting the heads of eight new product groups, all focused round the customer, make key decisions themselves.

By making all major decisions and a host of minor ones, Gates and Ballmer had slowed down responses and created dissatisfaction – not only among employees, but customers. In the mid-1990s, Giga research found that Microsoft customers were very dissatisfied, and that some would 'do anything to get away'. Microsoft people were typical of managers in general: they refused to accept such evidence. Like IBM in the 1980s, they wouldn't listen to messengers who brought bad news.

A vital difference between the entrepreneur and the manager is that the latter pays lip-service to the customer, while the former truly meets the customer's requirements. The entrepreneurial manager, moreover, listens to what the customers say, seeks out criticism, never suppresses it – and acts on what has been heard. Microsoft has been trying to do precisely this, but it goes against the corporate grain.

The Microsoft life-cycle is typical. It runs from entrepreneurial to managerial and then to strenuous attempts to become entrepreneurial again. That third stage occurs when, as at Microsoft, the original markets become saturated. The first temptation is to try to screw more revenue from the market, whether the customers like it or not. To bolster its revenue growth, Microsoft duly resorted to 'conduct unbecoming' – charging more to existing customers, while giving them less.

The true entrepreneur, knowing better, seeks to provide new products and/or services to the customers already served, and to find new buyers for both old and new offerings. There are growth opportunities galore in Microsoft's markets, but they do not arise from the PC operating systems and tied applications that have powered the company's surge. According to Ron Enderle, a Giga vice president, the age of the personal computer is drawing to an end. 'Appliances' will take over, meaning phones and palm-top computers that connect with the Internet and set-top boxes that will do the same. That shifts control of the market to the service provider – and away from Microsoft and Intel.

In this turbulent e-world, nothing is fixed for long – and that is the world in which all managers are compelled to seek their futures. You cannot build change on unchanged foundations. That doesn't make a case for the classic reorganisation, in which job titles, responsibilities and jobs are shuffled and reshuffled in a deadly serious game of musical chairs. The organisation, and the methods of those at the top, have to be fluid and fluent, able to adapt organically to achieve changed purposes.

That's the typical mode of the entrepreneurial business. The structured reorganisation is characteristic of the corpocracy, whose chains of command act like leg-fetters on any would-be entrepreneurs within. That's no way to get the right answers to three tough questions which Gates asked himself:

1 Are we making what customers want and working on the products and technologists they will want in future?
2 Are we staying ahead of all our competitors?
3 What don't our customers like about what we do, and what are we doing about it?

Organisational change should only stem from the answers. They will tell you whether the company is set up effectively to achieve its goals: and where the organisation must adapt to eliminate its failures. It's common, but not inevitable, for the management and the methods built by entrepreneurial success to eventually solidify and become deadweights. The original entrepreneur starts from scratch, and that is the solution and the test for manager/entrepreneurs: to restart the business as if from scratch.

CHAPTER FIVE

emulating the e-economy

How to add new dimensions to the old business of being an entrepreneur

Much depends on what conclusions managers draw from the utter collapse of the dot.com boom, and the partial collapse of the dot.com businesses. Those who conclude (and there will be plenty of them) that the Internet really doesn't change everything should take a second look at the evidence. Sure, a large number of dot.com businesses failed, and failed abjectly. But, as noted on page 11, so do most start-ups (90% on some estimates). And these were start-ups with a vengeance.

The mistakes made by the lost dreamers did not include the dream itself. The opportunity of the Internet is real. The risk is the risk of all enterprise – that you'll do the wrong thing, or do the right thing badly. It's perfectly true that you can avoid that risk by doing nothing. But nothing leads to nothing – and the managements which have pulled back from their investments in the e-future (including Rupert Murdoch, the pre-eminently canny media tycoon) risk being proven none too canny in time.

It's Fusion Management again. The need is to combine the venturesome spirit of the new entrepreneurs with the disciplined systems of the old establishment. The digital baby is too big and growing too fast to be thrown out. Fusion demands keeping both baby and bathwater, for even the primary changes now unfolding impact any business in three ways that go deep into their cores:

- First, you can carry out essential internal activities in much more efficient and economical ways.

76

- Second, you can achieve similar benefits in your contacts and communications with the outside world.
- Third, you can set up wholly new entrepreneurial businesses, or radically reshape an existing business to widen its reach and develop new streams of profit.

As an example of the first, elementary type of change, you can replace printed internal directories with an intranet that not only saves printing bills, but provides a continuously and cheaply updated listing with far more functionality – for instance, you can find out where the people in the directory are that day, what their department does, to whom they report, etc. This simple stuff must become universal.

The second type of change, impacting the outside world, affects everything from marketing information to processing orders and payments. The activities concerned can be speeded up and made more effective by IP (internet protocol) technology. One of the biggest areas affected is purchasing. By combining with others in the same industry, or setting up your own purchasing site, or using one of the many exchange sites, you can make enormous savings in transaction costs (30–70%) and great gains in speed. Any sophisticated company will move in this direction.

But the transformation in routine internal and external processes is not where the greatest gains lie. The big bonanzas must come in the third change category, business creation and transformation. What's happening is a rerun, over a far shorter timespan, of the earlier development of information technology. The computer age began with number-crunching, moved on to systems like airplane reservations, then to integrated process control – and finally to transformation of the business.

That last stage was in relative infancy when the mainframe and the minis – the mainstays of the earlier revolution – were overtaken by the PC and the Internet. At last it became possible to fuse all aspects of the organisation, from the individual desktop to the boardroom, from design to customer satisfaction and service, from information to implementation. The problem remained the same: to transform the managers who alone can lead business transformation.

This isn't a problem that troubles the young, especially those driven by dreams of success. Once, students flooded to the Harvard Business School for MBA passports into top consultancies, Wall Street investment banks and blue-chip companies. Instruction in scientific management was the order of the day. But webwise graduates wanted, instead, to develop their skills as entrepreneurs and hone their business plans, ready for a leap into the deceptively golden waters of e-flotations.

Two of these grads, runners-up in the School's Business Plan Contest, raised a stunning $48 million in venture capital. The pair designed their website, Suppliermarket.com, to give industrial buyers one-stop shopping, posting requests for price quotes for items like screws, fasteners and packaging. The idea was to match the quotes with the capabilities of registered suppliers, host a bidding process – and pocket 2% on the transactions.

That's cheap at the price, judging by the experience of one user, Simmons, which saved $400,000 on polyethylene film used to protect its well-known mattresses. The transaction took just 30 days. But what did the young CEO and his president, whose Suppliermarket baby soared to 100 employees in six months, learn from their Harvard alma mater? 'Our objective', they say, 'was to create a long-term sustainable company that values integrity, respect, honesty, commitment, teamwork and loyalty.'

And so, no doubt, say all of them, although in this case long-term hardly applied. After a year or so, Suppliermarket sold out to Ariba, one of the business-to-business leaders, for $580 million in shares. It has to be said that the Suppliermarket model sounded more immediately rewarding than other would-be stars from the HBS. They included GetConnected, founded by two girls whose on-line service was designed to help consumers to get connections to the Internet that best suit their purpose and purses. Then there was eFrenzy, whose business plan involved access to valuable services such as house-cleaning, garden care, tax preparation, moving, etc.

That might not sound too valuable a service in itself. But this start-up website, which had 80 employees before even opening its electronic doors for business, seemed to be neither up nor running in May 2002, whereas GetConnected could boast an imposing list of customers and (just as important) investors. Note that there's nothing special about these three businesses, apart from their use of the Web. Customers have been getting their lawns tended, buying screws, getting best-buy advice and so on for decades.

According to Professor at the School, Amar Bhidé of Columbia Business School, author of *The Origin and Evolution of New Businesses*, this is par for the course. He found that successful start-ups begin with commonplace, not very original ideas – 'ideas that are, at best, minor modifications of somebody else's idea'. This ties in well with my own research into hot 'new' products. They are almost all covered by what I have called 'The Seven Satisfiers'.

The winning products studied did not fit the usual idea of great innovations – wondrous breakthroughs of inspired tech-nology and brilliant leaps into the unknown. That applied to only one of the Seven Satisfiers. The products fitted one or other of these descriptions. They . . .

1 Met an unfulfilled need . . . or . . .
2 Overcame disadvantages in established products . . . or . . .
3 Filled gaps in otherwise well-served markets . . . or . . .
4 Extended proven lines or presented them in new formats . . . or . . .
5 Exploited technological breakthroughs . . . or . . .
6 Transferred established successes to other markets . . . or . . .
7 Supplied more economical ways of satisfying needs that were being met more expensively.

Just as new products do not live up to their mythology, nor do the start-up pioneers. This person is commonly supposed to be, wrote Daniel Penrice in *New Business*, 'a highly creative, fiercely single-minded individual who combines (somewhat paradoxically) great vision and foresight with a heroic appetite for risk'. If that were true, ordinary people would have to pack up immediately. Bhidé's findings are therefore highly encouraging. This is a game that anybody can play, because . . . 'most entrepreneurs begin with mundane ideas, initially risk few or none of their own resources, and rely heavily on their ability to react to unforeseeable events'.

So you do not require great creativity, bold risk-taking, and exceptional powers of vision – at least, not at the start-up stage. 'What does make a difference above and beyond all else', according to Bhidé, is having an entrepreneur's 'tolerance for ambiguity.' These people are prepared to exploit opportunities 'that other rational persons ought to want to pursue but frequently don't'. That explains why people working in established or large organisations have such trouble in adopting entrepreneurial ways. They don't like, and find it hard to tolerate, situations where they cannot anticipate or quantify risks and rewards. The entrepreneurial type is exactly the opposite.

Moreover, managers tend to take a cut-and-dried, black-and-white approach to issues. That is the source of many mistakes, some ruinous. Andy Grove of Intel avoids the trap by following an essentially simple approach to decision-making.

- First, you have totally free discussion, uninhibited by rank, seniority or any other factor that has nothing to do with ability to contribute.
- Second, you make sure that the decision is taken and expressed with total clarity.
- Third, all those involved must accept the decision and act accordingly.
- Fourth (and equally important), if you find you have made a mistake, go back to the beginning and start (with free discussion) all over again.

Demonstrating the fourth principle, a start-up named Factor Direct originally offered direct-mail services to non-profit organisations. When that didn't work (because the non-profits wouldn't risk spending the large sums involved with a mere start-up), the founders changed tack. They moved on to success-fully provide telemarketing. You could put this willingness to switch under the heading of 'open-mindedness', which Bhidé ranks as an important characteristic.

More important still is double-mindedness: 'successful entre-preneurs seem to have an almost schizophrenic capacity to act in the moment and fully believe in their idea, while at the same time having somewhere else in their minds a sceptic'. This Doubting Thomas whispers the words, 'Well, this may not be working – I might have to try something else.' If that in fact happens, no stigma is involved. Whether you're working in a big company or a start-up, the worst wound that can befall you is self-inflicted: the thought that your failure in one instance means that you are a failure all round.

The typical dot.com flop committed suicide. The faults were so gross that their correction is correspondingly easy. The losers . . .

1 Failed to define a business model which would generate revenues in excess of operating costs.
2 Spent large, even enormous sums on non-essential items.
3 Ran small start-ups as though they were large companies.
4 Confused raising capital (easy in those heady days) with running a business (hard at any time).

Any business, not just a dot.com, would have flopped under that four-fold burden. In sober, sad fact, though, the established companies that climb on the e-bandwagon often make similar errors. Even the giant of the contenders, AOL Time Warner, pursued a business model that yielded no visible profit, and did so at gigantic expense. E-business has to be approached with the same objective determination that lies behind all big company breakthroughs, combined with the iconoclastic enthusiasm that explains why the Harvard and other start-ups find openings.

They approach a business sector without any prior concep-tions. That is much easier said than done. But remember GE's original 'destroyyourbusiness.com' initiative, in which every division was told to establish a start-up to challenge the existing business system, just like a hungry newcomer. The motto must be that of the Hill Street Blues police sergeant on TV: 'let's do it to them before they do it to us'.

Never forget, though, that the normal rules of business apply. The apparent exceptions of the dot.coms, which thunderously broke the rules of sound financing and rational market valuation, turned out to be exceptions that proved those very rules. The new rules that the dot.coms thought they were writing sounded very convincing – but they could be dangerously seductive. For example, it sounds wonderful to aim for 'winner-take-all dynamics', to be the first-come first-served clear winner, like the eBay auction site: but aiming and achieving are very different matters.

Tom Eisenmann, a Harvard professor, points out that three factors (which eBay has in high degree) have to be present for this strategy to work: first, increasing financial returns; second, economies of scale; and third, ease of customer retention. Many businesses, lacking these characteristics, lack any chance of emulating eBay. Moreover, even if the three factors are available, they will be vitiated if several inspired hopefuls rush full throttle into the market.

Every gold rusher can't win, as entrants in sectors like furniture, pet supplies and on-line trading have found, to their great pain. Only one or two will make it, if they achieve a sensible fusion between seeking rapid growth and maintaining corporate focus. It's dangerous to grow too indiscriminately, Eisenmann warns: just as it is to grow too slowly. But in the new age, it's the latter threat that confronts most non-start-up companies. The fusion recipe for them is no more, but no less, than applying old principles of management excellence in the new context:

1 Set up a small steering group with strong leadership.
2 The more sacred a cow is, the sooner it needs
   examination and possible slaughter.
3 Use digital means to raise internal and external
   communications to the highest possible standard.

4 Get task forces to look at, and rectify as needed, every basic of the business.
5 Use going digital to symbolise that you are deadly serious about change.
6 Set tight deadlines for every report, decision and action, and insist that they are kept.

The programme won't turn pig's ears of e-businesses into silk purses. But it will help to turn threats into opportunities, and to avoid the stupidity of one large bank, which invested heavily in four e-businesses, and closed them all before they could prove (or disprove) their potential. The question for established managers is huge. How many real opportunities did you spot, create or exploit last year – and how many are you pursuing now? If they don't spot, create and exploit effectively, by fusing their traditional strengths with the new opportunities, the consequences could well destroy them – dot.com.

PART III: THE NEW IMPERATIVES

What must be done in order to seize the new and endless opportunities – and to defend the base

CHAPTER ONE

creating the e-corporation

Every company and every manager can master the
three-stage ascent that turns Internet promise into reality

Was there ever a New Economy? Or were the wonders once
hymned by politicians, managers and gurus, all pointing to
alleged results like the surge in US productivity, just another
expression of a hysterical age that saw 'the unscrupulous rewarded, the dimwitted suckered, and the ill-qualified enriched
at a pace greater than at any other time in history'? The quote
comes from Joseph Nocera and Tim Carvell, writing in *Fortune*
magazine. It reads like an epitaph – but it wasn't.

The authors went on to say . . .' despite all that, [the Internet]
still changes everything'. They were writing, however, before
scandal enveloped Enron, the megastar of the alleged New
Economy, and its discredited auditors, Arthur Andersen: and
before three suicide planes crashed into the Twin Towers and
the Pentagon, signalling a sea-change in the US economy. In
fact, the boom had already turned into slowdown before these
awful events – the dot.com disasters were a symptom and to
some extent a cause of the sea-change.

The US had been in the grip of a stock-market fever unprecedented since 1929. The 50 largest companies in the US were
'worth' $840 billion in spring 1991. In mid-2001, that number
had swollen to a stupefying $4,008 billion, a rise that couldn't
be justified by any other yardstick. In company after company,
the ephemeral figure for market value rose much faster than
either profits (some grossly exaggerated) or sales. The New
Economy leaders and the Old Economy laggards alike had no
logical basis for the paper fortunes they were creating.

The doubters were also right to point to an undeniable fact – that the revolutionary new technology of information and communication has had relatively little impact on the management of most businesses. The best advice, though, is still to join the revolution. Even if future events prove the nay-sayers right, which is improbable, you cannot afford to risk the business or your personal future on ignoring the threats and the opportunities. You cannot carry on playing to your strengths while allowing your weaknesses to continue. This sermon is especially powerful at a time of Quadruple Revolution.

I used to talk and write about a Triple Revolution, one that combines an information revolution, a management revolution, and a global one. The fourth leg, however, has become just as important: a customer revolution. All these developments were under way for reasons that were independent of cyberspace, before the first website was created in 1993. In summary, the spectacular growth of computer networks was already being exploited by progressive managements to transform their internal and external relationships across the frontiers of both countries and industries, and also to transform the interface with customers.

You cannot discuss one of these upheavals without the others, since they are interdependent. The phenomenon is Fusion Management writ large. The growing importance of the customer, and the big shift in the balance of power towards the purchaser, have been given a tremendous forward push by the Net. Markets have more transparency when purchasers can compare prices so readily; and service enters a whole new dimension when the customer can achieve a permanent connection with the supplier in both retail and wholesale markets.

The consequences of the Quadruple Revolution are burgeoning on all sides. Supplier partnerships have led companies to communicate by linking their computers. Business operations are becoming flatter and often much faster. Aggressive competitors are becoming global forces by using the Net to disrupt existing industry structures to their advantage. Direct selling is threatening middlemen and producers in market after market. Global sourcing has become a fact of life. Airlines are dealing with their customers over websites in preference to travel agents or the telephone. And so on, and on.

Given that all this is true, what went wrong with the New Economy? Jerry Useem, writing in *Fortune*, delved thoroughly into the experiences and destroyed a dozen myths. First, the New Economy is the Old Economy. There has been some serious disruption, and more and more serious assaults will be made on established firms. But the vast bulk of economic activity, and of those conducting it, is continuous, not discontinuous. This is Fusion Management again: discontinuity in the midst of continuity.

Second is a lesson that nobody should ever have needed to learn: that you can only make money by selling goods or services for more than they cost to supply. The corollary to this eternal truth – or triteness – is that marketing costs are not capital investment, but running expenses. The e-retailers especially spent far more money on recruiting customers than they could recoup by any likely level of sales. Their breakeven points soared out of sight, and only inane injections of venture capital kept them afloat.

The millions of subscribers attracted to 'free' websites are only valuable if they can be converted, at some reasonably near point in time, into paying customers. The longer the delay, the greater the consumption of capital and the further away the breakeven point. That gives established firms the time to catch up, adding e-commerce to conventional channels and perhaps finding (as stockbrokers have and retailers will) that clicks-and-bricks can fuse perfectly well.

Even purchasing, which is under the biggest e-threat of any activity, looks likely to run the old alongside the new. A great deal of procurement, especially of commodity-style goods, will pass over the new B2B exchanges. Vertical set-ups serving specialised sectors or supplies will flourish – but only those that get in first and fastest. This new-fangled necessity for speed of entry and development hasn't gone away, but it doesn't remove the old-fashioned need to build a business methodically and well on all the required foundations.

One of those foundations is the brand. The importance of

branding, that of the company and of its goods and services alike, is obvious. But as Useem trenchantly observed, the dot.-coms adopted a wildly mistaken strategy:

1 Spend your venture capital lavishly on 'building the brand' up-front
2 Score a large and increasing number of 'hits' and 'eyeballs'
3 Then sell your offering to your enormous, supposedly lucrative customer base.

This model was encouraged by the success of Amazon (and before that, Netscape). But these two breakthroughs were based on important offerings that both attracted and served the customer. They were not brands in search of a business. If you want to be a true brand-builder, follow a quite different routine:

1 First build a profitable customer base
2 Broaden the base with new markets and lines
3 Only boost marketing expenditure to create brand strength as sales and profits rise.

In other words, the laws of business economics have not been suspended for the benefit of e-entrepreneurs. But media coverage since the dot.com crash, while suitably sceptical, has been by no means downbeat. On the contrary. *Fortune* quotes well-informed people who say things like: 'Anyone who thinks the Net is not transformational is dreaming.' You will get the same message from the *Harvard Business Review*. According to Richard Wise and David Morrison of Mercer Management Consulting, the B2B future involves, not simple exchanges, but five new models:

• the mega-exchange, processing large-scale transactions
• the specialist, handling complex and relatively expensive products like electronic components
• the 'e-speculator', chancing his arm on things like replacement car parts

- the solution provider, to whom you might turn for speciality chemicals, say
- the 'sell-side asset exchange', acting as broker between suppliers and buyers in relatively fragmented businesses.

All these are evolved forms of today's wholesalers and brokers, but with their functionality greatly enhanced by the Net. Remember that this is still a nascent technology. Many assumptions about its application may well prove to be false. The basic principle of the website, for instance, is that the company is essentially passive and depends on an active customer for results. The future could revolve instead around exploiting new technologies that 'will enable businesses to reach customers whenever and wherever they want to buy'.

This is called 'contextual marketing' by David Kenny and John F. Marshall of Digitas, who argued in the *HBR* that massive spending on developing corporate websites – in the tens of billions – has so far been deeply unprofitable. In fact, about half of the sites generated 'no commercial return at all'. They also generate little customer loyalty, a defect shared by some of the best-known dot.coms. *Fortune* noted that CDnow had 83% recognition among on-line shoppers, but a mere 17% loyalty rating.

Some analysts believe that Amazon will have to keep its customers for a full dozen years to make economic sense of its massive investment in the site. You cannot rely on the customer to make your website work – but you don't have to, according to Kenny and Marshall, if you shift your point of contact to the new mobile world. In a world of few certainties, one surefire development is this: before long, everybody will be connected to the Net by anything from a Palm Pilot or a wireless phone to an 'e-wallet' or an Internet-enabled POS terminal – or an interactive TV, for that matter.

They will have access wherever they are and whenever they want. The right marketing strategy in these new circumstances will be radically different from either traditional patterns or those favoured by most websites. The authors say that you must:

- Focus on context, rather than content.
- Build a ubiquitous 'agent' that travels alongside your customer.
- Master technology that tells you when you're needed.
- Be where your customer is ready to buy, and when.

Being translated, this means that General Motors, say, might capitalise on all the information carried within every one of its vehicles on the road. Each car would tell oil firms how much petrol there is in its tank, warn restaurants that its travels have brought it nearby, give mechanics service information. Frankly, this example is deeply unconvincing – but you can see the germs of a powerful idea.

Its power isn't much increased by the authors' closing advice, which is (1) become a direct marketer (2) master new technology skills quickly (3) measure everything for relevance to customers and market penetration. Forget the Internet for a moment. If you're not already doing these three things, you should be. In fact, that's the overriding reality. The Net accentuates the positive and magnifies the negative.

Nobody knows what consequences Net ubiquity will have, but there's nothing imprecise about the correct course of action, anyway. Use the risk-free stuff, where the benefits are gross and net, described below. It provides the basis for becoming an e-corporation – and remember the wise words of Intel chairman Andy Grove, 'All companies will be Internet companies, or they will be dead.' As the survivors-to-be complete this conversion, so they will find that the necessity for Fusion Management becomes overwhelming. Therefore every company should have an e-strategy. The essential start is to recognise that the right strategy doesn't come singly. It is tripartite.

Part One is symbolised by nothing more complex than internal e-mail: as in that example, it means using the Internet to improve any of the corporate processes where greater speed, efficiency and functionality can be won. Part Two of the tripos extends similar gains into the outside world and back again. Communications and processes involving customers and suppliers can be transformed at relatively little cost which is far outweighed by gains in speed and efficiency.

In time the cooperative exchanges will presumably be spun off, yielding easy billions for the car mammoths and other sponsor/users. These lucrative corporate by-products fit into e-strategy Part Three: either a wholly new business that can only exist in cyberspace. or a wholly new method, like Internet banking, that supplements or maybe supplants the existing core business. Part Three is where imagination, vision, courage and risk-taking are required, and where conventional managements may be seduced into silliness.

Leaping into this promising but problematic third stage without having the other two in place is certainly silly. You need the risk-free gains, not only to help finance the risks, but to provide both an effective infrastructure and an educative experience for the whole company. It's like a staircase. You walk up it before you run, climbing from internal re-engineering to external interdependence to the initiation of a brand-new business model.

Conventional management will do well to study the ascent of their unconventional rivals. The dot.com start-ups have the luxury of passing through all three parts at once. They have no legacy systems (or legacy managers) to worry about. They don't have to change the corporate culture, because none exists. In contrast, established companies that want to run the entire gamut of e-strategy have intimidating stairways to climb.

The ascent becomes easier if you adopt every available method of improving information flows and (even more important) mobilising information to improve decision-making. This is a key process which most companies don't even recognise as a process. Using intranets and e-mail, senior management can consult more widely and more rapidly than ever before. And those lower down the pyramid can then criticise and contribute to decisions with much greater freedom, if allowed and encouraged to do so.

There's thus a better chance of removing those banes of corporate life, the great ideas that disappear into black holes, the action plans that don't get actioned, the follow-ups that don't get followed, the decisions that don't get implemented. Unless these loopholes are closed, the opportunities, internal and external, will be squandered – and they are getting bigger, not smaller. Whatever true wealth the e-corporation has already created by 2003 is as nothing compared to the real wealth creation that lies ahead.

CHAPTER TWO

the thinking manager

Why the four thinkers behind GE, Microsoft, Intel and
Berkshire Hathaway are key models for all managers

Managers do not commonly regard themselves as thinkers. They
are doers, men and women of action. All the same, managers
seem to be more susceptible to ideas than most other groups of
professionals. Only look at the serried ranks of management
books and the endless stream and range of newcomers. If you
want a book on the tools of leadership, maximum success, or
the science of success, there they sit on the bookstore shelves.

Some volumes are more recondite than these: like a book on
'the global me', which deals with 'new cosmopolitans and the
competitive edge'. As those few, random titles indicate, there
is an infinite market, and therefore an unending appetite, for
an infinite range of ideas that promise to defeat competitors
and achieve success. The promise is by no means deceptive. The
books nearly all contain valuable nuggets, even whole lodes, of
knowledge.

The same is true of the countless seminars and the numberless
articles. So managers not only appear to believe in the power
of ideas; they are right to do so. Every manager should analyse
the best ideas of the best thinkers, check them against the hard
facts of experience and evidence, and select the most valuable
advice. Their chief problem is the sheer abundance of choice –
a flood only challenged by books on self-help and psychology.

But nearly all business management volumes share one significant feature. They are mostly not written by managers, or
even by people with substantial experience of managing. Anybody who has spent real time in a senior position has developed
considerable knowledge, both practical and theoretical. Yet few

95

managers write down the lessons from that knowledge, seeking to build on their own understanding, and to turn it into useful guidance for others.

Yet Fusion Management requires the combination of words and deeds, of understanding and execution. These are not opposites, but partners in the essential business of generating superior performance. There really are business champions whose intellectual stature matches any business academic, and academics whose insights are invaluable guides to management action. The two worlds are not two separate cultures, but two complementary approaches to the same end.

That is clearly demonstrated by the career of Jack Welch, who bent the vast General Electric to his will by force of personality and ideas (he brusquely instructed GE's managers that in this new century they have to win by ideas, not by whips and chains). Welch only started planning – for his impending retirement – to put his thoughts on paper in 2000. However, in his teaching at GE's Crotonville management college, and in his practice as a manager, Welch's ideas wielded great influence long before he wrote his bestselling *Jack*.

His most powerful thought was expressed in a stark injunction to the managers of GE's many and mostly unrelated businesses: be Number One or Number Two in your market, or get out – by sale or closure. This was later modified to cover global markets and has since been further modified to encourage GE managers to seek new markets. But in its original form, it was music to my ears, because it chimes with Heller's Law: that most markets will only support two profitable leaders and one specialist.

This Law was derived from observation of companies and markets as a business writer. It was a theory tested against observed realities, generalising from the particular. Welch's injunction sprang from his experience as a GE manager; he had noted that his corporation combined companies with high returns and others with low profitability, and that this discrepancy correlated with their power or weakness in the marketplace.

Like any natural businessman, he found the imbalance an affront to common and financial sense. Welch's edict, and the actions that enforced it, were based on the same concepts as Heller's Law:

1 Optimising return on assets is an essential aim of management.
2 Resources should therefore be allocated to activities offering the best prospects of exceptional returns.
3 Other things being equal, market share correlates with profitability – small goes with small, and large with large.

The Boston Consulting Group catapulted to fame and fortune by codifying the same three ideas. It produced a seductive matrix based on profitability and growth. High growth and profitability were achieved by 'Stars', which were to be fed with investment. 'Dogs', with low growth and profitability, were to be killed. Low growth and high-profitability businesses, the 'Cows', were to be milked – and, receiving no nourishing investment, they probably starved to death in the end.

That left a fourth box, the '?' companies, with high growth but low profitability, which might either become Stars or degenerate into Dogs. These possibles, it was suggested, should receive ample investment until the issue was decided, one way or another. Hundreds, if not thousands, of managers seized on the Boston Matrix as if it were Holy Writ. The reason is obvious in hindsight: it did their thinking for them. Far better, though, for managers (see Welch) to think for themselves.

In truth, the Boston Matrix, while an excellent consultancy tool, had grave intellectual shortcomings. For a start, putting businesses into categories doesn't and can't manage them; allocation of resources is a beginning, not an end. It's what you do with the resources, not the characteristics of the business, that ultimately determines the results. More important still, giving Dogs (and Cows) a bad name was a self-fulfilling prophecy that no doubt slew many a perfectly good business.

The wiser managers, who did their own thinking, used the Matrix to judge the existing shape of their businesses and to decide where the portfolio needed to be reshaped and strengthened – in the manner of Welch at GE. In other words, you use the ideas of others to stimulate your own thought, and you test that thought by its results in action. If you think consciously and continuously about your deeds, their rationale and their consequences, and alter course as you receive feedback from the real world, you are in effect writing your very own management textbook.

That was certainly true of Welch. His textbook has been developed and expounded down the years in many ways. I thus had no trouble in writing a book on his thought, using interviews, GE reports, speeches, etc., for a series called *Business Masterminds*. The miscellaneous sources added up to a cogent and coherent body of thought. Plainly, Welch's phenomenal success as a wealth-creating manager was partly linked to his ability to set his deeds in a thinking framework.

That's also been true of some great Japanese managers, like Ryazaburo Kaku, the preeminent architect of Canon. In his prime as a CEO, Kaku still carried in his pocket a chart which dated back to his days as a young manager in the finance department. He had spotted that whenever Canon introduced new products, profits shot up. When innovation lagged, so did earnings. The analysis convinced him to adopt innovation as Canon's driving force if and when his personal moment came.

Other practising managers who are also thinkers include Warren Buffett, the mega-investor whose Berkshire Hathaway, both a conglomerate and a financial investor, is another legend of wealth creation; Bill Gates, the inspiration of Microsoft; and Intel's Andy Grove, by all odds the most effective hardware manager of the digital revolution. All three doers have strong intellectual credentials.

At university, Buffett sat at the feet of Ben Graham, the teacher whose theories on 'value investing' inspired and informed Buffett's own theories and practice. Gates has written two books on his explosive industry and its technological workings. Grove was an academic before going into business, wrote a well-respected textbook on microelectronics, and has produced two good management books. One, *High Output Management,* can hold its own with any other text on how to manage.

The second, *Only the Paranoid Survive*, is a deadly serious study of managing under high pressure in a high-tech business.

But these four men are very much the exceptions, not the rule. Search as you may, it's not easy to find other managers, especially successful ones, who have followed in the footsteps of Alfred M. Sloan, the genius of General Motors, to make powerful contributions to management thought and thus practice. Lee Iacocca's best-selling account of his life and times at Ford and Chrysler, *Iacocca*, like most other books of its type, is not in the same class. On the other hand, non-managing gurus are in abundant supply – too abundant, some might say.

I featured four such thinkers as *Masterminds*: Peter Drucker, Stephen R. Covey, Tom Peters and Charles Handy. Even though two of them (Covey and Peters) are successful businessmen, you wouldn't place either in charge of a major corporation. But that by no means invalidates their teachings. All these writers have the advantage of a broader view than the vast majority of businessmen. The experience of managers is limited by their particular jobs: and they don't, by and large, study other companies – including competitors – with an unprejudiced, open mind.

More important, though, they do not generalise, seek patterns, or impose philosophies. In contrast, generalisation, patterning, and philosophising are meat and drink to the thinkers. This addiction has its dangers, since thinkers tend to select examples and facts that support their theses. That is the opposite of the properly applied scientific method and leads to embarrassing misjudgments – like the choice of IBM as the arch-hero of *In Search of Excellence*, which Peters wrote with Robert Waterman.

The philosophies, moreover, may have a strong moral content. Covey, a devout Mormon, believes that eternal natural laws of ethical behaviour are the guides to success. Handy favours the evolution of new organizations that disorganize in order to free individuals from the immoral chains of traditional employment. Peters similarly advocates liberation, calling for 'chaotic' management, not only to cope with chaotic times, but to enable individuals to make the best of themselves, and companies to make the best of individuals.

Only Drucker has no overriding theme, except to urge the pursuit of rational ends in rational ways, rigorously testing every alleged truth (including the three above). He also expects the conventional wisdom to be profoundly unwise. Like the others, he has always operated within an intellectual framework which directs attention to key issues and gives coherence to practical ideas. The practicality is striking. Each of the four tackles aspects of business management which are definitely down-to-earth.

Thus Drucker teaches readers how to manage effectively in many ways: like setting objectives, organizing groups, motivating and communicating, measuring performance, and 'developing yourself and others'. The last category includes 'developing a relationship responsibility' for those you work with, asking:

1 Do I know what everybody else does?
2 Do I know how they perform?
3 Do I know what they contribute and what results are expected?
4 Do I trust the people I work with?
5 Do I treat each of them as individuals?
6 Do I know their strengths?

Whatever your answers, the questions are an excellent example of how intellectual stimulation should make you think about your role in a different, positive way. Peters is especially good at challenging 'the way we do things round here' and acting as a corporate or personal gadfly. For example, one of the Peters teachings demands to know whether or not you are a 'skunk' – meaning a rule-breaker, innovator and individualist. If not, why not? Becoming a skunk is quite easy:

- Break rules if that is necessary to achieve what you want to achieve.
- Experiment all the time to find better ways of operating.
- Seek out and join forces with people of like, iconoclastic mind.

- If you see decisions or actions that you think are wrong, challenge them.
- Welcome change, and act as a change agent.

The issue is not whether managers should be stimulated by such advice, but whether they will respond to the stimulus. Move to the doers, like Gates, and that's the crucial difference. Thinking merges into action. For instance, every manager must have heard by now that you should strive to make the future happen. Gates did just that – he shows how to pursue 'big, hairy audacious goals' and 'manage by fear' (believing that the opposition is capable of doing the impossible, defeating you and destroying your success – as it may well be).

The first thought of the thinking manager, in other words, is that thought alone is not enough. As noted, you bring it to bear on your practical requirements, use the thinking process to learn from results, and feed back that learning into deeper understanding of your work. Study what Buffett has to teach on buying companies, for instance, and the value of directed thought becomes abundantly clear. In his case, the worth is measured in the tens of billions.

The value is also apparent from the performance of the thinking-managers' equities as a whole: $100,000 invested equally between GE, Microsoft, Intel and Berkshire Hathaway in 1989, after doubling every two years, would have grown to $3.2 million in 1999. Whether the thinkers pay off equally well depends on you. Approach their teaching as you should approach your own experience. Practice Fusion Management: test what they advise against the realities of your job and incorporate what works into your own managing philosophy. Make sure you have one.

Think of yourself as a thinker who acts on the ideas which fit and improve the real world, and learns from them. The more you live up to that ideal, the better you will think – and, more important – the better you will do.

CHAPTER THREE

the age of innovation

Established managers are being forced to think and act like genuine start-ups

Creativity and innovation have become the supposed guiding lights of 21st-century business. Virtually all managers kneel at the altar of new ideas and new businesses. But very few companies are actually organised to achieve the requisite flow of inspiration. Nor is it only a question of ideas. By far the most important aspect of innovation is translating ideas into action – and that is still the fatal stumbling block in business after business.

There will never be a sadder example than that of Xerox. An inspired top management established the Palo Alto Research Centre (PARC), appointed brilliant leaders who in turn recruited the brightest and best minds in electronics, and gave these people carte blanche and ample finance to follow their own predilections. PARC duly produced, not only the key innovations which made the personal computer possible, but also a working prototype. Their benevolent parent thereupon ignored the brilliance completely.

No Xerox PC was forthcoming. None of the innovations was incorporated into Xerox product lines. Tiny upstarts like Apple cheerfully made billions out of PARC's inspirations. PARC operated in independence from operating divisions which were coining money from copiers and other familiar technology, and it also lacked a powerful champion on the board. It's a classic dilemma of Non-fusion Management. The people who have the ideas don't have power. And the people who have the power don't have or appreciate the ideas.

The dilemma achieved alarming new proportions with the

102

advent of the Internet. The new go-getters – the Interpreneurs – are wholly committed to innovation. They have no established products or services to defend or enjoy. Rather, their success in raising investment funds depends substantially on the novelty and uniqueness of their selling propositions. Amazon is a perfect example. Nobody else was selling books over the World Wide Web: and in Webworld, the prime mover's pole position can become a permanent victory.

E-sceptics will wag fingers at other prominent aspects of Amazon – its continuous and serious losses and the plummeting of its share price when the dot.com bubble burst. That raises a second crucial point about innovation. You must turn a unique and powerful idea into action, but must also turn the action into profit by constructing a business model that leaves you with nourishing gross margins. That may require (Amazon could again be an example) considerable trial and error. But this is where the traditional business, averse to experiment and wedded to profit, may be at a significant disadvantage.

Clayton M. Christensen rammed this point home in his brilliant book, *The Innovator's Dilemma*. His case studies showed that, time and again, major innovations in an industry threaten existing profits and are therefore ignored – as at Xerox. The evangelistic Tom Peters has long urged the use of 'skunk works', innovative groups which operate outside of, and are physically remote from, the parent organisation. That's fine in the development phase. But the Xerox case makes it devastatingly clear that the skunks' achievements will wither on the vine without effective plans for creating a major business round the innovation.

In the first days of 2000, Wal-Mart made an historic announcement of just such a plan. It signalled the strength of a new trend for a new era. The world's biggest retailer was spinning off its online shopping, creating a stand-alone company under independent management. Sited in Silicon Valley, far away from the giant's commercial and spiritual centre in Bentonville, Arkansas, the operation was mandated to seek its own global destiny.

As one commentator observed, Wal-Mart had seemed

'hopelessly confused about the Internet'. In that confusion, Wal-Mart was not (and is not) alone. Not only in retailing, but in banking and other financial services, publishing, telecoms and many other businesses, managers have looked into the e-maelstrom and hesitated to plunge, or just dipped into the water, unsure how or when to move. Christensen doesn't criticise them for this confusion. As he says, it reflects their strengths, not their weaknesses.

Good management looks after its existing customers superbly, upgrades its products and processes constantly to give them a bigger and better bang per buck, invests its capital where it earns the fattest returns, and goes after markets offering the largest sales. This very excellence, however, makes the excellent giant almost incapable of matching brash new disruptors. They have no customers and offer different products and processes that are less profitable and have tiny or non-existent markets.

Even worse, the established management, sitting on the fat cash flows of the established business, is bound to give the old and rich priority, and to resist the costly, contrarian demands of the new and unproved. That's why Wal-Mart not only went West, but, looking for new blood and ideas, brought in a minority partner, venture capitalists Accel Partners, to assist in recruitment and execution. Execution, in the Death Row sense, may be the right word, since much of Wal-Mart's e-business will not be additional: many of the existing 100 million weekly customers will transfer their business from the stores.

One estimate is that a mere 15% loss of turnover would drive many stores into loss. If such prospects frighten you, inactivity is no solution. There's no guarantee that others will not attack your business with their own e-companies. Cannibalisation, or eating your own business, is a better option than being eaten by somebody else. But it's still a choice any businessman would rather not have to make. Whatever way you look at it, the dilemma in Christensen's title is excruciating for established companies.

If they don't, in his words, 'focus all their energy on upgrading their product line, and on being more and more competitive through existing customers, they'll fail'. But if they don't adopt the new technology, they'll also fail. Since it's out of the question to do both, the innovatory solution, he argues, is to set up a different company that has a different focus and then let it go after the disruptive technology. The mainstream company can keep doing what it does well. In Christensen's view, 'It's got to do that in order to survive, and you don't want it to lose that focus.'

How do you achieve the right balance? Researching with Michael Overdorf, Christensen concluded in an article in *Harvard Business Review* that 'three factors affect what an organization can and cannot do: its resources, its processes and its values'. It follows that, to know yourself as you really are, you need to answer three questions:

1 What are our key resources – both tangible (people, equipment, technologies, cash) and intangible (product designs, information, brands, current relationships with suppliers, distributors and customers)?
2 What are our key processes – how do the people who we employ interact, coordinate, communicate and make decisions?
3 What are our values? (By this the authors do not mean ethical principles, but the standards by which employees set priorities in making their decisions, both large and small.)

Christensen and Overdorf stress that resource analysis (the place where most managers look first) 'doesn't come close to telling the whole story'. Processes, on the other hand, can be decisive. It doesn't matter whether the processes are formally laid down, or are informal 'routines or ways of working that evolve over time'. Nor are disabilities most likely to crop up in the visible processes like logistics, development, manufacture or customer service. Underlying processes 'that support decisions about where to invest resources' are the more likely causes of failure.

As the two authors say, there are only three ways in which 'when an organisation needs new processes and values –

because it needs new capabilities – managers [can] create a new organisational space where those capabilities can be developed':

1 Start up a new division within the existing organisation to tackle the innovation.
2 Start up a new operation, right outside the existing organisation, and give it real autonomy.
3 Buy a business that fits your needs and entrust the innovation to its management.

All three approaches can work. The conditioning factors are the fit with the existing processes and the fit with the existing values. If both fits are good, you can happily keep the innovation within the organisation. You'll still need a team, but it can be 'lightweight', which cuts across functions in its membership, but whose members are still controlled by their own managers.

That won't do if the fit with processes is poor – that is, you need to do important things that are new to the organisation. You can still keep the innovation inside, but only if the values fit is good: that is, this isn't a disruptive innovation, but a 'sustaining' one that improves on your existing technology for the benefit of your existing customers. Give that to a 'heavyweight' team. Its members spend all their time on the new project, work in the same place, and accept full responsibility for successful completion.

You risk failure, however, if you attempt disruptive innovation in-house. By definition it has a poor fit with the existing business values and will almost certainly require new processes. Spin it off, with a team in charge, another group of genuine heavyweights. If new processes are not required, the heavy fellows may stay in-house, but the authors warn that taking innovations to market in this way will almost always mean spinning them off.

As for acquisition, the rules are simple. If your target's strengths rest on its processes and values, absorbing the buy into your own organisation will kill it stone dead. 'A better strategy is to let the business stand alone and to infuse the parent's resources into the acquired company's processes and values.'

Resource analysis, as the *HBR* article says, is the easier part. Process analysis is tougher, because you may never have thought about processes like decision-making at the top; or you have taken for granted processes lower down like dealing with orders, deliveries and invoicing. Do not underestimate the lower processes, though. General Electric found that it was alienating its biggest lighting customer by far, Wal-Mart, because their two corporate accounting systems didn't mesh. Process analysis, information technology and investment produced a vast payoff in customer satisfaction and millions of dollars.

Geographical separation is a great help (like that location of Wal-Mart's e-commerce in Silicon Valley). Would-be interferers have less leverage at a distance. But the dead hand of the established business can be exercised over any mileage – as the progenitors of the IBM PC found to their (and the company's) cost.

The original crash programme was almost completely insulated from head office in Armonk, New York. The team established down in Boca Raton, Florida, accomplished wonders to launch a superbly successful project in little more than a year. Their success was their undoing. Legions of IBM-ers descended from Armonk, independence was lost, and – worst of all – IBM failed to recognise that the PC was a deeply disruptive technology, and not a mere 'entry system' from which people would progress to buying real, bigger computers.

The world is moving so fast that there is no time to argue corporate conservatives of this stamp out of their positions. By the time they understand the threat, it may well be too late to mount an effective counter-attack. Even if you do that, however, running the two sides, the old and the new, in harness is no answer. Christensen is plainly right to stress the impossibility of doing both. But there's a snag with his solution – spinning off the disruptive technology on its own: the parent cuts itself off from the future.

It's hard to remember now, but Vodafone, which was turned briefly into Europe's highest valued company by merger with Mannesmann, was once part of Racal. Pre-merger, the child was worth some one hundred times more than its erstwhile parent. It has emerged as a potential superpower in the Internet world, because of the certainty that mobile phones will be a prime source of Web access. Nobody, insider or outsider, believes that Vodafone would have accomplised its transformation inside Racal.

If a parent company sets up independent centres of innovation, followed by the successful exploitation of the innovators' ideas, the parent's own culture will change. That remains true if the new business gets spun off, wholly or partially, and creates fortunes for its stars: others will be stimulated by their example. Such stimulus is a key element in invigorating the culture, injecting new and richer blood into the organisational veins.

The impact of in-company breakaways should be doubly innovative, for the skunk-works approach requires a different kind of management control. The skunks have targets expressed in deadlines and break-points, rather than return on capital or sales. The leading skunks are left to their own operational devices, with their spending controlled, but their activities untrammelled. This contrasts vividly with the typically over-controlled corporation, where second-guessing and vetos of initiatives are commonplace.

The skunk-works ethos, though, is spreading into the bureaucracies (or corpocracies). Much more work is being conducted by project teams, not only within divisions, but cutting across them. The objectives are very similar to those of the breakaway, primarily completion to specification, on time and within budget. Some companies now place the introduction of new products and/or services high among the factors by which managers are judged when the time comes round for bonuses and stock options.

All this demands acts of abdication by senior management, whose role changes from day-to-day directorial (and often dictatorial) overlords to that of year-to-year mentors, guides, recruiters and financiers. The new role supplies internally what venture capitalists have provided externally for the dot.coms and other gee-whiz start-ups. Failure to surrender day-to-day powers comes hard: but that is one reason why established companies have lagged behind the pace in innovation – even when the old-liners have turned to new recruits as a source of fresh ideas.

Without fresh ideas on organisation and control, the old-liners will fail. With those new ideas in place, though, you can go on to tackle what truly matters. The Web is more pervasive still. It demands innovation in areas that are by definition strange and new. Established companies moving into the e-economy are thus being forced to think and act more like genuine start-ups. Do that, and you can have your creative cake and eat it, fusing the fruits of innovation into a continuing business that can expand securely into a richer future. The alternative is to have no cake.

empowering the business

Truly fused management creates a family of teams

Management is a seamless web. No one skill – not even finance – can exist by itself. This truth provides another definition of Fusion Management. The skills fuse, interrelate, interlock; and weaknesses in one will very possibly undermine strengths elsewhere. That applies to individuals and companies alike. In both cases excellence demands continuous all-round improvement or *kaizen* accompanied (another fusion) by occasional *kaikaku* – radical change.

Radical, all-embracing, joined-up, fused change is needed to escape the Augean Stables Syndrome. Hercules, you will recall, had to grapple heroically with a filthy stable that was no sooner clean than it again became dirty. Companies customarily concentrate on whatever Augean Stables confronts them most painfully, only to find that, with the old problem solved, a new and equally serious horror has emerged. By the same token, what succeeds obsesses them, sometimes to the extent that they fail to notice that the winning light has failed.

A fascinating example and awful warning comes from Boeing. As noted on page 27, the company had achieved phenomenal, rich expansion in two 20-year periods: averaging 15% growth in earnings per share in 1960–80 and 1970–1990. It was the only mainline American manufacturing giant to achieve such results. Boeing exploited its unchallenged leadership in civil aviation with a series of blockbuster jetliners. But circumstances changed in 1980–1999, when Boeing at last met serious external challenge.

The crunch problem of the later 1990s was the excessive loss of sales to the challenging Airbus. So the company powered up its sales drive and duly won enormous orders. There was a fatal catch. The internal challenge was even more serious than the external. The orders swamped the production capacity so hugely that Boeing ran into a full-scale manufacturing crisis. Production lines had to be shut down, the company reported its first annual loss for decades – and, rubbing salt into the wounds, Airbus, anyway, overtook Boeing's sales in 1999.

A further irony is that Boeing heavily discounted its selling prices, relying in part on expected cost savings. These were to come from the planned success of an attack on the company's grossly inefficient and extravagant production processes. Plainly, the manufacturing incompetence vitiated the sales drive which in turn caused production to crash. But the disaster does, of course, raise a further question. Why was Boeing, America's flagship aerospace company, so massively incompetent? As I observed:

> It's better management by far never to reach the Boeing Bind, which means that the highest criteria of efficient use of manpower must be built into the system . . . high productivity isn't the product of high physical effort, or even mainly of high morale. It's the consequence of inte-grated management that knows what it's doing and what it wants – and uses its will, know-how, and investment to achieve the most in output with the least in manpower.

Without that integrated management, manpower may still have to be cut back, but in the most painful way possible: lay-offs. Hence this Seattle gibe: 'Optimists who work at Boeing bring lunch. A pessimist leaves his car running.' Boeing's headcount has been slashed by a third since 1998. But that bitter jest didn't relate to the company's recent travails. Like the passage above, the gibe dates back to 1984. That's when I wrote about another ghastly Boeing year, 1969, when manpower had been slashed by 46,000 souls – a full and dreadful 30%.

If the 1969 severances hadn't been made, Boeing would have gone bankrupt. That year the company lost $14 million on sales of $2.8 billion. A decade later it made a profit of $875 million.

You can readily understand the difference by comparing two figures. In 1969, Boeing used 25,000 workers to produce seven 747 jumbos a month; a decade later it needed just 11,000. Great stuff, but wait: in the late 1990s, Boeing was at it again. Man-hours per 737 had soared to a horrible 30,000. They were then cut – all the way to 6500.

What had been happening? What can explain this appalling cycle of incompetence, reform, renewed incompetence and repeated reform? The vicious cycle, like the overmanning, arose from managerial failure. It was only one symptom of the same fell disease: the curse of disintegrated management. In 1969, the curse meant that the 747 jumbo was put into production before the engineering was good and ready. In 1997, the curse caused the 737 and 747 lines to be shut down, after managers had tried to double production rates long before they had resolved the latest bout of shopfloor problems.

You can recognise the disease by one dead giveaway. People tackle the dreadful snags on the fly – hiring extra people, or 'buying your way out of a problem,' as one Boeing manager put it. In 1998, according to *Fortune*, workers called 'expediters' were sent (sometimes on bicycles) to fetch missing parts. Consequently, 'factory floors were covered with huge tubs of spare parts worth millions of dollars'. In 1969 half-finished planes had been taken off the line and left outside to wait for missing parts: in that year, there were some 1600 parts shortages per day.

Not only were the signs of disintegrated management much the same 30 years apart: so were the remedies. Both times, managers as well as staff lost their jobs (the losses included, in 1999, the man who had led the far too successful sales drive). Both times, too, new programmes were forced through to identify and reform areas of inefficiency. Both times, too, the remedies sounded thoroughly plausible.

In 1969, for instance, parts shortages were to be relieved by computer cataloguing of all 100,000 parts used in the 747 – and every employee who used them. That sounded nothing but wise. Yet five years later Boeing was still using a manual numbering system to keep track of an aircraft's 4 million parts and 170 miles of wiring: 'there had been attempts at automation', wrote *Fortune*, 'but by the early 1990s they had metastasized into 450 separate computer systems, few of which could talk to one another'.

The study of this bizarre story is important. It shows in exaggerated form what happens inside many organisations and what explains their own recurrent Augean bouts of big problems, cure and renewed failure. In these unhappy episodes, management and other systems are heavily reorganised until the CEO and his cohorts feel that proper control is again being exercised. Greatly improved results seem to support their case. But these improvements come from gathering the 'low-hanging fruit'. They leave unresolved the root causes of the crisis.

In a nutshell, Boeing has been persistently under-managed and over-engineered. You could express this as an issue of culture. Designing new best-selling aircraft was the be-all and end-all at Boeing. Other equally important concerns took second place (or third) because nobody considered these matters to be equally important. In 2000, engineers were grumbling that the emphasis on greater efficiency was losing Boeing's lead in aeronautical innovation – as if the two were incompatible, instead of being complementary.

The only safe bet is to give due weight to everything that matters at all. That applies to both companies and to individual managers. The latter dare not be a one-note man or woman. The need for individual fusion becomes obvious when you ask which is more important: delegation, motivation, or leading teams? Obviously enough, delegating to unmotivated people is pointless, and teams cannot work effectively as teams without delegated powers and high motivation. The same type of interdependent relationship applies to all other management skills – communication, decision-making, problem-solving, time management.

Time management perfectly illustrates, at the individual level, the overriding problem of the Augean Stables: that managers know perfectly well what to do, but don't actually do it. They know that managing time is fundamental to everything else. Unless you, as a manager, control your time effectively, you

the new imperatives

must fail on other counts. Time management is what determines your effectiveness by balancing your workload.

In this context, delegation meets one of the prime requirements for the Fusion Manager. It enables you to exercise personal responsibility for the delegated task, without having actually to do it. That being so, you would expect every Fusion Manager to ask Peter Drucker's three famous questions, which richly deserve repetition and application:

- What am I doing that need not be done by anybody?
- What am I doing that somebody else could do?
- What am I doing that only I can do?

The correct course of action is wonderfully clear. First, stop doing the unnecessary things. Second, delegate everything that can be delegated. Third, organise your time and your priorities around what you, and you alone, must do. Yet when you spell out this catechism to busy executives, even those who claim to be overworked are often strangely reluctant to ask the questions, let alone act on the answers. Like managers caught in the Boeing Bind, they avoid or evade the obvious. There are four main (and very bad) reasons for their reluctance.

1 Each of their activities, even the unneeded ones, feeds their sense of personal importance.
2 They fear that the delegated activities may be done better, which may undermine their own position.
3 Conversely, they fear that the delegated work will be badly done – thus again damaging their position.
4 They shy away from the task of deciding how best to use their time – preferring to react to whatever circumstances are thrust upon them.

Phil Condit, the CEO of Boeing, appeared to buck the four barriers by appointing one Harry Stonecipher as president. He gave his new delegate carte blanche to attack the operating inefficiencies and 'equally creaky financial practices'. But if you want to achieve integrated management, delegation must carry on down the line. The new man came, not from Boeing, but from its acquired rival, McDonnell Douglas. His hard ways and harsh tongue alienated the unions and, more important, the union members – and, no doubt, their managers.

According to *Fortune*, in 2000, 'When asked to rate Boeing as a place to work . . . only 39% of respondents rated it positively, compared with 61% two years ago.' So appalling a slump in morale poses great dangers, not only to internal workings, but to relations with customers. This is a key arena for joined-up, fused management. Delegation creates motivation which breeds teamwork which builds delegation, and so on round (this time) the virtuous cycle.

The well-known, unbreakable link between employee satisfaction and customer happiness is another demonstration of joined-up management. You cannot expect workers and staff to serve the clientele to the latter's satisfaction when the company people feel badly served by their management. Boeing's management had failed in its prime purpose, which is the same for any management: to so direct the strategy and operations of the company that it provides security and progress for all parties – the employees (including managers), the customers and the shareholders.

Managers in bad times often blame a demotivated workforce for their troubles. The great W.Edwards Deming would have none of it. As noted earlier (p. 61) he put 85% of productivity problems down to management. The shop floor at Boeing wasn't responsible in any way for the sorry computer bungles, the inadequate financial reports, the pile-up of orders, or all the other blatant errors. Everything was the fault of a management that hadn't 'got its act together'; or rather, hadn't got all the various acts together.

Yet Condit's people actually put money and muscle behind a new slogan (much-ridiculed internally) that read 'Not Family, but Team'. That's especially hilarious given the resentment and bad blood between Boeing people and the various executives moved over from McDonnell Douglas. Since teams depend so vitally on morale – or team spirit – and on delegated authority, a top-down management that has nearly halved worker morale is only wasting words when it talks of 'Team'. Good teamwork won't actually materialise in these sorry circumstances.

Without the fusion of activities inside a company, the switch-back cycle shown at Boeing is very likely to reappear. By concentrating on one aspect of its Augean stables – operations – the company (as in the previous crisis) produced short-term improvements of scale and importance. But that same concentration produces a basic imbalance that, over time, erodes the efficiencies and lands the company back where it started. The Augean Stables Syndrome strikes again – and always will unless you ignore a persuasive old cry: 'You can't do it all.'

Omnicompetence is, of course, difficult. But 'do it all' is the only option in the present era, when the market pressures are strong and getting stronger. Boeing couldn't afford its management laxity even when it enjoyed a virtual monopoly. After the attacks by Airbus, the Seattle firm was left even more grievously exposed. Yet the Fusion Manager really can do it all – if you do it all.

There's no paradox in this tautology. You divide and conquer. By working through highly motivated teams of many sizes (right down to a 'team' of one person), and giving them fully delegated powers to tackle their fully delegated, highly specific tasks, you can hope to cover every problem, opportunity and operation. Boeing's 'Not Family, but Team' were in fact the right words, but used in the wrong way. Truly joined-up management creates a family of teams, working together internally and externally. If they work well, then the Augean stables will be clean, and stay that way.

CHAPTER FIVE

meeting the threats

You won't beat the new competitive challenges until the old system's command-and-control aspects are swept away

Imagine this nightmare scenario. You have long had a marvellous, specialised business. After spectacular early growth, it has became the biggest in the market, with by far the best-known name. The company has not been able to keep up its early momentum, though, partly because of competition from a much larger, non-specialist opponent, who has sadly stolen your market lead.

As if that wasn't bad enough, smaller rivals are nibbling away at your market share. Then, suddenly, the nightmare: a major start-up competitor confronts you with a new and apparently serious threat. The newcomer, another specialist, not only undercuts your prices, but has distribution just as broad as the nationwide system that you have so painstakingly and expensively put together. How do you defend yourself against the attack?

Can you and should you retaliate? The firm under assault in this real-life nightmare was Toys 'R' Us, which first lost its sales lead in toys to the gigantic generalist, Wal-Mart, and was then assailed by the Internet seller, eToys. The latter threat eventually collapsed completely: eToys went under, drowned by the weight of its own incompetencies. But a similar danger, to a greater or lesser extent, is either real or pending for many businesses right round the globe – and it isn't confined to e-commerce.

The problem is actually as old as business, but it was intensifying long before the first website appeared in 1993. Businesses – even monopolists and quasi-monopolists – are rarely left alone indefinitely to enjoy a market in which they face restricted or stable competition. Nature abhors a monopoly. All private monopolies eventually founder, and not only because of political intervention. They face an inherent dilemma that is shared by non-monopolists.

Suppose a new competitor appears, using a new approach (in technology, marketing, etc.) and under-cutting you on price; the choice is between three difficult options.

- First Option: sticking to your current business model, suffering some loss of sales and profits, and putting longer-term prosperity, even survival, at some risk.
- Second Option: shunning the new approach, but matching the lower prices, and taking an even larger hit on revenue and earnings without removing the long-term risk.
- Third Option: starting your own operation to confront the new challenge head-on, cannibalising your own business, but hoping to regain the initiative.

E-commerce adds a new dimension, simply because the attackers can start so easily and so fast. During the dot.com hysteria, this ability was grossly exaggerated by resounding, instant success in another area: capital value. To give a bizarre illustration, Toys 'R' Us had $11.3 billion of sales in the year to end-January 2001, on which it earned a tolerable $404 million of net income. The sales were 100 times those of eToys, which actually contrived to lose more money than its revenues. That didn't prevent the shares from rising to a capital value of $5.2 billion at one point. The equivalent number for the Toys 'R' Us heavyweight was $4.8 billion in spring 2001.

To add insult to injury, Toys 'R' Us itself had Web-sales that were little below those of its all-Web rival. So, at that lunatic time, if you had regarded the eToys market value as a significant figure, the whole of the Toys 'R' Us business, with its 700 outlets across America, was in the share price for less than nothing. That highlights the prime difficulty of the Third Option, meeting the challenge head on. By definition, you are coming late into the market; you will be seen as a follower; and your chances of success may be rated far below those of the pioneering challenger.

Following doesn't guarantee failure, any more than leading guarantees success. You couldn't ask for a more conspicuous example of threat being turned into opportunity than the eventual Third Option reaction of Microsoft to the rise of Netscape. The latter owned the Internet browser market until the software giant counter-attacked with its own Explorer product. Microsoft now has overwhelming dominance of a market which once belonged totally to the newcomer.

Microsoft's circumstances, however, were unique: its ability to bundle Explorer, free of charge, into the Windows package gave the champ an unbeatable (and according to the US Justice Department, illegal) advantage. Despite that inbuilt advantage, Microsoft's winning edge was nearly thrown away. To begin with, it behaved like most threatened companies: Microsoft persuaded itself that the new competition was insignificant and irrelevant.

Brushing the Internet aside makes King Canute's attempt to turn back the tide seem positively pragmatic. The time lost in wishing away unwelcome competition gives an invaluable present to the attacker. It's far better to follow the First Rule of Resistance. Assume that the new competitor – any new competitor – is strong, well-managed and a serious challenger. Second Rule: always assume, too, that it will succeed, unless you can find a way of resisting the attacker and drawing its teeth.

Once he had woken up to the threat, not a moment too soon, Bill Gates reacted in a way that exemplifies the Third Rule of Resistance: look for key weaknesses in the challenger's business model and for key strengths of your own. Then exploit both to alter the nature of competition to your advantage. But Gates, with his war-chest of billions, could easily afford a full frontal assault. In business wars, as in real wars, success only comes by outflanking, going round the side – unless, like Gates, you have a three-to-one or greater advantage.

When IBM (again belatedly, this time by four years) retaliated to the rise of Apple by launching its own Personal Computer, it also overmatched its upstart rival with huge assets:

three-to-one was left far behind. The advantages included the much greater strength of the brand, the no-contest dominance of IBM's sales force in large corporations, and its ability to leap-frog Apple with the newer 16-bit technology. Like Microsoft with its browser, IBM had unique powers to put behind its venture.

All the same, starting up its own wonderfully successful PC business did not avert the threat to IBM's long-term prosperity. In hindsight, it's clear that the PC revolution was bound to undermine the giant's richly profitable markets in mainframes and mini-computers. IBM was unable to sustain its old pro-prietary dominance in the new technology, partly through its own many-sided errors (which included giving Gates an effec-tive monopoly in operating software that could be sold to all third parties); partly through the nature of that technology.

Taking the Third Option was plainly right. The fact that the threat materialised all the same, despite IBM's unique power and wealth, raises a lesson that applies generally. Companies genuinely threatened by new competition are between a rock and a hard place. As a Toys 'R' Us executive told the *Wall Street Journal*, 'You're damned if you do and damned if you don't.' You cannot afford Option One, ignoring the challenger, whether it arrives via the Internet or along some non-cyberspace route. Yet the strategy required to compete with the brash newcomers may well conflict head on with the established business.

In the case of Toys 'R' Us, that existing profitable turnover, remember, was 100 times the size of its e-business in 1999. Setting up your own e-business is the easy part of the proper response. But just establishing a website and selling over the Net is only half the battle, if that. Toys 'R' Us, typically enough, put little energy behind the new venture, yet demand over the Web still swamped the company's ability to fulfil orders. That was doubly unfortunate, because Toys 'R' Us had approached e-commerce with some intelligent, fused strategic thinking.

For a start, the operation was launched in partnership with a venture capitalist. The latter expected the on-line business to evolve into an independent and highly valuable company, competing against eToys blow for blow in exactly the same

120

territory. How else can you counter your basic disadvantage? Unlike you, the attacker, who starts from scratch with no fixed ideas or habits, has the built-in benefits of relative small-ness: notably focus, agility, ambition, and, of course, autonomy. Its management can't face any conflict with the established business, because there is none.

That conflict, however, crippled Toys 'R' Us when it came to the crunch. A new man hired to galvanise the Internet business almost immediately saw that he needed to compete with eToys and the other on-liners on price. The bosses at Toys 'R' Us refused his request, on the grounds that the existing franchisees and store managers would object. So, only a few months into the job, the new man exited – and the venture capitalists promptly bowed out, too, asking themselves (understandably enough) whether Toys 'R' Us was 'serious about developing an independent on-line business'.

The burning, fundamental issue is independence. The dilemma is being faced by many companies. It confronted Compaq in its efforts to combat the rapid rise of Dell, with its galloping success on-line. Compaq's own rise had been built on close, exclusive relationships with its dealer network. The dealers were naturally dead against Compaq's moves to sell direct. Their opposition seriously slowed the company's responses – with severe effects on its growth rate, profits and chief executive (who was fired by the board).

The logic of the dealers is very clear, but their logic imposed an irrational policy on their supplier. The Third Rule of Resistance is that, if you don't make the sales, somebody else will. In other words, pulling your punches (as both Toys 'R' Us and Compaq did) will merely divert your business to the competition. You will gain nothing, but will certainly lose market share. To quote the *Wall Street Journal*, 'the rules of the Web play havoc with existing business relationships and economic structures. Retailers who aren't willing to rip up their old rule-books risk missing out on the Web's huge promise.'

The dilemma doesn't only confront retailers. All businesses have to react to the rules of the Web, which will affect them in different ways, and at different times, but will affect them nonetheless. To repeat, this is a general issue, not one confined to cyberspace. Changes of many kinds will alter the rules of every game as the new century develops. The issue is how to structure and manage the organisation so that it can mutate rapidly enough to make change its ally rather than its enemy.

Being 'serious about developing an independent business' raises issues even wider than coping with new competition. John A. Byrne, writing in *Business Week*, says that 'the Soviet Union collapsed because its command-and-control economy couldn't keep up with the West's free market. In the 21st century, the same fate will befall companies whose CEOs attempt to control everything.' The decision not to discount the on-line prices of Toys 'R' Us was a typical piece of command-and-control interference with a subsidiary operation.

The Fusion Manager will know that such policies are unsustainable. All organisations are entering an era when the very word 'subsidiary' will become meaningless, because each part of a flat structure will be equally important in its own right. Byrne argues, too, that 'In a world that is becoming ever more chaotic and dependent on brainpower, teams at the top will make more sense than a single outrageously paid CEO . . .'.

He approvingly quotes John Chambers of Cisco Systems. Neither the company nor its boss look so heroic after their 2001 setbacks, but Chambers is dead right on this point: 'I learned a long time ago that a team will always defeat an individual.' Apparently, Chambers has three times as many direct reports as the typical CEO and thus forces himself to encourage greater autonomy. The new technology helps to generate genuine independence, because it keeps ultimate controllers, like Chambers, fully informed of what's happening as people pool their knowledge, decisions and action plans in real time.

The trends to flatness are plainly visible. In 1987, 280 of the 1000 largest US companies had some self-managed groups. According to *Business Week*, research by Edward E.Lawlor III, of USC's Centre for Effective Organisations, showed a massive expansion to 780 as long ago as 1996. However, you don't need research to see that the companies mentioned in this chapter – IBM, Wal-Mart, Microsoft, Toys 'R' Us, even Cisco – all have or have had dominant CEOs with extravagant pay and strong urges to control, if not all things, at least most.

In the past, this dominance has created wonderful results. But the control culture can then move on to turn long-term success into long-term relative failure. Even though Toys 'R' Us saw off the competition from eToys, its sales fell in 2000, while its return to investors over the past decade was a negative 2.9% p.a. Chambers must be praying that the sudden shrinkage of his sales growth (from 58% to 5% or less) doesn't reflect a similar long-term weakening before new challenge – led by Juniper and Nortel in two of Cisco's four key markets.

If so powerful a force as Cisco in telecommunications equipment can be rocked by new threats, so can anybody. Companies won't beat the new competitive challenges, from whatever source, until the command-and-control aspects of the old system are swept away. People who are free to shape their own destinies will nearly always outperform those still in thrall. Independence for the Fusion Manager is how threats can be turned into opportunities, and nightmares into dreams come true.

PART IV: ACQUIRING REAL GROWTH

*Why organic growth demands senior management
reform – and better ideas*

trouble with takeovers

Mergers and acquisitions are only as good as their fusion

The easiest task in management is offering to buy another business. You only need to identify the target, work out how much you want to pay, and make your bid. True, complications may follow. The other party may resist, forcing you into a costly takeover battle. Investors may not take kindly to the proposal. But since some investors (those in the target business) will benefit, you will not be acting in a uniformly hostile climate. Like BMW buying Rover, or Daimler-Benz buying Chrysler, you can hope to complete the transaction to general hosannas.

As both those cases, Chrysler as much as Rover, showed dramatically, the cheering can soon change to jeering. The market capitalisation of Daimler Chrysler, whose chairman, Jurgen Schrempp, had nailed his colours to the mast of 'shareholder value', shrank by 60% in a single year. As for BMW, it invested £2.8 billion in a business which before long was losing £360 million annually. And neither management, note, was plunging into strange industrial waters. This was their very own industry – and they were deluged.

These remarkable events merely stress that doing the deal, the easy part, leads directly into making the merger or acquisition work, which can be the hardest task for the Fusion Manager. The difficulty starts with the strategic objective. Why do you want the other business in the first place? If the objective is wrongly chosen, the next logical question, whether the chosen purchase will help to achieve that aim, is irrelevant. The deal is bound to fail. Yet there's nothing wrong with buying a business in principle. Practice is another matter. But some of the perfectly acceptable purposes are:

- to acquire new turnover (and probably new customers)
- to obtain new facilities, from factories to shops
- to add new products
- to broaden product ranges
- to diversify into new product areas/markets
- to purchase new technology.

All these laudable aims could be achieved by organic means, but acquisition is quicker and easier – provided you obey the rules. Any deal should be able to pass stringent tests. Would-be purchasers, no matter what the size of company that's buying or being bought, need to answer these questions:

1 What strategic aims must be achieved for this purchase to be justified? Why do I really want it?
2 If those aims are achieved, what financial benefits (making profits and/or preventing losses) will be realised? Have I done my sums properly?
3 Do the benefits represent an attractive return on the costs? Does the deal make financial sense?
4 What are the chances of the aims not being achieved? Are the risks acceptable? Can I live with the worst possible outcome?
5 If the proposed purchase vaults the above hurdles, how is the merger to be implemented and by whom? Do I have a convincing, carefully wrought plan?
6 What framework will be established for the combined venture? How will the buy be fitted in?
7 How quickly can the buy be integrated and the benefits start to be won? Will I have to wait too long for it to work?

The last question is clearly critical. If you're buying to save time, it makes no sense to get tangled up in a long and costly process of integration. The risks involved in mergers are intensified if this question and the other six do not get proper answers. In the BMW-Rover case, the strategy was to broaden the buyer's product line. But the first combined product, the Rover 75, was directly competitive with BMW's existing mid-range models. The other Rover cars were too old and uncompetitive to broaden anything: and the task of replacing them was left far too late – the new Mini, for instance, only appeared in 2001.

The task of getting any financial benefits, let alone adequate ones, was made exceedingly difficult by the fact that Rover's reported profits, when submitted to BMW's accounting principles, were turned into large losses. If the Germans did sufficient 'due diligence' before buying Rover from British Aerospace, they must have taken a sublimely optimistic view of their chances of achieving their financial aims.

That optimism, of course, flew in the face of all evidence from past mergers. Successful fusions are outnumbered by the horde that either fail demonstrably or produce inadequate returns. It's an interesting reverse of the demerger coin. When a company sells a business which, under new management, proceeds to establish a far higher capital value in only a year or two, what must that mean? Either the vendor management undermanaged the business, or sold it too cheaply – or most likely both.

Vodafone, the mobile telephone supplier, for instance, was spun off from Racal. Even in mid-2002, post-slump, it was valued at $61.8 billion, which is 61 times the price its erstwhile parent got for its telcoms division in 1999. The value in Vodafone was unlocked by unlocking the business. In fact, the record of spin-offs looks to be far better than that of acquisitions. ICI and Zeneca provide another example where the parent is now worth far less than the child: £48.2 billion against a mere £3.4 billion.

Both these two mighty ex-mites, interestingly, got engaged in massive mergers: Zeneca with another drug company, Astra, Vodafone with its US counterpart, Airtouch, and with Mannesmann in Germany. The deals could extend the companies' triumphant runs: more likely, the great increase in size and the complications of any acquisition will offset some, if not all, of the benefits (for which Vodafone grossly overpaid).

Why should this be the case? Sheer enlargement provides part of the answer. The management span at the top becomes much wider, which imposes new strains. The managers' chances of coping successfully with their new burdens are reduced by the inevitable difficulties of fusing two different cultures and pushing through cost-saving (or downsizing) measures which are bound to be resented by those affected – including some of those who stay behind.

The upheavals of the early negative measures then exhaust the appetite for change, and needed positive action is postponed. Delay is deeply dangerous after acquisitions. In Rover's case, as one senior BMW manager told the *Financial Times*, 'We set our targets, but left them to get on with it. But nothing much happened.' That applied across the board, including the development of new models, without which Rover could not possibly have hoped to meet any worthwhile targets.

Here Rover had made far too little progress before BMW moved in. The expert acquirer, buying a business with such evident problems, plans the onslaught on the deficiencies before the takeover. The taker-over then implements the planned actions with ruthless speed as soon as closer inspection has confirmed the plans. However, Walter Hasselkus, the German installed at Rover by BMW, was far from ruthless. He took much care in handling the 'very strong culture' at Rover – probably excessive care.

Hasselkus told Elizabeth Marx, author of *Breaking through Culture Shock*, that:

> At Rover we set our goals very high with the expectation that we will not quite hit them. If we hit 80%, that's OK. This is completely unacceptable to BMW. At BMW (maybe typical of a German organisation) the goals are clearly defined, and the expectation is that you reach these goals. Your goals may not be as high, but they are realistic.

Frankly, this passage does much to explain just why Hasselkus lost his job, to be followed in a now celebrated boardroom putsch by the BMW chief executive who appointed him, Berndt Piechetsrieder. Setting goals which you never meet is low-grade management in any language, and in any situation, including merger. Allowing such behaviour to continue is simply unacceptable. A company that meets only 80% of its goals, and is allowed to do so, will operate well below 100% in all aspects of its operations.

The 80% phenomenon helps to explain the success of spin-offs and the unsuccess of large multi-business companies. Subsidiary managements, even in growth businesses like mobile telephony and pharmaceuticals, negotiate the easiest targets they can. If the group management imposes higher numbers, the chances are that the targets will be missed. The group then faces an unpleasant choice between replacing the failed management or putting up with failure. Even if the numbers are on target, they may well conceal poor performance in some of the subsidiary operations.

This was the case with Zeneca, where one £930 million division was making only 2.8% on sales under ICI management. That can't have been the only case of under-management within the sprawling chemicals empire. So you had to wonder about the chances of much the same ICI managers successfully executing their master strategy: spin off Zeneca to take advantage of the inflated market value of pharmaceutical shares (which worked); and switch out of bulk chemicals, where margins are intrinsically low, into speciality chemicals, where customers are relatively indifferent to price (which didn't work).

The strategy sounded perfectly sensible. Strategies nearly always do. The boardroom strategists are saying that, if all goes according to plan, the company will gain a far superior business. Because outcomes lie in the future, nobody can prove them wrong: BMW might conceivably have made a success out of Rover. But what ever goes exactly according to plan?

The assumptions may be wrong. The market may change. The implementation may be flawed. If the strategy has been effected by acquisition, moreover, you may have hung a financial albatross around the company's neck. BMW, after paying its £800 million for Rover, invested the extra £2 billion mostly in the wrong places (the factories, not the products), with no sign of let-up in the annual losses. The investment was all wiped out.

All this failure stemmed from the assumption that BMW,

with its concentration on executive cars, produced in relatively small quantities, was strategically vulnerable in an industry dominated by far larger entities. Events since the buy saw BMW get much richer and the giants get larger still. Their gigantism didn't prove the strategic thesis. What if Ford, General Motors, Daimler, Renault and the rest of the industry were and are wrong?

Two erroneous beliefs come into play. First, that all those great brains, if they come to the same conclusion, can't be wrong. Second, that bigger is better: bigger resources and greater economies of scale ineluctably mean better results and still better resources. But BMW was a tiny player surrounded by giants when its wondrous ascent began. Honda's is an equally relevant example of relatively small size, and smashing success. In fragmenting, customer-led markets, should sheer size rule?

As for believing that great minds think not only alike but right, shared grand strategies often fail. In pharmaceuticals, giants like Smithkline Beecham had to sell recently-bought US drug distributors for half the huge purchase prices. The received wisdom, that owning distribution would strengthen holds over the prescriber market, turned out to be nonsense. The buyers bid up prices in the competitive struggle to jump on a band-wagon that was heading nowhere.

Bandwagon is the word. A top American manager, avidly bidding for a smaller financial services company, was asked by his advisors why he was so interested in the pursuit. 'Aw, shucks, fellers,' he replied, 'All the other kids have got one. . . .' Childishness lies behind much of the excuses explaining why large companies have to reshape their strategies around mega-buys. Some, as in telecommunications, are vying with each other to create networking supremacy. Many more are reorgan-ising round 'core businesses', disposing of superfluous interests and buying new ones, allegedly to strengthen the core.

The new groupings thus created (as at ICI) still have no genuine coherence. For such a strategy to work, managers have to demerge on a far more thorough-going scale. The model is Nokia, which made its exit from paper, tyres, metals, electronics (including PCs), cables and TV sets to devote itself to mobile telephony. The Finnish company proceeded to knock Motorola off its perch, and has also outpaced and out-innovated Ericsson. Unlike these two diversified rivals, Nokia concentrates on its core – which is a real core, not just wordplay. The reverse merging enabled it to manage brilliantly.

The ease of acquisitions is thus highly misleading. Making the deal does not require management: making the deal work is a tough exercise for the Fusion Manager, both in the initial integration and in the subsequent joint development. It doesn't matter that the deal is supposedly the building block of a carefully planned new structure. The structure must still be made to operate as planned. You may plan to transform the business by imaginative fusions of formerly separate activities. The blend must still be made to appeal to the market – the real-life customer market, not the stock-market dreamland.

Whatever the motivation, mergers and acquisitions are only as good as their management. There are innumerable books on corporate strategy: hardly any on overcoming the management problems of using mergers in pursuit of strategic ambitions. Just how do you guide managers towards the overriding goal – using amalgamation to achieve superior organic growth?

If they have done their work properly before the acquisition, the managers will have done their utmost to prove that they have sound, logical reasons for the purchase – which is a key principle in itself, 'Aw, shucks, fellers, all the other kids have got one' leads but to the grave. To check the logic of any buy, try a SWOT analysis.

- What new Strengths will the buy bring to the company?
- How will management capitalise on those Strengths?
- What are the Weaknesses of (a) the buyer (b) the target and (c) the combined businesses?
- How will management eliminate the Weaknesses?
- What Opportunities are available to the combined businesses that are not already available to the buyer?
- How will management seize those Opportunities, if any?
- What Threats will the buy avert?
- What new Threats will be created by the acquisition?

- How does management propose to overcome the Threats?

This analysis dovetails neatly with the key questions already detailed. Both analysis and questioning tend to encourage caution, which raises a real problem. Buying a business excites the animal juices in each of the three types of management personality. The Conservative thinks that the buy confirms the company's strengths. The Pragmatist believes that it will eliminate weaknesses and deal with threats. The Visionary lusts after new vistas of seized opportunities.

So the normal, uneasy balance between the three at the top of companies vanishes, to be replaced by hazardous unanimity. In other circumstances, the Conservative wants nothing but the preservation of the status quo; the Pragmatist will accept change, but only after it has been tried and proven somewhere else; and it's left to the Visionary, often battling against the odds, to try and drive the company into the future.

If organic ventures won the same unanimous enthusiasm and commitment as acquisitions, the latter would be needed far less as engines of growth. The reason why some Silicon Valley wonder-companies have enjoyed acquisition success far beyond the norm, despite whopping prices, is that mostly small targets have been picked off against a background of dynamic growth in the existing businesses. The buys, moreover, have been slotted into a receptive culture, in which new ideas are the key currency and Visionaries dominate, led by a visionary chief executive who has delegated all operating duties to others. Let these attributes be a lesson to everybody. It's one which can be easily learnt.

CHAPTER TWO

exploiting the slowdowns

*Why the crunch test of enterprise is to seize on slowdown as
an opportunity to create your own upturn*

The 21st century ushered in tougher times for managers – and
uncertain ones, which made matters worse. Even sadder, their
present fix compares with a very recent past in which the world
economy enjoyed a purple patch that (to the optimists) seemed
likely to last forever. Indeed, the worst that the pessimists could
(and did) say was that nothing does last forever. One day, as
sure as death and taxes, lovely boom turns to horrible bust –
but since nobody in a purple patch knows how or when, who
cares?

The uncaring optimists always have a plausible story to support their blind faith. This time round, the old economic order,
they argued, had been swept away by new, powerful and permanent developments. Low inflation and high growth were
being powered by advanced technology and inexhaustible
markets that were generating, and would go on generating,
unexampled rises in productivity. Enron was their model company, an apparently (but most deceptively) profitable growth
engine whose prime assets were not physical, but mental – the
all-conquering intellectual and trading skills of its perpetrators.

Just as Enron's fraud was exposed by application of the old,
orthodox accounting methods, so the iron laws of orthodox
business economics have resumed their rule. One of those laws
is that success breeds excess, and that the excesses invariably
have to be corrected. The longer the boom, and the larger the
bubble, the sharper and deeper the eventual, inevitable correction.

But Fusion Managers are no more carried away by downturns

than they are by booms. They look for trends – and those of today happen to be unusually clear, very powerful, absolutely irresistible and by no means gloomy. The trends of Fusion Management affect every aspect of every company and every manager's life with sweeping changes. They affect . . .

- how companies are managed (e.g., flat structures and bottom-up decision-making)
- how they compete (e.g., strategic alliances in which they 'co-opete' with competitors)
- where they do business (e.g., by direct participation in global markets)
- how they serve customers (e.g., through multimedia 'contact centres')
- how they communicate (e.g., by interaction over active websites and e-mail)
- how they operate (e.g., by optimising the efficiency of the entire, end-to-end business system)
- how they win competitive advantage (e.g., by disrupting markets to change the rules and unhorse competitors).

These changes started to work their way through against a late-century background of remarkable economic growth – though the general perception, thanks to the stock-market bubble, exaggerated the actual rate of expansion. The duration of the upward cycle in the US was exceptional, but the underlying pace in the real economy was not. The upturn was also highly predictable for followers of the great Soviet economist, Wassily Kondratieff. He detected long cycles of 20–25 years in economic history in which (much like the Seven Fat and Seven Lean Years of Biblical Egypt) slow growth alternated with faster expansion.

The oil price crisis of 1973 triggered a marked Kondratieff growth downturn which (as I used to predict to unbelieving audiences) was likely to give way to faster expansion in the mid-1990s. That Kondratieff upturn could last all the way to 2020 or so. Moreover, the last two cycles – the slow period and the fast – share two important characteristics.

First, the pace of creation of significant new businesses and new technologies quite plainly accelerated in both periods. Second, the pillars of the traditional economy (the smokestack and other capital-intensive old-line businesses) entered a process of general relative decline that is clearly still continuing.

The reason is equally plain. The economic gorillas once had a near-monopoly of capital and valuable skills, including managerial and technological know-how. They now compete on virtually equal terms with corporate chimpanzees. To return to the trends highlighted above, companies of any size can compete with any giant in . . .

- the speed and the efficiency of their communications
- their service and retention of the customer
- their competitive edge
- their cost of production
- their global spread
- their strategic alliances and joint ventures
- and, above all, the excellence and excellent performance of their managers.

The enormous impact of this change is shown by the startling transformation of IBM, from the world champion of high technology to also-ran in most of its markets. I wrote long ago that the old IBM was nibbled to death by mice. When Microsoft inflicted the deadly blow of Windows on its erstwhile PC partner, Bill Gates's baby had half-a-billion dollars of sales, a tiny percentage of IBM's massive market. One after the other, led by Gates, the mice took control of the markets that should have belonged to IBM in perpetuity.

Its managers believed that their market ownership was indeed perpetual. But the mice became huge, sometimes savage beasts, devouring new markets which in wealth and growth came to match even IBM's fabulous mainframes. Two exogenous forces determined this amazing, unpredicted outcome. First, the technology expanded and diversified at a pace that made it impossible for any company, even one as wealthy and multi-faceted as IBM, to control all, or even most, avenues to the captive customer. Second, that customer no longer wanted to be captive.

For all manner of reasons, supply in most sectors has become super-abundant, perhaps permanently, and suppliers have proliferated. The great brands are still great, but their owners can no longer – in most cases – use the brands to produce and protect lush margins. In this new world, a brand is only as good as its last sale. The trend can only be contradicted in those areas (Microsoft in operating and bundled software, Intel in microprocessors) where the supplier has achieved a quasi-monopoly, either by conditions of trade (Microsoft) or by dominance of supply (Intel).

It would be unwise to predict that even the quasi-monopolists have an iron grip on their futures. Microsoft is vulnerable to unforeseen technological breakthroughs that certainly lie ahead: already Linux is nibbling away at its operating system monopoly. Intel is under unprecedented pressure at the bottom, the middle and the top of its market as growth shifts from the PC to hand-held devices and servers. Both brands are vulnerable to strategic error

Like the iron laws of business economics, and probably because of them, this vulnerability has an uncanny knack of asserting itself at awkward moments – quite often, interestingly, on the retirement of the architect of the previous success. Under Jack Welch, for example, GE recorded impressive financial results, like his last decade's solid rise in earnings per share of 12.1% a year. Return to shareholders – reflecting a sevenfold rise in market value – was something else, though: a huge 28.7% annually.

The $449 billion increase in market capitalisation for GE duly achieved Welch's ambition to make it the world's most highly valued company. But in April 2002, GE lost over $100 billion of that market value – an amount greater than the total capitalisation of General Motors and Ford combined a year before. There were specific explanations. Welch had left the command centre after an episode of conspicuous failure – the aborted takeover of Honeywell – which expensively cracked the image of irresistible success and immaculate judgment.

Then, his unfortunate heirs almost immediately ran into the backwash of the Enron debacle. Investors have begun to query the wondrous (and logically quite impossible) smoothness of GE's earnings per share growth, quarter after miraculous quarter, under Welch's expert ministrations. That previous achievement owes much to his managerial skills, to be sure. But the Kondratieff upturn, and far more the upward valuation of all companies, the deserving and the undeserving alike, were indispensable conditions of Welch's and GE's rise.

Fusion Managers can learn (and teach) a lesson from all this. GE was and is good, but not so good as that $449 billion rise in market value. You should always seek to disentangle your own achievements, which have everything to do with you, from the effects of the environment, which you don't control. Ask yourself these annoying, but soul-searching questions.

- What is the baseline for my performance – the level of turnover, revenues and unit sales that is the minimal benchmark?
- What improvements over the benchmark figures resulted from external influences outside my control?
- How did my performance truly compare with that of the competition?
- What was the real contribution of any initiatives of ours towards differentiating our performance?

This analysis is a very tough procedure. It's a safe bet that most managers will be very disinclined to undertake such a post-mortem after a successful year. This is a big mistake – similar to that of managers who fall foul of Charles Handy's Sigmoid Curve. As described on page 39, the Curve describes the life-cycle of companies, most of which blithely and fatally miss the critical point, well before the cycle peaks, when only the start of a new and different cycle will sustain growth.

It takes a genuine Fusion Manager, one who can combine optimism with realism, to see that the acme of success may mask the onset of failure. Continued high profits, sales and cash-flow blind managements (see IBM again) to the fierce reality: that their underlying strengths are diminishing. When the impact of this deterioration finally breaks through, it's usually too late to undo the damage – and the abundant money and lofty morale of peak performance have probably given way to much worse finances and demoralisation (especially if the company starts downsizing in the usually forlorn, knee-jerk effort to restore its fortunes – trying to move foward by cutting back).

In sum, you need to search out the unpleasant truths before you begin to congratulate yourself on the pleasant ones. If a particular strategy or tactic is succeeding, by all means pile on the pressure and the pleasure, repeating and (if possible) improving what has worked. The New Zealand entrepreneur who gave his name to, and made millions from, Macleans toothpaste was a firm believer in heavily backing success. But Sir Alexander's simple and effective formula had another part: never reinforce failure. If a product didn't sell, Maclean simply scrubbed it from the portfolio. In doing so, he obeyed a literally simple instruction: Keep It Simple, Stupid (or KISS).

The growing uncertainties of the early 21st century, dominated by the tug-of-war between necessary cost-saving and unmissable opportunity, make it vital to adopt the Maclean approach. Keeping It Simple, Stupid actually requires the exercise of intelligence. Thus armed, you can see, for example, that taking out any superfluous processes or stages has the same impact as cutting down (see Maclean) the attention paid to superfluous products. Costs come down and margins go up.

You plainly don't have to be super-intelligent to grasp the rationale of such results. Stupidity only comes into the picture if, having understood, you ignore the lessons – as do all too many managers. The iron laws of economics revolve round three words: Revenues, Costs, Quality. The laws lay down that management must fail unless it raises revenues, reduces costs per unit of output, and notably improves the quality of internal processes and external perceptions. Those rules, moreover, must be obeyed all the time, and for ever.

The RCQ formula is essentially simple, but involves asking penetrating questions and not resting until you get answers which imply and demand action. For example, you can't hope to win market acceptance unless you know . . .

1 Who are the customers?
2 What are they like?
3 What do they need?
4 How do we persuade them?

The simplicity is deceptive, but only because most managers have not considered these basic issues in any kind of depth. The second question, for instance, is answered by 'value mapping'. You divide the people or firms targeted into three groups: Visionaries (the entrepreneurs and innovators), Pragmatists ('I'll see whether it works for other firms') and Conservatives ('it will never work/sell'). There's a parallel division, coined by marketing guru Simon Majaro, between Philes (who love you and your products and/or services): Phobes (who hate you and all your works): and Promiscuous buyers, who jump into bed with any supplier who catches their fancy.

The consequences of this simple analysis are equally simple. You concentrate maximum effort on trying to convert the Promiscuous into Philes, who you look after with the most tender loving care, and you don't waste time on the conservative Phobes. It's a policy that conforms to Pareto's Law, whose iron insistence that 20% of any activity accounts for 80% of the outcome has been proved again and again in all fields of management – production, marketing, inventory control, design, human resources, and so on.

Without this type of analysis, you will lack the RCQ foundation for moving forward, even in stagnant times. Remember that the formula is self-sustaining and circular. Expanding Revenues when costs are falling generates the higher resources from which to finance improvements in Quality. The enhanced perceptions of Quality in turn help to expand Revenues, and so the benevolent cycle continues. You thus eliminate the conflict between cutting back and moving forward. By doing both you improve both sides of the equation. The conflict ends, the cake is both had and eaten, and Fusion Management wins.

It can still win big, very big. Just as the years before the Kondratieff upturn showed unprecedented vigour in the creation of new businesses, processes and products, so does this period after the dot.com crash and the Twin Towers catastrophe. That definitely includes the e-world, *Red Herring*, the magazine devoted to the 'business of innovation', has it right: 'there is nothing wrong with e-commerce in and of itself'. On-line commerce is evolving and is more than the Web, says the magazine, which concludes that 'the failure of the first wave . . . simply demonstrated that a new technological vehicle is worth nothing if its driver doesn't focus on customer satisfaction'.

As for the slowdown, 'the winnowing of bad businesses will simply create better conditions for the good companies' which are now creating the second wave of e-commerce. This observation applies across the business board: other people's pain can be your gain. The crunch test of enterprise is to see and seize slowdown as an opportunity in itself to create your own upturn while others are sitting on their hands. 'Simple'-minded, really intelligent, truly enterprising Fusion Managers won't sit on anything. They will move, move first – and move fast.

CHAPTER THREE

transforming the theories

Transformation can't be achieved unless managers truly want themselves or their organisations to be transformed

Managers love ideas – especially big ones. Or so you might conclude from the output of academics, other management writers, seminar organisers, consultants and the rest of the managerial support industry. Few of the supporting theorists, though, ever question how much impact their theory-peddling has on the great majority of practising managers – or even on the minority who determine the fate of major organisations.

How many managers, for example, have been directly influenced in their actions – day-to-day, month-to-month, even year-to-year – by the Six Forces theory on strategy formation? Or the 'core competencies' concept? Or the idea of disruptive technologies? Or the description of 'emotional intelligence'? The ideas made the fame, respectively, of Michael Porter; the duo (now disbanded, but writing individually) of C.K. Prahalad and Gary Hamel; Clayton Christensen; and Daniel Goleman. But have the ideas made anything else for anybody else?

The first point to stress is that all four theories are based on observations of purported fact. The resulting insights are not necessarily earth-shattering. Porter specified familiar forces which appeared to be dominating strategic action. Prahalad and Hamel concluded that what you do particularly well is the determining basis of organisational success. Christensen, more originally, noted that concentrating effectively on what you've done well in the past debars market leaders from competing successfully in new ways. And Goleman, less originally, saw that how people feel has more influence on their actions than how they think.

Now, there's an important role in bringing people's attention to the obvious. All the same, stand up anyone who thought differently on any of these points. Also, stand up anyone who has knowingly applied any of the ideas in practice. Yet all of them are identified in the *Harvard Business Review* (May 2001) as 'truly big, paradigm-shattering ideas' that 'don't just advance the conversation; they permanently alter it'.

Even if that's true of these supposedly big concepts, altering conversation and altering action are very different activities. Remember, too, that the 'paradigm-shatterers' begin with descriptions: if these are inaccurate, then what? It's well-known that the companies which management writers (including the present one) select as wonderful examples often turn out to have feet of heavy clay. But generalised observations can equally unravel as real life unfolds.

Michael de Kare Silver, for illustration, has written an excellent critique (*Strategy in Crisis*) of strategic thinking, including Porter's. From his observations, the latter identified three 'generic strategies'; lowest cost, differentiation, and focus (or 'niche'). By the mid-1990s, Porter himself had recognised that cost leadership through economies of scale was a dwindling alternative. Silver added that Porter had also 'begun to blur the distinction between focus and differentiation'. But did any true distinction ever exist?

Focus means concentrating on a segment of a market or industry by placing a distinctive offering before the customer. Silver pointed out that today 'most companies are compelled to focus anyway on particular buying segments . . . rather than aiming to compete with advantage across a whole industry'. Porter actually gave IBM as an example of industry-wide differentiation. But 'computers' hardly amounted to a distinctive description. If anything, Porter was identifying, not IBM's strength, but its weakness – its failure to differentiate its market into powerful segments.

That leaves precious little of Porter's three generic strategies for managers to follow. Anyway, Silver was right to point out that, even before demolition, the strategies didn't actually help managers to decide what to do or how. He scored Porter high

only on encouraging managers to take a longer-term view –
and rated him very low both on starting the value chain at the
customers' end (the raging fashion of the early Millennium)
and on 'reflecting business realities'. The obvious question is
whether any theorist writing about 'what is', and getting that
wrong, can be a useful guide to 'what should be'.

'Should be' is another concept in itself – the idea that managers impressed with a theoretical idea or ideas, can, by acting
accordingly, alter the fortunes of their organisations in successful ways. That is no doubt true – if you can find the right theory.
But which to choose? The choices are by no means easy. To
take the *HBR* list, how do you reconcile the development of
core competencies with the encouragement of disruptive technologies that may fracture that core? Christensen comes up
with a convincing solution: you spin off the new disruptive
enterprises from the main corporate body. But what's the
answer if the core is rotting?

There are precious few examples of companies that have sacrificed their cores in favour of creating something wholly new
– as Hamel would recommend in such circumstances. When
asked for an example of such mighty transformation, Hamel,
speaking at a public seminar, nominated Monsanto. But that
company's decision to switch all its emphasis to bio-science led
straight into the public-relations horrors of the world-wide fight
over genetically modified foods. The company lost both its
reputation and its independence.

With few exceptions, total transformation is rarely achieved.
Managers don't *truly* want themselves or their organisations to
be transformed. Odd as it may seem, they are often happier
with what they have, even if its results are miserable, than with
undergoing deep change. That being so, transformational ideas
have little chance of being translated into transforming action.

The *HBR* editors inadvertently illustrate the difficulty, in the
same issue, by moving on from 'paradigm-shatterers' to high-
light 'five provocative concepts that are shaping management
now'. All five do challenge earlier concepts once thought to
constitute 'breakthrough ideas'. Here are the old ideas with the
new challenges:

1 Every company establishes a 'business model' which determines its strategies and tactics . . . *BUT nobody has really defined 'business model' – and the new thinking is to concentrate on the basics and on 'simple rules' that 'govern key processes'.*

2 Companies must reinvent themselves or die . . . *BUT reinvention (or the 'radical change imperative') can destroy what is truly valuable without creating anything of equal value.*

3 Effective leaders follow a distinct pattern of transferrable, strong personality traits . . . *BUT ego is less important for effectiveness than the 'authenticity' of the leader.*

4 Managing people as individuals is the key to corporate achievement . . . *BUT connections between people matter more for effectiveness than individual nurture.*

5 Physical science is determining the speed and force of technological change (viz, the Internet and all its works) . . . *BUT the current century looks like being the era of biology.*

Blinding glimpses of the obvious abound on both sides of this list. First, every company actually does have a business model. It isn't optional, and it isn't theoretical. It describes the business. The phrase presumably stems from information technology. You can 'model' any business process or set of processes – right up to the national or even the global economy – on any computer. At its simplest definition, the business model establishes the relationship between how a company earns its revenues and how it generates the associated costs.

Compaq, for example, had a highly successful model that rested on selling highly (and expensively) engineered products at high prices, just below those of market-leading IBM. The model generated gross margins of 50% from sales limited to only part of the market and to dealer-only distribution. This earthly paradise was shattered by competition from other, numberless PCs, which, like Compaq's, cloned the IBM product, but were able to offer the same Intel microprocessors and Microsoft software at prices that savagely undercut the high Compaq charges.

New management adopted a brand-new model: Compaq would supply the whole market, not just a few segments, going through wider channels at lower prices, and aiming at all competitors – including those at the mass end of the market. This change of model halved gross margins, but targeted much greater volumes: Compaq was able to match and then surpass its former record levels of sales and profits. Model Two left the huge success of Model One far behind as Compaq soared past IBM to become the world leader in PCs.

The relationship between margins, volumes and profits is simple, basic and easily modelled – with pen and paper, never mind a computer. You can quickly model how much volume has to rise to justify a price cut, for example; or (*vice versa*) how much a price rise can cut volume without reducing profits. Compaq's changed management had the courage to act on this logic. In the process, they radically transformed the company. The baby was not thrown out with the bathwater, as the *HBR* feared – because every change had a specific business purpose in view and was carefully monitored to ensure that the purpose was well and truly served.

So two of the five *HBR* challenges prove to be illusory. What about the next two – 'leadership' and 'people relationships'? For a start, they plainly belong together. The leader, whether or not driven by a vast ego, can only lead through causing and directing relationships. The leader cannot lead by force of personality alone: nor will effective communication do the trick. You can no more have effective leadership that doesn't communicate effectively than you can have effective communication that doesn't spring from an effective personality.

Nor, except in very rare and remote circumstances (like a researcher marooned in a mountain-top lab), can you have an individual who works in isolation – or whose work stands alone, without any need for contributions from others. The *HBR*, in fact, specifically makes this point. So why does the *Review* think that 'social connectedness' is a 'new focus'? What's the difference between 'fostering stronger connections among people' and the age-old emphasis on teamwork – and team leadership? What is meant by 'social networks and the norms of reciprocity and trustworthiness that arise from them' if it doesn't cover people working in teams?

That last quote above comes from a 1995 tome, *Bowling Alone*, written by sociologist Robert Putnam. Its theme has been followed by several authors who likewise look at management in terms of 'emotional intelligence'. Once again, these ideas put new clothes on old and familiar concepts. Take emotional intelligence itself. Who ever thought that effective management was an exercise in intellect alone, or that intellect was the principal determinant of managerial and business success?

To return to Compaq, Eckhard Pfeiffer, the German saviour, may or may not have been brainier than Rod Canion, the founding CEO. But Pfeiffer wasn't blinded, like Canion, by emotional attachment to Compaq's first success. When his own moment of truth arrived, as the company came under threat from direct-selling and his fateful purchase of Digital Equipment, Pfeiffer got stuck in his own emotional trap – and fell in turn.

The lesson from these episodes is that all successful managers face a similar threat: that a time will come when, for whatever reason, they have outlived their usefulness. If they are identified with a failed business model, a counter-productive change programme, over-dominant leadership, or dissension at the top, the solution is strictly clear: change the leader. That's what BMW did when its ventures into a broader product range, buying Rover and LandRover, paid no market dividends, but cost huge losses (see page 130).

The Bavarian company dropped its pilot, and under a new leader returned to a model built around excellence and concentration on executive cars – and won industry-leading profits. As an idea, removing people identified with failed policies and execution is hardly new: if it 'shatters' a paradigm, that's only because the reluctance of boards of directors to act in good time has itself become a paradigm.

BT, for example, only fell into losses, a passed dividend, halved share prices and massive debts because of top management policies dating back several years. Yet the chairman, Sir Ian Vallance, was only replaced on the eve of the dividend cut: and, still more oddly, the chief executive, Sir Peter Bonfield, was left *in situ* (but not for long). There can't be any theoretical justification for this reluctance – though Bonfield's boardroom colleagues may have thought, or felt, that his knowledge of past decisions and present problems was too important to be sacrificed.

This has usually proved to be a dumb idea. The episode makes the point, however, that business is not 'driven by smart ideas', as the *HBR* wrote, but by deeds – clever, foolish and neutral. The big books and interesting articles don't actually direct events, but flow from them. In the practical world of business, managers are coping with hard facts that result from changes outside their control – like these:

- Business isn't as usual anymore. Management needs to develop the company's direction and purpose anew on a continuous basis.
- Fulfilling that purpose requires concentration on a well-defined market – and rules out diversified and uncoordinated interests.
- Technologies and markets have become so volatile that innovative attack is the best, maybe the only form of defence: and that means innovative corporate organisation.
- People are asserting their individuality more throughout society: you need to use that individuality to innovate and to animate the new corporate forms.
- Those forms are becoming much less rigid because of the need for broader inter-relationships, crossing boundaries inside and outside the firm.

Note how these five developments mesh with each other. They are dominant characteristics of Fusion Management. You don't need to read tomes (Putnam's *Bowling Alone* runs to 544 pages) to recognise that the developments are realities of your managerial existence. But don't be like Canion, Pfeiffer, Vallance and Bonfield and turn your back on the realities. Do suit your actions to the real requirements. That means starting with an intense examination of your business model (which exists whether you know it or not) and asking whether it still meets your objectives.

If not, revise or replace the model and make all consequent changes as necessary. But never forget that management is essentially paradoxical – it's the fusion of opposites. Thus, the *HBR* quotes a banal definition of winners by Michael Porter: they 'display the discipline and focus necessary to establish a distinctive competitive positioning and then stick with it, no matter which way the winds blow'. A mere paragraph later, the editors observe contrarily that 'None of this means that companies should become rigid: flexibility still matters.'

The Fusion Manager knows that neither of the above statements is valid by itself. You need both flexibility and rigidity, working in harness. Your guide out of this management maze is to remember that no single theory works in all circumstances – with one possible exception. Stick with what works well. Before it doesn't work any more, change it, no matter how much change hurts, for something that will work even better.

curing power complexes

Having an all-powerful CEO can be a driving force for success or a quick road to failure

Chief executives are more than ever the pinnacles of the management system. They have immense power, subject only to the confidence of the board of directors. That confidence, still too often misplaced, is somewhat less easily retained than in the past. This is not because boards are any keener on exercising their authority, or any stricter in demanding acceptable results, but because investors have become far more restless about 'under-performance'.

But what performance should be expected from the people at the top? The general approach is to vest them with total responsibility for the success or failure of the organisation. That applies all the way from a global corporation to local government. But the vesting is vague. Appointees are hardly ever given, or asked to provide, a list of objectives or criteria by which they can expect to be judged. In well-run companies, that is, of course, how delegation works.

Why should the delegator-in-chief be exempted from the same accountability? In fact, common objectives and criteria, while generally unstated, do exist for all CEOs in all businesses. They must be able to answer, with a resounding Yes, questions such as:

- Is the company providing only profitable goods and services that customers want and at prices that they readily pay?
- Are the goods and services being supplied at highly

competitive and constantly reducing costs, with
continuous improvements in physical efficiency and
productivity?

- Does the business rate more highly, on all the aspects
  most important to the customer, than its very best
  competition?
- Is the business tapping the widest possible markets,
  geographically and by segment, for its existing products
  and services?
- Are new products and services coming onto the market
  that will add significantly, as and when needed, to the
  company's competitive strength?
- Are there powerful reasons, in the customer's mind, for
  buying the company's products and services rather than
  anybody else's?
- Are policies, plans and strategies in place, and being
  continually renewed, that should sustain the company's
  strengths into the indefinite future and go on giving Yes
  answers to the above six questions?

Those Seven Critical Questions, note, involve a number of trade-offs and compromises; but you neglect any of them at your peril. The harm done will offset much good done elsewhere. This, however, generates the paradox which Fusion Managers come to know and love. By concentrating on all the critical seven areas, you significantly improve your answers to each. A clear example is quality. You should more than cover the cost of quality by reducing the cost of waste.

Another deeply significant aspect of the Seven Critical Questions is that all can be translated into measurable objectives and criteria. The CEO must be said to under-perform if these targets are not met. That is not because the incumbent has personally failed to 'make the numbers', but because those working lower down the organisation have not been adequately motivated, organised, managed and resourced. Ensuring that this demanding set of needs is met is an intimidating but essential task, and top people who fail to meet the needs cannot be left on top. Leave them, and the under-performance will become systemic, and immensely difficult to eradicate – even under new leadership.

That danger would seemingly justify the new century's more numerous executions of 'under-performing' CEOs. But under-performance for these victims does not mean losing market share, or missing great innovative opportunities, or allowing quality to decline, or mismanaging the workforce, or falling behind in customer satisfaction, etc. A company under-performs in this context when its shares, for whatever reason (and usually over too long a period of toleration) lag the stock market as a whole, or fall behind its own sector.

Sometimes the above-mentioned sins (lost share, etc.) are present and plainly responsible for this market under-performance. But the stock price is, of course, one parameter over which nobody, including the CEO, has any control. The surge in media valuations, for example, both before and after the now ailing AOL-Time Warner merger, had nothing to do with the efficiency of the CEOs involved or the excellence of their strategies. Media shares were simply in fashion, just as retail stocks were unfashionable. But, leaving that aside, is it fair to saddle the executive-in-chief with all the blame for failure in the stock market?

There is an element of rough justice, true. The reward systems load riches on to these bosses as if they truly were the architects of all success. If the CEOs want the rewards of assumed omnipotence, they must in fairness accept its penalties. But the award of exclusive praise and blame is evidently absurd. Management expert Henry Mintzberg once pertinently observed, after quoting a passage heaping praise on the miracles allegedly achieved by Lou Gerstner at IBM, 'All by himself?' Even Gerstner would not claim that the truthful answer is Yes.

Any success in management, as in war, is the work of many hands – and in recent years that truth has become more powerful (or should have done), for several reasons. It creates the supreme requirement for fusion: blending the need for strong individual leadership at the top with maximum contribution from the bottom all the way up. The four factors below are all ways in which Fusion Management has been necessitated and implemented:

1 Most businesses have become more complex, and one man or woman cannot possibly command all the expertise involved.

2 The need for teamwork and fusion at all levels, including the design and implementation of strategy, has made the leader's role as CEO facilitative rather than prescriptive.

3 Most companies are now organised into discrete, autonomous units with individual leaders who are held fully responsible for all of their results.

4 Much of the crucial work of companies is now carried out in interdisciplinary, cross-functional project groups, to which the principles of autonomy and accountability apply with equal strength.

Since all that is undeniably true, why does the cult of the CEO ride so high? The answer lies partly with the men and women themselves. Having reached a position of authority, they want to exercise it, to enjoy the feeling of having near-total power – and its disproportionate rewards. In the biggest companies, these anti-fusionists have already earned so much money that their riches reinforce their natural ego drives – as in the extraordinary case of Coca-Cola's Doug Ivester.

According to a fascinating account in *Fortune* magazine, Ivester left the company after a disastrous two years as CEO with $318 million in shares and options. That vast sum dwarfs a final-year salary of $1.25 million. He also received a $1.5 million special bonus, paid because of his 'leadership in difficult times'. Since Coke's net income had fallen by 22% and its return on equity from 57% to 35%, the remuneration committee must have been very easy indeed to please – though little easier, probably, than most such committees.

But Coke has two non-executive directors who are hard men to gratify: Warren Buffett and Herbert Allen. The former, speaking for 8.1% of the Coke equity, takes a strict and strictly pragmatic view of the CEO's duties, which emphatically do not include presiding over a sharp fall in return on equity. Allen is a powerful investment banker who also speaks for a significant number of shares. He no doubt endorses Buffett's view that the

CEO is a proxy for the owners and must protect shareholders' interests as if they were his own.

Few, however, can pass Buffett's triple test: that CEOs should 'love their businesses . . . think like owners and . . . exude integrity and ability'. It's a tricky piece of fusion: thinking like a proprietor while acting as a hired hand. Even when CEOs fail the triple test, as Buffet remarked in one of his wonderful annual reports, their positions 'nevertheless, are usually secure'. At his own Berkshire Hathaway, which owns an immense clutch of enterprises, each with its own boss, that security has been earned by performance. That is by no means the case elsewhere. In fact, as Buffett says, 'it is far easier for an inadequate CEO to keep his job' than an inadequate subordinate.

He calls this plain truth the 'supreme irony of business management'. Buffett blames the lack of performance standards; in the rare cases where they do exist, they might as well not; the standards for the CEO are 'often fuzzy or they may be waived or explained away, even when the performance shortfalls are major and repeated'. In a telling metaphor, Buffett describes the boss 'who shoots the arrow of managerial performance and then hastily paints the bullseye around the spot where it lands'.

As noted above, in describing the Seven Critical Questions, suitable criteria and objectives can easily be found. That is surely the responsibility of the board. But non-executive directors are even less accountable than CEOs. Buffett and Allen did not demand the departure of their fellow board members of Coca-Cola – who, remember, actually voted the erring Ivester that absurd special bonus for his non-existent achievements. Non-execs should be Fusion Managers *par excellence*; providing (like Buffett) friendship and support for their CEOs while also being their severest critics.

Anyone with substantial boardroom experience, however, knows that relations between the CEO and his board are very far from adversarial. Pungent as ever, and deeply experienced in the matter, Buffett notes that, 'At board meetings, criticism of the CEO's performance is often viewed as the social equivalent of belching.' It would hardly be welcomed, anyway. When director Don Keough, the retired president and a great man in

Coke's previous upward march, sent Ivester six pages of suggestions for improving Coke's lagging business, he got a one-line letter of thanks – and that was the sole response.

Far from passing Buffett's triple test, Ivester had a self-centred set of priorities, as his unwise actions showed. One of them, offending Keough, who for good measure is chairman of Allen's company, was especially ill-judged. Worse still (from Ivester's point of view), Keough is a Nebraskan friend of Buffett, the Sage of Omaha. Furthermore, Ivester offended the powerful Coke bottlers (whose numbers, suicidally, include Buffett's son) with his verbal blunders. Much more hurtful still, he abruptly raised the price they paid for the magic syrup, the secret of Coke, by 10%.

Inside Coke, Invester instituted rigid, bureaucratic controls which revolved around him personally. He believed that good management depends on good information, which is true, but also that the more and better the information, the better the management, which is false. However, the theory misled *Fortune* in mid-1998 into writing as follows: 'Ivester may give us a glimpse of the 21st century CEO, who marshals data and manages people in a way no pre-Information Age executive ever did or could.'

In fact, deceived inside the forest of data, Ivester lost sight of the people inside and outside the company. He also lost touch with the consumer marketing which is Coke's lifeblood. Further, he failed, as one high-placed informant said, 'to give people a sense of purpose or direction'. Still, remember Henry Mintzberg's question: 'All by himself?' If CEOs can't justifiably claim all the credit for success, they don't deserve all the blame, either.

They think they rule the system, when in reality the system rules them. The Fusion Manager builds on the best of the past to achieve excellent present performance which serves as foundation for an even better future. Anti-fusionists, in contrast, find it desperately difficult to extricate themselves from the past. One reason is the depth of the holes that they and/or their predecessors have dug. Kodak's loss of market share in film to Fuji, and its failure to develop powerful new businesses, turned it, perhaps permanently, from leader to follower; sales fell by a quarter over the 1990s.

The hole-diggers, moreover, customarily ignore the shifting earth beneath their feet. Senior managers commonly complain about resistance to change among the lowest orders. In fact, resistance among middle managers is both stronger and harder to eradicate. Many are wedded to the post and fearful for their jobs (often with reason). But their conservatism is generally outdone by their seniors. Top executives not only lived under the previous dispensation: they created its failures, and then denied their existence. The denial delays response, and slow reactions invariably make bad much worse.

That is why the over-familiar Supertanker Myth is so dangerous. Corporate captains like to compare their vessels with bulk oil carriers that can only turn at lugubrious speeds. That misses the crucial point. The transformation which they need changes the supertanker into a fleet of smaller, fast-moving (and fast-turning) motor boats. This metaphor was actually used by Heinrich von Pierer, CEO of Siemens, to explain his plans for corporate revolution. Three years on, his flotilla was no more impressive than the supertanker it supposedly replaced, earning half of Hewlett-Packard's profits on 50% more sales.

The moral is that, to become speedboats, supertankers need different crews, Fusion Managers who can achieve dynamic synthesis between past, present and future. General Motors may have got lucky with the new CEO, G. Richard Wagoner, a 23-year veteran, appointed in 1999. He promptly called on other veteran managers to 'shake off GM's complacent, cautious traditions and take more risks'. You can only sympathise with the analyst who told the *Wall Street Journal* that, without someone to pressurise slow-moving management, 'there's no such thing as a p/e too low for a company [GM] with these kinds of characteristics'. However, Wagoner's GM proceeded to improve on all counts, leaving Ford behind in the dust.

Fast fusion is of the essence. Yet the departed CEO of Procter & Gamble was berated for trying to force through too much change too rapidly. That seems odd, if not unfair, given that his company's 'restructuring' programme was a five-year marathon, excessively long in any era, but an eternity in the Age of the Internet. Unless change comes fast and runs swift and deep, led by CEOs who understand and apply the lessons of Fusion Management, companies will go on limping from one stage of under-performance to the next – which will one day be the last.

The brief purple passages in between serve only to delude. Restructuring, the euphemism for closures, cutbacks and lay-offs, nearly always pays dividends in the short to medium term. True transformation, however, will not be achieved unless everybody in all the businesses supports the strategy and its purpose, and is fully and personally involved in its execution – from bottom to top. Note the inversion. At the top, those who have the absolute power are powerless to create change, except by genuinely devolving and sharing that power.

Should that absolutism exist at all? Organisations can get lucky with their absolutists. In two decades at the helm of General Electric, Jack Welch gave the company the great 'sense of purpose or direction' mentioned above. He changed the way GE worked. He spent much time talking to managers one on one. He ended these sometimes fierce exchanges with a written summary of managers' commitments; he followed up to ensure that they were met. His managers naturally emulated this model in their own dealings with subordinates.

But Welch knows that, 'To be vital an organisation has to repot itself, start again, get new ideas, renew itself.' That means he has still to pass the last test failed by Coke's Goizueta: to quote Welch, 'My success will be determined by how well my successor grows [GE] in the next 20 years.' That can't be left to luck. This doesn't refer solely to the selection process, though that at GE is famous for leaving no stones unturned – Welch claims to have begun the work a decade before his scheduled retirement. Outcomes depend more on how effectively your successor shares power, fusing supreme authority with genuine democracy, and reserving unto himself or herself two key tasks above all: stopping the bad, and encouraging the good to be done. That's plenty.

doom at the top

Why boards would do their jobs properly if they followed the wise ways of Warren Buffett

Managers are faced with paradoxes that make fusion essential. But one of the recurrent and greatest examples goes to the heart of any organisation, or rather to its top. As noted in the previous chapter, since the mid-1990s, chief executives, especially in the US, have been fired more frequently, and sooner into their reigns, than ever before. The departed have failed to fulfil their investors' desires for enhanced stock-market performance – and have been given little time, perhaps only a couple of years, to make their marks.

These dismissals, harsh or fair, are short-term judgments. The first half of the paradox is that managers are supposed to be thinking, planning and acting with long-term aims in mind. The second half of the paradox lies in this heavy reliance on one man or woman, the CEO, in an age when power and responsibility are supposed to be devolved down the line, and when management is seen as a group activity to which teamwork is fundamental.

This isn't a pious hope: it is the actuality of managers' lives. Managers are working more and more in genuine, task-oriented teams. Even if that were not the case, it's never true that bad results stem solely from bad individuals. There must also be serious failures of the system. Of course, that system and the effectiveness of its operation are among the prime responsibilities of the CEO (although very few of them show much interest in the task). The CEO is, however, certainly responsible for the key systemic actions:

- setting up the roles
- staffing the key roles
- determining relationships
- monitoring the effectiveness of performance.

Boards rarely, to their shame, spend much time with CEOs on these issues, even though they are transparently crucial. So what do boards (and the large investors whose interests they are supposed to protect) most consider? The answers are relevant to all organisations, which in every country will have some form of governance, exercised either by an owner (collective or individual) or some statutory body, like the board.

These bodies rarely answer to any higher authority, except that amorphous, supine mass known as the shareholders. Their most important personnel role, again rarely much influenced by external pressures, is plainly to appoint the CEO. No doubt after due deliberation, the nine collective wisdoms of Mattel, Lucent, Newell Rubbermaid, Campbell Soup, Coca-Cola, Gillette, Procter & Gamble, Maytag and Xerox settled on men who were eminently qualified for their overpaid jobs – but who left them in the 2000s after tenures ranging from a mere thirteen months to a scant three years.

Exactly why did the nine boards celebrate the Millennium by ousting their own appointees so soon? Part of the answer is that all nine companies, often right up to the succession of the unfortunate victims, were universally admired corporate wonders. The inimitable Warren Buffett had long sung the praises of Coke and Gillette as two of his star investment holdings, while Rubbermaid was once voted America's most admired company by its peers. P&G had (and has) an immense reputation as the monarch of fast-moving consumer goods. Lucent shot to stardom after its spin-off from AT&T.

The nine wonders turned into nine flops. In all these cases, the successors had extremely hard acts to follow. In some cases, they had no hope of repeating the once-for-all successes that powered their predecessors into the Hall of Corporate Fame. At Coke, for example, Roberto C. Goizueta had transformed the company's fortunes by imposing stern demands for return on capital and reorganising the crucial relationship with the bottlers. There were no similar masterstrokes available to his hand-picked successor, Doug Ivester, who only lasted for a miserable 28 months (see the previous chapter).

But the encore problem was not that of the CEO alone. 'Encore' refers to that well-known question, 'What do we do for an encore?' Xerox has been thrashing around for years, trying and failing to follow up its original and smashing success in xerographic copying. P&G has long badly needed to find a brand-new recipe for FMCG (fast-moving consumer goods) marketing in the face of mounting evidence that the markets are changing rapidly, and that even exceptionally famous brands are not enough to generate truly exceptional success on their own.

The boards in all these nine cases must share the responsibility for failure. They all made the fatal mistake of leaving the encore problem entirely to the new CEO. Sometimes the hero will get it triumphantly right, like Coke's Goizueta or Jack Welch at General Electric. But in both these cases, the new men had a priceless advantage: the two companies were not in crisis, but were under-performing for such clear and simple reasons that massive uplift was possible without breaking stride.

The key contribution was to see this vast room for improvement when the board previously could not. The pressures on boards have mounted so heavily from one particular direction – the stock market – that the directors concerned are in the position of the farmer who killed the goose that laid the golden eggs. Stephen R.Covey, author of *The Seven Habits of Highly Effective People*, uses this very metaphor to explain why Fusion Management is essential – striking a balance between production and production capability.

The farmer destroys the balance by killing the goose to get at the eggs more quickly, and thus loses the supply. In like manner, a board wants to gratify the stock market with a soaring share price (which also brings more than welcome uplift to directors' and executives' stock options). But the managements take, and the boards approve, actions that undermine the only reliable foundation for share price growth and thus golden eggs: a strong and viable long-term strategy.

For example, there are few better ways of undermining a share price than embarking on a takeover binge. Yet boards time and again vote in favour of deals that are all but guaranteed to permanently weaken the shares. The case against conventional mergers and acquisitions has been argued unanswerably by Buffett, even though he may personally be much the most successful acquirer of the past hundred years.

The great man has explained the failures of other buyers in convincing manner. They behave in a way that precisely contradicts the simple formula which governs his own purchases. Buffett only looks (and so should you) for targets that are large enough to be worth the trouble. Targets should also fulfil six criteria:

1 They have demonstrated consistent earning power.
2 They earn good returns on equity.
3 They have little or no debt.
4 They have good management in place.
5 They are simple businesses.
6 They are available at a known price.

The sense of these stipulations is glaringly obvious. Yet most CEOs on the hunt for higher earnings (and a higher share price) through acquisition ignore several of the criteria – if not all. Rather than study past records, they look at projections of future earnings: 'of little interest to us', says Buffett, who cares just as little for turning round companies in trouble. Acquirers love to believe that their brilliant management will right the acquired wrongs. Buffett's tiny staff can't supply management and is thus immune from this dangerous temptation.

Nor (unlike so many corporate investors) will he buy high-tech or other businesses that he doesn't understand. This looked like a bad mistake when the dot.coms and other whiz-businesses were soaring, but reads like the soundest of policies today. When you buy a share at the market price, you are endorsing the valuation of the entire company. The dot.com valuations were beyond any sane endorsement. Ask yourself, would I really pay 160 times earnings for the pleasure of owning the whole of any company, no matter what its business? Or huge sums for a company with no earnings at all?

It's the price issue that divides Buffett from the acquisitive floppers. No investor likes to overpay for a block of shares, which constitute a small fraction of the total equity. But Buffett is just as averse to over-paying for an entire business as for a block of shares. Failed acquirers are often so indifferent to the price that they (or rather their shareholders) have to pay, that the management not only makes the first approach, open cheque-books in hand, but is first to name a price.

They may well raise that offer, sometimes more than once, in order to secure the deal. The whole acquisition process is emotional rather than commercial, for reasons that, in Buffett's view, are all too plain: 'You don't get to be the CEO of a big company by being a milquetoast. You are not devoid of animal spirits. And it gets contagious.' In the twenty or so companies of which he has been a director down the years, Buffett has noted a recurrent phenomenon: 'the conversation turns to acquisitions and mergers much more' when competitors are on the warpath – especially in buoyant stock-market conditions.

These booms encourage companies to pay for their purchases in shares, a practice to which Buffett is firmly opposed. As he argues, with most deadly logic, the purchased company will probably change hands at the full intrinsic value of the business, at the very least. The purchaser's shares, however, will be valued at market, which could be much less than the intrinsic worth of the business. Buying for shares in these circumstances is a mug's game.

If the acquirer is paying more in value than is being received, wrote Buffett sharply, 'a marvellous business purchased at a fair sale price becomes a terrible buy'. Buffett's views are so well-known that Coca-Cola's attempt to buy Quaker Oats in late 2000 came as a great surprise. Buffett not only sat on the board, but he spoke for a major slice of the equity.

The new chief, David Daft, had good reason to covet Quaker: its Gatorade sports drink has a Coke-like hold over its market, and Pepsico, the arch-rival, had already made an offer. But neither of these arguments fitted Buffett's criteria: he snubbed

Daft and vetoed the acquisition. You will never, of course, be able to prove that the board was right to accept Buffett's arguments. Maybe Daft would have made a brilliant success out of Quaker: maybe not. But the burden of proof should always lie with the people putting forward a strategic initiative.

In all too many cases, the strategy wins by default. Nobody challenges the CEO, even if the strategic case is very weak. At Campbell Soup, for example, the ousted CEO had committed himself to winning an 8% annual rise in revenues. In old-established products facing heavy competition, the target was simply beyond reach. The efforts to boost sales were self-defeating. Price cuts and higher marketing spends merely resulted in lower revenues and still larger reductions in operating profits.

At Campbell, as at Xerox, P&G, Maytag, Lucent and Rubbermaid, there was an especially curious pattern. The displaced CEOs mostly came in from outside, and were all replaced by the men who had retired in their favour. Whichever way you look at it, this is an awful failure in succession policy – and that is surely one of the prime responsibilities of the CEO, acting in close collaboration with his board. So the return of the retired heroes is especially grotesque. If they had performed the culminating act of their tenures very well, the subsequent disasters would never have happened.

The systems of these famous firms collapsed because the new men were expected to work undefined miracles. That is never how lower appointments are made; at least, not in a well-run company. The task is clearly defined, the performance criteria are agreed, and the appointee's plans for carrying out the mission are agreed and monitored. Whoever makes the appointment must also be satisfied that the task is wholly within the person's competence. In other words, the board should only approve the appointments of CEOs, or any senior executive, after satisfying criteria that are strikingly similar to Buffett's six rules of acquisition.

1 Has the candidate demonstrated consistent ability to raise earnings?

2 Do those earnings represent a good return on equity?
3 Has the candidate shown the ability to optimise the generation of cash?
4 Has he or she put good management in place throughout the operations they have led?
5 Does the candidate follow the KISS philosophy: 'Keep It Simple, Stupid'?
6 Have the candidate's investments always generated an economic value higher than their cost?

It should always be easier to make these judgments about an insider – somebody you actually know, with a track record that cannot be falsified – than an outsider. Yet boards have been turning increasingly to the devil they don't know, much to the joy of the head-hunters whose expensive executive searches produce the candidates. The percentage of American CEOs hired from outside rose from 11% to 20% between 1990 and 1999, according to Watson Wyatt. Many of these appointments were total or partial failures, which may well be no coincidence.

Over this same decade, on the results of a survey by Drake Beam Morin, a third of CEOs appointed at 450 major corporations lasted no more than three years. Indeed, a quarter of the companies used up three CEOs in the period. That is a staggering indictment of the processes used for appointments to the most senior position in the corporation. There should be far better fusion between the collective wisdom and experience of the board and the knowledge which the CEO has of the business and his colleagues.

That knowledge, however, is far from wholly reliable. CEOs have their favourites, their own interests, and their emotional biases, which may include the subconscious desire to nominate a successor who won't outshine them. So the nine boards of the nine flops were not doing their true job. If that job is not being done well, the would-be hero at the summit is all too likely to fail – and the corporation will do just as badly.

PART V: THE NEW OLD ORDER

*How to perform management's traditional and essential
tasks in new and much more effective ways*

CHAPTER ONE

managing the managers

The aim of managing managers is to keep diverse people working harder for you than they would for themselves

The management of other managers is the key to success or failure in every company. The principles are the same whether a small business is making small money, or a giant is betting and generating billions. But the practice of manager-management varies enormously – and two phenomenal friends provide a most remarkable case study of two totally contrasting approaches.

They are two of the world's richest men, Bill Gates and Warren Buffett. The differences start with themselves, as for every manager, and with the amount of their involvement in detail and the degree of delegation. They have different answers to three vital questions:

- What work do I reserve for myself?
- What work do I delegate to other people?
- How do I control their performance?

The software czar, until he changed his role at Microsoft in 2000, kept his fingers in every pie and ruled the actions of his delegates by constant and fierce interrogations – which have often reversed the subordinates' decisions. The great investor still reserves only two functions for himself: allocating Berkshire Hathaway's capital (which he loves to do) and helping 15 to 20 senior managers to 'keep a group of people enthused about what they do when they have no financial need whatsoever to do it'.

The wholly owned companies managed by these people hold assets worth very much more than Buffett's marvellous stock

169

portfolio – in which seven major holdings from Coca-Cola to the *Washington Post* are dominant. The seven cost $4.4 billion: they were worth, at end-1998, $32.1 billion, out of a total share portfolio of £37.3 billion. The wholly owned assets, however, came at that point to $80 billion, with the companies concerned employing 47,566 people, which was 60% more than Microsoft's roster.

Buffett made some bad decisions (like selling McDonalds) during the last years of the bull market, but emerged with deep resources that financed another whole-company buying spree, acquiring unspectacular but solid companies like the engineering group, Allis-Chalmers. In one sense, Buffett makes no distinction between the two types of investment – stocks or businesses. Whether you are buying all of a company, or just a fraction, you should, he believes, be vitally concerned with the same criteria:

1 Is the company simple and understandable?
2 Does it have a consistent operating history?
3 Does it have favourable, and predictable, long-term prospects?
4 Is the management competent and honest?
5 Is the underlying business undervalued?

The need for predictability and understanding rules out companies like Microsoft. Buffett was not tempted by the soaring share prices of the Internet Bubble, despite his friendship with Gates. Look at Point One above. Buffett doesn't understand the technology of operating systems, the Internet and software programs and has no intention of learning how. And even Gates himself, before he nearly missed the Internet boat, saw clearly that the technology is not predictable, that it has a mind of its own.

His own titanic success has, however, been built on controlling the technology. By making MS-DOS and Windows the universal, all but inescapable entry into personal computing, Gates created a degree of market control that, until the Internet arrived, gave Microsoft's business a very high degree of predictability (and profit). The heavy way in which that control was exercised attracted the attentions of the US Justice Department, with historic results.

But control is basic to Gates's nature and his management practice. He has an obsession with detail and with checking up (he even used to sign expenses for his right-hand man, Steve Ballmer). The obsession is so well-known that few believed Gates's evidence in the Microsoft anti-trust trial. For astonishing example, when asked if he had ever read the complaint in the case, Gates said no. But did he know if the complaint made any allegations about a meeting between Microsoft and Netscape? Even though the latter's browsers were a huge threat to his business, his lame and incredible reply was: 'I think somebody said that that is in there.'

Thanks to the anti-trust case, the Internet and other developments, Microsoft's commercial (as opposed to technological) predictability has vanished. So, in theory, has the egocentric system by which the company was managed. Under the previous dispensation, groups (deliberately kept small) were continually formed and reformed to carry out specific tasks. Tight financial controls were applied, but the true organisational cement was Gates himself (backed up by Ballmer).

As *Business Week* put it, 'With decisions large and small funnelled to the top, the pair became a bottleneck. Worse, they undermined the confidence of managers below.' The 1999 reorganisation, which used the grand-sounding theme of 'Vision Version Two', has already been mentioned in this book. Microsoft was split into eight new, customer-oriented divisions, each under a top manager supposed to exercise delegated, autonomous power over his domain – thus applying the classic system, derived from the military, of divide and control.

Gates was supposed to stand clear of the day-to-day management of these divisions and to concentrate on broad strategy. The hope was that this would 'free Microsoft from its bureaucratic morass'. In the wake of the adverse anti-trust ruling, Gates stepped back further still, remaining chairman, but handing over to Ballmer as chief executive, and occupying the new role of Chief Software Architect. But even with the reforms, Gates's management is plainly going to stop far short of Buffett's practices and principles.

Buffett wants Berkshire Hathaway's managers to think like owners. Since many of his chief executives actually did own the businesses before selling them to Buffett, ownership thinking should come naturally. Buffett also likes to leave them with a significant stake (10% to 20%) to make the ownership practical as well as theoretical. Their rewards are tied exclusively to the achievements of their own businesses, not the progress of Berkshire Hathaway – a principle to which Buffett holds very strongly.

It's hard to argue with his view that managers must be judged only by what they personally influence. The only counter to this principle arises where divisions relate directly to each other. If you hold managers responsible only for their own results, that intensifies the natural (but heinous) tendency to ignore other divisions, losing the potential, and sometimes essential, benefits of cooperation. That was one reason for Microsoft's notorious inability to get people to work with each other across boundaries.

To avoid this trap, you may need to have a significant part of the rewards tied to overall performance. This need doesn't arise in Buffett's case, though, because See's Candies has no conceivable connection with the Nebraska Furniture Mart or the *Buffalo Evening News*. It's therefore easy to treat each business and each CEO on their individual merits. Buffett gets regular financial reports from them all, of course. Otherwise, CEOs can contact him (usually by phone) as they want (he rarely rings). They only have to follow some simple rules to retain their chairman's confidence.

One of these rules, possibly the most important, runs as follows: 'If there is any significant bad news, let me know early.' That is Buffett's 'only caveat'. He is clear that 'All of you do a first-class job in running your operations with your own individual styles. We are going to keep it that way. You can talk to me about what is going on as little or as much as you wish.' His other advice is of a piece with the above. 'Look at the business you run as if it were the only asset of your family, one that must be operated for the next 50 years and can never be sold.'

He adds that, 'We can afford to lose money – even a lot of money. We cannot afford to lose reputation – even a shred of reputation.' This humane, collegiate, commonsense approach is incomprehensible to many managers. The key to Buffett's ability to live up to his own credo is confidence in others. He truly means it when he congratulates his executives on their excellence. The more typical attitude elsewhere is:

1 You are not doing a first-class job, and will not do so unless I apply considerable pressure.
2 You will run your operation the company way (and my way), not your way.
3 I want you to keep me fully informed all the time, and will intervene forcefully if I don't like what you tell me.
4 If you bring me bad news, you may well be fired.
5 You will only run this business, or part of a business, for a short time and will be judged on your short-term results.

The great superiority of Buffett's system (or lack of it) is self-evident. A climate of confidence and freedom must surely generate better performance than one of suspicion and control. Yet in some ways, suspicion and control have ruled Microsoft – and its results have been sensationally successful. How can this paradox be resolved?

One answer is that both Buffett and Gates believe in financial incentives, in making their managers extremely rich. Buffett doesn't like to use stock options, but his purchase prices have the same effect: the man who sold Buffett a company called Dexter Shoe in 1993 came to own Berkshire shares worth $1.5 billion six years later. Even Buffett's generous bonus schemes – sometimes hitting six times the basic salary – can't compete with such rewards.

Nor can even Microsoft compete with $1.5 billion. Before the high-tech share slump about a third of its employees were thought to be millionaires: a few veterans were supposedly worth $100 million, but only a few. And the wealth isn't enough. According to the *Wall Street Journal*, in 1999, tired of 'gruelling deadlines, frustrated by the bureaucracy that has accompanied Microsoft's explosive growth or lured away by the boom in high-tech start-ups, dozens of Microsoft's most capable leaders, all around forty years old, have opted out – at least temporarily'.

Microsoft's response, to reduce Gates's span of command, and give the new business unit managers more autonomy, was partly governed by a hundred interviews with programme managers and team leaders. Listening to people's ideas on such issues and, far more important, acting on them is a huge step in the right direction. But stopping the brain drain will depend still more on the reality or otherwise of the autonomy that Microsoft's able, rich people understandably crave.

Meeting their wishes may come hard to a company which is accustomed, for instance, to having public-relations people sitting in on interviews and taking copious notes of what executives say to the media. Buffett can't do that: he doesn't even have any PR staff. It is, of course, unfair to compare a large, integrated corporation like Microsoft with a widely diversified holding company like Berkshire. But most companies can be readily split into discrete, free-standing businesses which can be managed and controlled along Buffett lines.

The secret is to treat the unit manager as a CEO in his or her own right. Don't impose targets, for a start, but let them tell and satisfy you about what they are going to achieve and how. Second, don't have a fixed idea of how long people (or yourself, for that matter) should stay running an operation. If they are happy and doing an excellent job, only move them if you both feel they are not living up to their full potential: or if you have another, more important post for which they are ideal – a view which they can be persuaded to share.

As advised on page 216, you should always have a reservoir of able internal candidates for any such promotion. Characteristically, Buffett delegates this aspect of his responsibility, too. Thus, his top managers are asked to 'send me a letter updating your recommendations as to who should take over tomorrow if you became incapacitated tonight. Anything you send me will be confidential.'

That degree of delegation, you may be sure, rarely happens at Microsoft or most other companies. It means treating subordinates as equals, as grown-ups who know their businesses and their people and who can be trusted with anything – from accounting honestly for their expenses to thinking about succession. Trust is what ultimately distinguishes the Buffett and Gates styles. On results, you would have to say that Gates wins: but that has depended far less on management style than on the ruthless exploitation of a monopoly position which was always unlikely to last, no matter what the trustbusters did.

For the long haul, though, Buffett's way must be best. As an associate says, 'Somehow Warren has been able to keep a diverse cast of characters working harder for him than they did for themselves. I see it every day – and I still don't know how he does it.' Having read all the above, though, you will have a good idea of the maestro's magic methods, and of their essential simplicity. Use them.

totally productive management

TPM and TPM2 – fusing superb management with superb technology of product and process – are not optional

Everybody's attention was focused as the Millennium began on the American recapture of leadership in the world economy (and thus in management) and on the relative failure of Germany and, above all, Japan. That focus went hand-in-hand with the new faith in the New Economy – the belief that old-line manufacture had gone into terminal decline, to be succeeded by services and the gee-whiz technologies of Silicon Valley.

The US and (on a smaller scale) the UK, on this highly debatable reading, have been leading the way to a new post-industrial world in which the most prosperous nations will owe their riches to the knowledge industries. That at least is true. Despite the high-tech setbacks of 2001, moreover, the observations in an earlier chapter also apply. The newcomers in the Valley and elsewhere really are pioneering the development of a new style of management, faster-moving, freer in style, non-hierarchical, anarchic. The necessity is to fuse the new style with the old.

The new economic style is certainly going to affect all industries – especially as more managements discover and exploit the potential of the new information technology. But the attention grabbed by the hot-shot entrepreneurs, with their unbelievable stock-market ratings, ignored two unarguable and all-important facts. The first, now recognised in hindsight by one and all, was that the stock-market bubble, like all such bubbles, would burst. The second fact is that hot-shots, like everybody else, depend on the products of traditional factories – and these are the sites of a different management revolution, which is still being led by Japan.

Mention new technology, and people immediately think of microelectronics, the Internet and associated marvels. But this vibrant sector, while pervasive and potent, is only a small area of the technological explosion. By far the greatest activity, often immensely successful, lies in sometimes despised areas of 'thing-making'. This is true both in industries of creaking antiquity – like shipbuilding and steel – and in brand-new enterprises, like those making silicon wafers and the lithographic machines, 'steppers', that print circuit patterns on the silicon.

Manufacturing is so unpopular in an alleged 'post-industrial' age that nobody takes much notice. After all, factory profits have suffered, employment has slumped, and over-capacity is chronic. But these vices stem from virtue. New manufacturing technology has hugely increased output per worker, sharply reduced costs, vastly cut materials consumption, and steeply raised efficiency. Inevitably, spare capacity and pressure on prices have risen malignly as this benign progress has speeded onwards. This post-industrial revolution is both industrial and truly revolutionary.

What's happening is embodied in the initials TPM, which stands for Total Productive Maintenance, and is a close relative of Total Quality Management. Everyone has heard of the latter – but TPM is the province of production specialists. You will find them in the oil industry, tyres, food, chemicals, liquor, packaging, trucks, nuclear fuel, cars, castings. All these are among the multitudinous suppliers of manufactured goods which are indispensable to every aspect of the modern economy.

Mobile phones, PCs, PDAs and Internet routers could not exist without these producers: and the greater efficiency of their production is underpinning economic growth. The greater productivity achieved in the digital economy is often a matter of speculation. But Eamonn Fingleton pointed out in his important book, *In Praise of Hard Industries*, that manufacturers have been accomplishing miracles in the same way that their predecessors did in the Industrial Revolution – making more with less.

In telecommunications, 'Just 70 pounds of glass in the form of optical fibres can transmit as much telephone traffic as one ton of copper.' Then, everybody takes CDs for granted: by end-1998, 11 billion CDs had been sold, about 10 for every household in the world. They are only an eighth of the weight of long-playing records, and cost a mere 30 cents to produce. And these are only two miracles among myriads.

The way in which these miracles are being made has lessons for all managers, including service industries. This isn't just Total Productive Maintenance. It's also Total Productive *Management* – TPM2. First, both kinds of TPM demand total reality about where you are now. For example, at the bottling operations of United Distillers and Vintners, the world's largest spirits company, the 'prevailing operating culture' read like a bad dream – and was realistically recognised as such.

Operators would stop working when there was a breakdown, and call an engineer, because engineers were the experts. All faults were treated as breakdowns, and left alone by the operators because 'I might make it worse', coupled with 'I might get hurt.' The operators lacked confidence and, anyway, didn't want to steal the engineers' jobs. As for the engineers, they were no better. They liked a breakdown, because it made them feel valued. They took comfort in the routine of being called in as the experts.

The engineers readily agreed that the operators would make things worse and would probably get hurt: and 'we'll be busier fixing their mistakes'. They feared the unknown and were also frightened (reciprocating the operators' view) of having their jobs stolen. The consequence was an inordinate amount of waste – intangible and very tangible. When the operators and engineers got together in a TPM programme, 12 skips of tangible waste were removed in six months. Line changeover, moreover, halved from 23 to 11 minutes: tools are now changed in 10 seconds – and you can't get much faster than that. Before crowing over UDV's stupidity, though, try this catechism.

- Do you have detailed information about the productivity of your operations – not just in manufacture (if any), but in the offices (right up to the executive suite), the shops, the service operations, etc?
- Do you know the cost of waste inside the business?

- Are you sure that there are no dysfunctional attitudes affecting productivity in your organisation?
- Do you know what opportunities for cutting costs and speeding up are available?

Daniel Jones, a professor at Cardiff Business School, cites some even more spectacular results than UDV's, like those in one Indiana location. Inventory turns improved fivefold, with a cut in lead-times from 4.5 days to 2.5 days. Over three-and-a-half years the organisation progressed from 21 people making 55 pieces each in 2300 sq.ft to three employees making 600 each in 1200 sq.ft. Moreover, injuries were almost eliminated – and the capital investment was under $1000.

You may think that these miracles are only possible in very poor plants. But Jones (co-author of the pathfinding book, *Lean Thinking*) has a striking analogy. The common snail, he says, travels at Mach 0.0000094 (0.007 mph). 'This is more than ten times the average velocity of the fastest part flowing through a fighter aircraft production system!' Before collapsing with mirth, however, ask yourself if you actually know how long manufacturing and/or other processes take in your business. If the answer also turns out to be a snail's pace, the cause may well lie in 'hand-offs'.

That refers to the transfer of work from one machine or desk to another. In the typical manufacturing outfit, there can be as many as 40 hand-offs in one operation. Using the TPM approach, you can cut that to 11, with enormous savings in time and costs. In non-manufacturing environments, hand-offs can often be eliminated completely, by letting one person handle the entire job (like issuing an insurance policy or dealing with a complaint or processing an order). Not only does the work get done faster, but the employee obtains more job satisfaction. The magic Jones formula is . . .

1 Stop focussing on the organisation and concentrate instead on outcomes.
2 Draw a clear distinction between operations that add value and those that create waste.

3 Reconfigure the whole value stream to eliminate time and steps that add no value.

4 Successively remove all constraints to a smooth workflow directed towards the desired outcome – supplying the customer.

5 Recognise that you are setting out on a never-ending path towards a perfection you will never reach.

Jones says that the path is never-ending because 'most of what we do is waste', and 'the more layers of waste you remove, the more waste you can see'. You judge your progress towards perfection by the rate of improvement in eliminating non-value-adding steps; while reducing defects, throughput time, inventories and the vast amounts of management time devoted to fire-fighting, expediting and negotiating.

You also set extremely high targets. How about doubling output and profits with the same headcount? Obviously, that can't happen without radical improvement in the value chain. So how high should you set your target for cutting throughput time and defects? Inventories? Space and unit costs? If you think that reducing them by a third is excellent performance, think again. Jones says that the potential gains are respectively 90% for the first two, 75% and 50%. And once you have achieved such startling gains, you don't rest on your laurels. You begin all over again.

Note that this is not a 'downsizing' exercise: the headcount in Jones's calculations stays the same. He says that heavy capital investment isn't required, either. The crucial lesson of TPM is that simply reforming the processes can produce great improvements on its own. Throw in investment in new equipment and technologies, and you have the phenomenon of rising manufacturing output and falling workers. But the remaining jobs add far more value – which is why in 1999 employers in the 'weak' Japanese economy could pay their workers $22.01 an hour and those in 'slow-growth' Germany $14.79. In the booming, downsizing America of that year, the rate was only $12.37.

The pace of growth in American per capita income was actually bettered by 12 other OECD nations in the 16 years to 1996. These and other statistics assembled by Fingleton hardly square with the following statement in *Fortune* magazine: 'America is the world's most competitive nation, thanks to the overall high quality of its CEOs.' The first thing wrong with that statement, as Fingleton argues, with plenty of support, is that in many manufacturing industries, the US has almost abandoned competition. It has simply exported its activities – either to American-owned plants abroad or to plants owned by global competitors.

That hardly suggests high-quality management from anybody, including the CEOs. The second fault, anyway, is the assumption that the CEO alone has the decisive influence on performance. But that's the starting point for the two authors of the *Fortune* article, consultant Ram Charan and journalist Geoffrey Colvin. They claim to have found 'one simple, fatal shortcoming' that explains why CEOs fail and get fired. Any expert in TPM and TPM2 (and TQM) would know that any such finding must be a fallacy. There is never only one cause for the fault actually named by the two authors: 'bad execution'.

In their minds, however, the answer is as 'simple as that; not getting things done, being indecisive, not delivering on commitments'. In other words, bad managers manage badly and lose their jobs – not exactly a statement of breathtaking originality or value. The authors are no more useful when they describe 'six habits of highly ineffective CEOs'. The Dirty Half-Dozen are:

- people problems
- decision gridlock
- 'lifer syndrome'
- bad earnings news
- 'missing in action'
- 'off-the-deep-end financials'.

Only the second of the Dirty Half-Dozen could be truly called a personal habit: the others are symptoms of broad corporate disorder, not TPM2 but TUP: Totally Unproductive Management. And that springs from precisely the same causes as those which UDV found in its bottling plants: mismatches between the objectives of the organisation and the mindsets of the people who alone could realise those aims.

Charan and Colvin produce an impressive list of CEOs who have failed (a fate which, according to one piece of research, is three times more likely than a generation ago). In many of these cases, the leaders at the top had failed to mobilise the company's people, all the way down to the bottom, in support of a strategy to which everybody had agreed. What they did is a reverse definition of TPM2:

1 They looked inward into the organisation, not outwards towards the customer.
2 They persisted with operations that destroyed rather than added value.
3 They stuck with value streams that wasted time and processes that added no value.
4 They allowed systems to function and malfunction that blocked the smooth delivery of excellent goods and services to the customer.
5 They started and then stopped improvement programmes without getting the full benefits.

Worst of all, they were in denial. They had not started with the basic TPM appraisal of what's wrong in the here and now. That means more than benchmarking performance against the competition (and non-competitors, if they are better than you at any function). It means listening to what employees at all levels, customers, suppliers and distributors have to say about your defects. TPM2 managers then act decisively to cure the defects – which they never deny.

Rather, the good manager half-rejoices when serious under-performance is documented: because he then knows where and how to achieve serious improvement. The writing is on the wall once these signs appear:

• You start to believe all the stuff the company writes about itself.

- You think (and say) that your company's shares are under-valued.
- You blame shortfalls in performance on external circumstances.
- You artificially boost end-quarter figures to hit profit targets.

A fifth fault (as Charan and Colvin wrote) is that, while befogging the truth with all this nonsense, you claim that you're a realist. Realistically, there is no alternative to TPM and TPM2, combining superb management with superb technology of product and process. Some words of Sony's late great Akio Morita need careful pondering. 'In Japan . . . almost every major manufacturer is run by an engineer or technologist . . . in the UK, I am told, some manufacturers are led by CEOs who do not understand the engineering that goes into their products.'

That must be a grave disadvantage in managing technological thrust. But manufacturing bosses must also master the fast-moving, customer-focused, collaborative, non-hierachical, fact-based management arts of Silicon Valley. That's where the old and new technologies can profitably fuse to return manufacturing to its rightful position – stage centre. The practitioners of TPM2 are deeply rooted in the real world. Their discipline is not glamorous. But it's the basic habit of highly effective managers – at every level in every organisation.

CHAPTER THREE

revolutionising the strategy

How to meet the hard strategic challenge of propelling a successful company onwards and upwards

The future has become an even riskier place. It's now more dangerous than ever to extrapolate past growth rates and strategies into the future. That will be won by companies which are ready to trade in the past for new horizons. This isn't a once-for-all task, moreover. Each strategic victory carries with it the seeds of its own defeat. One victory therefore creates the need for another. And if that need is not met, successful strategy will turn into incipient, if not actual crisis.

Witness the extraordinary twist of fate at Ford Motor, as described in the Introduction. Only a short time after it had forged ahead to became the world's highest-profit automaker, Nemesis struck. An apparently robust strategy went well beyond the once-triumphant Japanese emphasis on low cost, quality and variety. Ford sought its growth in a redefined auto market, building a broader business on a truly global platform. The plan was rewarded with record per-car profits. But in mid-2001, the glowing picture turned so black that *Business Week* headlined a cover story: 'Ford. It's Worse than You Think'.

Ford, it appeared, had paid a wholly unnecessary price for its profits – neglecting the basics. The company which had pioneered the use of scientific quality management and collaborative teamworking in the US had sunk to the industry's worst quality performance. The long-time laggard General Motors had soared past Ford's quality ratings. Its difficulties ran deep into a culture which now seemed inimical to progressive change, and the company faced horrendous problems over recalls – especially those involving Firestone tyres.

The Ford case illustrates in stark fashion how much easier it has become for organisations to get into trouble – big trouble. The CEOs mentioned on page 160, were ousted from companies with superb reputations. Mattel, Lucent, Newell Rubbermaid, Campbell Soup, Coca-Cola, Gillette, Procter & Gamble, Maytag and Xerox had all enjoyed market dominance, most right up to the CEO's appointment. Many other top managers, in companies of all sizes, have suffered similar sudden humiliation, and all for the same reason: strategic failure.

In consequence, great businesses like those above look diminished today. In some cases, the trouble is so deep (as at Xerox) that emerging into renewed success would be a miracle of turnround management. But I have long urged the merits of a wonderful formula for averting crisis and building long-term success.

MANAGE OUT OF CRISIS AS YOU WOULD IN CRISIS, AND THERE WON'T BE ANY CRISIS.

To put that another way, become your own turnround manager. The success ratio of turnrounds appears to be far greater than that of acquisitions – even though at first (and horrible) sight, the task of the turnaround expert is enough to make the strongest spirit quail. Some once-viable, maybe once-great company is so deeply mired in doubt and derision that its stakeholders, above all the investors, scream for salvation and, of course, a saviour. For the latter, nothing lies ahead but trials and tribulation, hard words, hard decisions and harder work. Who would willingly accept this burden?

Yet there's no shortage of willing souls. In British retailing, intrepid imports took on the long-term strategic failures at Marks & Spencer and J. Sainsbury. They presumably believed that the upside potential greatly outweighed the downside risks. That interesting equation applies to both the new chieftains and their corporate charges. The two fates are obviously linked. If the company turns round, the turnaround leaders' future is assured – and the odds are actually in their favour.

The paradoxical truth is that turnrounds are at once the most difficult and the easiest of management tasks. The difficulty is that many messes, which usually (but not always) include financial shambles, must be cleared up. The ease lies in the low expectations. If a company is flat on its back, merely raising the hulk to sitting position will elevate the share price, rejoice the hearts of financial analysts and journalists, and very possibly create a new business hero.

No matter that a company whose return on capital improves from negative to 10% is plainly worse managed than one which returns a steady 15% year on year. The former will look exciting, the latter stodgy, and the share rating will reflect the difference. Professional company doctors are adept at spotting the abundant opportunities for improving financial performance. But like managements in general, they are less skillful at seeing and seizing the openings for future, long-term dynamic expansion. Quick results are wanted, and badly needed. But they are not enough.

By far the harder strategic challenge is to take over a highly successful company and propel it onwards and upwards. Yet Sam Walton's successors at Wal-Mart will never win the heroic status of the founding father, even though their company's market capitalisation rose, post-Sam, to the astonishing equivalent – *before* the dot.com crash – of seven eBays plus eight Amazons. Similarly, Lord MacLaurin's followers at Tesco are on a hiding to nothing: condemned if they fail to keep up his great work, taken for granted if they do.

Tesco provides a classic example of managing out of crisis as you would in crisis. Acting in good time, MacLaurin turned an old-fashioned grocery retailer into a pace-setting would-be globalist with outstanding information technology. There's no reason why other company veterans can't strike out brilliantly in new strategic directions. They only need to be given the power and opportunity in good time. Put them in charge in bad time, though, and the chalice will be poisoned – as the unfortunate Peter Salsbury found at Marks & Spencer and the no less unfortunate Dino Adriano at J. Sainsbury.

By implication, the unfortunates compare less well than they would like with their generally very expensive replacements.

The pattern is for these new people to come from outside (even though Sir Peter Davis did have the benefit of previous experience at Sainsbury's). As Andrew Grove, the chairman of Intel, has remarked:

> I suspect that the people coming in are probably no better managers or leaders than the people they are replacing. They have only one advantage, but it may be crucial . . . They can see things more objectively than their predecessors did.

The person replaced 'has devoted his entire life to the company and therefore has a history of deep involvement in the sequence of events that led to the present mess'. In other words, the insiders' difficulty in turnrounds, as in strategy, is that they are wedded to the past – after all, they helped to create it – when only a violent breach with tradition will work. MacLaurin was a maverick at Tesco, as he proved when he faced down its founder, the potent and highly emotional Sir Jack Cohen, over dropping his pet trading stamps.

MacLaurin behaved more like the typical outsider: in Grove's words, 'unencumbered by emotional involvement and therefore . . . capable of applying an impersonal logic to the situation'. That impersonal logic is the essence of strategic success. Another famous insider, Sir John Harvey-Jones, was only picked to lead ICI out of its unheard-of losses because of his well-known, radical, logical and impatient views about the company and its poor management. How he accomplished that turnround provides a textbook, not just for company doctors, but for all strategists. Eight paramount questions must be asked:

1 Literally above all, WICH?: Who's In Charge Here? At the top, is there a clear leader, and is he/she backed by a small, tightly knit group of like-minded, free-speaking and free-thinking colleagues?
2 Does that top group regularly review the organisation's 'sacred cows' and kill those that are obstructing progress?

3 How are important decisions being taken? Is the process as fast as possible, and is it truly decisive?

4 Are firm and fast decisions followed by equally firm and fast action, monitored daily?

5 Is what is being done, why, and with what results communicated clearly and in real time inside and outside the organisation? (The Web removes any excuses on this front.)

6 Is physical, symbolic change being used to drive home the fact that things are going to be different round here?

7 Are programmes in hand to review and reform all the basics of the business so as to match or surpass the best benchmarks that can be found?

8 Is the top group delegating operational matters to the operators and concentrating on strategy, involving the whole business in the pursuit of medium- and long-term success?

It's the eighth question that causes the greatest trouble for strategists, especially turnround artists. When the City and Wall Street hail you as hero for moving a business from poor to middling, you're too busy collecting the plaudits (and counting your stock option gains) to worry about what comes next. That's why so many turnrounds never make the jump from middling to truly meritorious. The gap between short-term saviour and long-term strategic winner is as tough to cross as the notorious divide between proprietorship and professional management.

If, like MacLaurin at Tesco, you have a clear strategic objective in view, no difficulty arises. But there's today's rub. In his case, the correct strategic choice was relatively obvious. That is by no means a criticism. Most management errors result from blatant disregard of the glaringly obvious. Xerox needed to move from copying into desktop and portable computing, and never found the right strategy and strategist. Digital Equipment stumbled over a similar barrier. In contrast, Tesco responded successfully to the need to move up-market into Sainsbury territory and to pay for the climb by improved systems, management processes and in-store performance.

Tesco's strategy had the essential virtue of exploiting established trends in the marketplace. For today's struggling giants, however, the correct strategies are by no means obvious. M&S was built on value for money, providing superior quality, even if at higher prices. Sainsbury's customer-value proposition had some similarity. Both platforms have been weakened over time by mismanagement of these powerful retail brands. Today, the clock cannot easily be turned back. Quality is much harder to differentiate, and higher prices are much tougher to defend.

Inefficiencies can be slashed – both companies abound in 'low-hanging fruit', cost savings that can be won with relatively low expenditure of time and money. But the low-hangers will do nothing to set the companies on the high strategic road to new success. Many other markets are in similar upheaval; margins are under pressure, once-loyal customers are fickle, e-commerce is gaining ground, and there are no niches in which to hide. Nor, in these conditions, can the strategist fall back on the three standard options: cut costs, raise revenues, or (preferably) do both.

The first seems unpromising when everybody else is on the same tack, the second is very hard in the circumstances just described, and the third – given the difficulty of the previous two – is just a wonderful dream. However, the cost-cutting option needs more careful examination. If you just seek obvious economies, like cutting down staffing ratios or squeezing suppliers, you may well win better financial results. But this is not a strategy for competitive advantage, and may have counter-productive side-effects (like shortages of people to stock shelves or man check-outs).

Nirvana can only be reached by being different and better – achieving lower costs through genuine strategic initiatives, making intelligent, comprehensive internal changes that streamline and eradicate business processes with the willing help and input of everybody involved. That's Fusion Management. Competitors may see what's being done, but are unlikely to imitate the strategies: because everybody believes that their *modus operandi*, 'the way we do things round here', is the best (even when it obviously isn't).

That self-deception is a major reason for slides into difficulties (and the arms of a would-be saviour). People in the upper echelons of M&S and Sainsbury's must surely have believed in the superiority of their ways even when those had become manifestly inferior over time. Nothing at M&S was vaunted to the skies more than its handling of the supplier relationship. But the chain's problems with quality and delivery indicated unmistakably that this old management magic no longer worked. Business processes are like machines: over time they become relatively slower, inappropriate to changing needs, and very possibly rusty.

That is why the true strategist looks closely at the three prime constituents of the company – customers, employees (including managers), and suppliers – and discovers what they really feel about the strategy and behaviour of the business. Real strategy experts value this tripartite evidence far more highly than their own opinions and those of their boardroom colleagues. True, the evidence consists of perceptions. But, in the rightly and often repeated phrase, 'perception is reality'. Unless the new strategy changes perceptions in ways that favour the company and increase its long-term profits, the operation will ultimately fail.

The change process has to be completed at speed. The factors that necessitate a new strategy are usually well-publicised and much-rehearsed. Ignoring criticisms benefits neither the share price nor the in-store performance. Customers are inevitably deterred by a company whose demerits are regularly aired, which is panned for lack of strategic direction, and whose offerings reflect that absence. The morale of employees is similarly affected, and that again has an adverse effect on the customer. By the same token, suppliers' commitment to the company is vulnerable to strategic failure.

These risks cannot safely be left to fester. Yet if the business has large sales, good cash flow, and a strong balance sheet, the temptation is to take the long view and make reforms slowly and cautiously. The kings in these vast empires seem to think that time is on their side. It actually works against them. When a new chief executive warns that so many years are needed to turn his company round, what makes him think that years are available? Anything from a sudden explosion in e-commerce to a takeover bid may strike while the company is still lumbering upwards.

Another most cogent reason for speed is that the competition will not be standing still. In the US, Al Martinez won rich praise for his turnround of the ailing Sears Roebuck. But others, notably Wal-Mart, were growing faster from a stronger base. Sears sales have since stagnated, earnings per share are lower than a decade ago, and the market value drooped to a twentieth of Wal-Mart's, which has four times the sales. Tesco has done much the same damage to its British rivals. You cannot afford to give such powerful competitors the invaluable present of time.

They have, after all, already benefited from that gift during the years wasted by competitors as their underlying businesses deteriorated. That fate would be avoided if more companies threw up fusion managers like MacLaurin, people who out of crisis are prepared to apply the eight crisis-busting principles with passion and impersonal logic, while radically rebuilding the relationships with customers, employees and suppliers. In other words, turn the company round when it doesn't need a turnround – and then, with luck, it never will.

CHAPTER FOUR

breaking the bonds

Today's great opportunity must break with yesterday. If that means cracking the old order – crack it.

There's a form of cynicism that comes easily to business managers, the attitude that they've been there before, seen it, done that. This is a form of living in the past, which sounds better than nostalgia, but also embodies a desire to have things stay as they were – and still are, or so these cynics hope. That hope, though, involves turning a blind eye to what is actually happening today.

The Internet is an extraordinary example. The facts of its growth are phenomenal and undeniable. You can find convincing illustrations of this unprecedented step-change at random, wherever you look. Thus, all of the large firms sampled in Sweden in 2000 had intranets, while 61% had extranets. As for B2C (business-to-consumer), 33% of Sweden's Internet users already shopped on-line. Since the Net users represent over half the population, that is a great deal of shopping.

Now, there are two possible reactions to such facts (the numbers, of course, have only grown since the survey). One is a form of denial. The Swedes are different, and it won't work here (wherever 'here' is). The other view is the exact opposite – that what is happening in Sweden very probably will be repeated in other markets as they catch up with Swedish levels of penetration by PCs and the Net (with the latter no longer accessed only by personal computers, its exponential growth must even be accelerating).

It's perfectly clear which of the two courses is the safer and sounder. The analysis is simple and unarguable. If you bet against change and lose the wager, you may lose the whole business. If you bet on change, and the bet fails, the cost of failure will be contained and bearable – on the assumption, that is, that the change investment was made with a reasonable degree of prudence. That means using analysis and judgment.

The management technique known as Best World, Worst World is an example of both. It's an elementary form of the 'scenario planning' that is used by sophisticated planners to accommodate the one certain fact about the future: that it holds no certainty. You don't know what tomorrow holds, and never will. You therefore draw up a set of internally consistent possible scenarios and devise your plans so that, whatever happens, your company is prepared for the event. In Best World, Worst World, you ask only:

- What is the very best result that can be even unreasonably expected?
- What is the very worst of all possible results?
- Can the company live with the Best World scenario?
- Can the company live with the Worst World Scenario?

'No' to either of the last two questions spells 'no go', or 'back to the drawing board'. The many examples of Best World calamities include the British company EMI. Swamped by huge demand for its medical scanners (a brilliant, world-beating innovation), it proved unable to meet the required quality or quantity of production. Then, Boeing (see page 110) was nearly drowned by a flood of airline orders that over-loaded the system as the 1990s ended.

As for Worst World, look no further than two recent British cases. The publisher Dorling Kindersley was stuck with 10 million unsold copies of its Star Wars books, a catastrophe which cost the company £18 million and its independence. And the Millennium Dome, hooked on a Best World projection of 12 million customers, was financially crippled by a Worst World result of little more than half that hyper-optimistic total.

You don't need such harrowing examples to teach the virtues of this very basic form of analysis, which forces you to clarify your expectations. Note that this isn't a matter of hindsight, or being wise after the event. Dorling Kindersley had never sold even 3 million copies of an equivalent project. The Dome management could – and should – have asked what consequences would flow from a halving of the Best World attendance: and they could – and should – have observed that the breakeven point was perilously close to the Best World projection.

Indeed, the Dome's management probably didn't even think of its 12 million number as a Best World figure. It looks suspiciously like working backwards from the numbers required to meet the financial targets. Realism about attendance would have demanded equal realism about the finances – but that would have been unacceptable to the Dome's political masters. They still had to foot the ludicrous £1 billion bill.

Realism is the key word in that last paragraph. The basis for advancing into the future (which, of course, cannot be avoided) is deep understanding of the present, which can easily be dodged – and often is. That's calamitous in two ways. First, true knowledge of the present, what people are doing and buying and why, sometimes gives cast-iron guides to the future. Second, lack of realism about your own strengths and weaknesses in the here and now must lead to irresponsible error about your future capabilities.

So lack of intelligent foresight isn't responsible for Dome-like failures – mere lack of realistic, current, commonsense judgment is to blame. The plot thickens, however, in cases like the Internet, where the evidence will stay scanty and ambiguous for many years to come. Electronic banking is an example. In 2000, even in the US, only 1.4% of the population used e-banking, while in Germany, the figure was half that. In France and the UK, the numbers were smaller still: 0.3% and 0.2%.

The numbers are certainly higher now. As Internet use continues to rise everywhere, so does the number of banks offering Net transactions. True, there are many stories – no doubt accurate – of Web customers who have already deserted their e-banks, disappointed by cumbersome websites and time-consuming transactions. Therefore the Worst World e-scenario is that banking websites do not improve their ease of use and efficiency, and that e-banking peaks at a single-figure percentage of the market.

Just to state that scenario reveals its extreme unlikelihood. But even Worst World offers no cause for relaxation, let alone rejoicing, inside the traditional banks. A rise to 9% e-banking would represent a sixfold increase from the year 2000 penetration in the US, and a 45-times rise in Britain. Momentum on that scale will attract and sustain new e-banks, whose low overheads should generate large profits in time. But what if a Better World scenario comes about, and e-banking takes, say, half the entire market?

The better strategy for the established banks must be to plan for that possibility. It's clearly in their best interests, for the cost of an e-banking transaction is one-hundredth that of branch banking. In fact, acceptance of Better World would probably be a self-fulfilling prophecy. The more money the banks pour into websites, and the more effort they make to convert customers to the Web, the higher e-banking penetration must mount.

Banks would thus be inventing their own futures, just as recommended by the PC pioneer Alan Kay. Their failure to invent an Internet future arises partly from denial of the present. The e-banking potential contradicts one of the industry's basic sets of assumptions: that conventional banking dominates the market because customers much prefer dealing with cashiers over counters, that this preference and dominance will continue, and that the spotty start of e-banking proves the point.

Every business has such basic tenets, which tend to be shared by all competitors. That accounts for the sameness of their strategies. Thus, all telecoms companies (telcos), seeing that the more aggressive giants were increasing their size with gathering momentum, mostly by acquisition, agreed that this aspect of the present was the future. They reacted in the early century as if under irresistible orders to enlarge their networks by a further wave of acquisitions, mergers and new licences – no matter how grotesque the cost.

The compulsion was purely internal. 'Biggest is best' is conventional wisdom, not established fact. The telcos were trapped by their own assumptions. The assumptions trap can be escaped, though. The key is to write down the trends and patterns that you take for granted and that are widely shared by competitors and commentators. Then write down your reasons for holding these beliefs (because that is what they are, faith not facts). In some cases you will find no logical reasons for believing as you do. The assumptions are just that: assumed.

Where beliefs are supported by apparently factual evidence, moreover, the same facts and the same story are often served up in many different guises. The evidence, on examination, proves to be highly selective. People are looking for facts that justify their conviction that this is how things are now, or have always been, or both, and ever will be. Never forget: ALL ASSUMPTIONS ARE OPEN TO CHALLENGE. So challenge them. The three key questions are:

- What facts could invalidate this assumption?
- What would be the consequences?
- How far are my assumptions creating a self-fulfilling prophecy?

This is not a negative exercise. You are not trying to knock down the old, but to build a new and better business. Look at the banks again. They are weighed down by fixed assets, which cost a great deal to maintain and, still more, to staff. Their efforts to cut costs within this structure only result in less customer service and more customer complaints. Worse, rivals are muscling into the traditional banking territory – insurance companies, mortgage companies, on-line upstarts, etc.

Going whole-heartedly on-line themselves would dramatically lower the banks' cost bases, enable the rapid start-up of new services, establish a new dimension of customer relationships, and revolutionise perceptions. By challenging the dominance of traditional banking themselves, the banks would ask new questions: above all, how to hasten the growth of Internet banking, which must be in their interest – so long as they are prime movers, leaders and not followers.

If you take a similar route through your own business, new and valuable ideas will be generated. The key question, however, is whether you will have the courage of your new convictions. Suppose you had been working for the world's largest booksellers, Barnes and Noble. Your counter-factual challenge might well have shown that, maybe, Internet bookselling would dramatically overtake any store-based bookseller. You put an e-proposal to the board. Pre-Amazon, would the senior executives wielding command and control have leapt to release and risk the necessary finance?

Everybody knows the likely answer. Such disruptive projects are nearly always turned down, for several specious reasons. The customers will not accept it; it will cannibalise the traditional business; it will just lose money. The root cause is not obvious, but very potent – the fact that, in most companies, top-down decision-making is controlled by older people. They have grown up in the traditional business. They are deeply attached to its past achievements and to their part in creating that success. They also tend, because of their age and experience, to be more cautious.

They are not reluctant to make huge investments, but only where these strengthen their own prestige and power and preserve the status quo. Mergers and acquisitions, half of them doomed to failure, serve that purpose. New organic ventures do not. The way to win in cyberspace is to select profitable customers, deliver a compelling software-based experience, link to suppliers over networks, and cannibalise your existing business. Assuming (a very big assumption) that the established companies can master these arts of execution ('compelling experience'?), severe damage must be done to the status quo.

They will not, to repeat, find new customers to compensate for all the diversion of the old. Nor can they counter all the attacks which will come from newcomers. Take Paypal as one brand-new but fast-growing example. Fund transfer is among the most tiresome banking services, and can be very costly. Paypal does it instantaneously by allowing you to transfer the money between e-mail addresses. The facility is free to the sender: Paypal (now bought by EBay) aims to make its money by investing the cash float.

To be sure of failing against such inspired attacks, the recipe is simple (and has been proven many times). Take a bundle of separate, current Internet activities and put them under one leaky umbrella. Name a suspiciously round number for your future investment, and double it, even more suspiciously, if that cuts no ice with the stock market. Place a manager from the existing business in charge of the Internet umbrella, but retain tight boardroom control of everything this lucky person wants to do. Make sure, moreover, that nothing on the Internet menu subtracts from the powers, privileges and portfolios of the non-Internet managers.

The key to the future, though, lies in attacking that legacy of prestige and power. Starting your own start-ups outside the mainstream business can achieve precisely that. These small internal start-ups are the opposite of their large parents, direct and informal, without rigid hierarchy, but with speedy, adventurous reactions, inclusive 'can-do' cultures, and rewards linked to results. These qualities are plainly virtues: indeed, virtues that big companies ideally want. But the virtues are not consistent with the bossism that dominates even established 'new economy' groups (like the telcos).

MBB (Management by Budget) rules the bossist culture. MFF (Managing for the Future) demands different thinking and organisation, based on radical reappraisal of the present. Making the future happen rests not on control or command, but on opportunity in two senses: opportunity for capable, very possibly younger managers who are set free to seize the great present business opportunity that breaks with the past. If that means breaking the old order entirely, break it.

CHAPTER FIVE

new century management

If you don't believe in the need for radical change, you won't change, thus proving your own weak point

Managers are being told from all sides, not least by this book, that their world is being turned upside down, that revolution is in progress. This is no passing *coup d'état*, either. The revolution is seismic, and companies and management will never be the same again. Yet the managers at the epicentre of this earthquake seem oddly detached. Talking to them, speaking to their conferences, studying their companies – you don't see much reflection of the management mayhem described in the media.

There's a parallel with the electronic revolution, which is, of course, basic to the predicted remaking of management and commerce. The media were far quicker than managers to cotton on to the enormous implications of the Internet for every aspect of corporate activity. In magazines like *Fortune* or *Business Week*, the 'electronic' coverage became dominant, occupying a vastly higher proportion of the editorial space than the still tiny share that e-commerce held of world trade.

Why were journalists so much quicker on the electronic draw than managers? Writers and editors are always on the lookout for new and exciting stories, and they are quick to seize on news and interviews that make the good new story run on and on. Managerial mindsets are less prepared to spot the new, less ready to draw new conclusions. That's because they have to act on those conclusions. But it's also because what delights the journalistic mind threatens the peace of the managerial one.

The journalistic argument is that the balance of power has shifted permanently to creative companies that are best at turning ideas into reality and whose decisive capital is intellectual, not physical. 'To thrive in this new century', wrote John A. Byrne in *Business Week*, 'companies are going to need a whole new set of rules.' Are you and your organisation poised to thrive? If you can answer the following 18 questions with a true 'Yes', the 21st century will be your Happy Hunting Ground:

1 Is your company organised as a web or network, and not as a pyramid?
2 Is its focus external, not internal?
3 Is management style flexible rather than structured?
4 Does the company draw its strength from change, and not from stability?
5 Does its structure consist of interdependent entities, not self-sufficient units?
6 Are its key resources 'bits' of information, not physical assets?
7 Are operations 'virtually' integrated, not vertically integrated?
8 Are products mass-customized, rather than mass-produced?
9 Is the company's reach global, not just domestic?
10 Are financial reports real-time, not quarterly?
11 Are inventories measured in hours, not months?
12 Is strategy created bottom-up, and not top-down?
13 Is leadership inspirational, not dogmatic?
14 Are workers treated as both employees and free agents?
15 Are job expectations built round personal growth, not security?
16 Are people motivated to build the business, and not only to compete?
17 Does the company look for and obtain revolutionary gains, and not just incremental improvements?
18 Is quality a no-compromise, total 'must', not merely the best that can be afforded?

There may be some 18-yes companies around, but I have yet to meet one, and don't expect to. The problem is not only that the weight of the firm's history pulls in the opposite direction, but that human nature is often inimical to the new order. For example, leaders love to lay down the law: it's easier and quicker than inspiring a consensus to which all levels contribute. At the receiving end, letting somebody else take the major decisions lets you off the hook. Then, most people are uneasy in unstructured situations; in a hierarchical pyramid, at least you know where you are.

For much the same reason, stability reassures and change is worrying. In fact, people are so wedded to established ways that relatively few companies have made some purely technical changes that would save costs and improve management quality without causing any major disturbance or demanding an onerous investment spend. Examples are real-time financial reporting; reducing inventories by just-in-time and other methods; or using the full potential of the Internet to network the company internally and externally.

What stops managers from picking these easy plums? Their strange inertia is well-known to consultants, whose problem (to change the metaphor) is not leading the horse to water, but getting him to drink. Inertia springs from a deep, sceptical conservatism that has some foundation in current realities. The scepticism has been well-expressed by Andy Grove, the guiding light of Intel and thus one of the information revolution's great pioneers. He gave *Business Week* a definitely sober view of the degree of change involved for management:

I've lived through 40 years of management, and people haven't changed in those 40 years, so I'm a little sceptical. Our fundamental organizations haven't changed on paper. On the fringes, there is more looseness in the organization. But more hasn't changed than has. Things have changed, but the left brain [the technology side] says they should be galloping. The right brain [a manager's brain] says there have only been slow, gradual changes in the way we operate organizations.

In historical terms, Grove is correct. Great changes come about in long, slow evolutionary waves, even if the changes are marked by ferocious revolution from time to time. Thus the French, Maoist and American revolutions can all be seen as steps in the long progress of mankind from political and economic slavery to personal independence and democracy. All the same, there was no comfort for Marie Antoinette, Chiang Kai-Shek or George III in knowing that their disasters were only incidents in the long march of history.

Managers who relax before the challenges of the 21st century risk similar fates. Being lulled by a Grove-like belief in continuity can bring total disaster in discontinuous times. For that view, which is the essence of Fusion Management, there is no better advocate than Grove himself. His excellent book, *Only the Paranoid Survive*, is built round his theory that vastly powerful '10X' forces produce 'strategic inflection points' that companies ignore at their deadly peril – like all the mainframe computer firms which failed to see the 10X implications of the microprocessor (the key to Intel's and Grove's stupendous success).

Maybe there are more similarities than differences in the ways that Unisys, Digital, IBM, etc., were managed before and after disaster struck. But the degree of change and decay in their fortunes (even IBM's) was so catastrophic that the continuities dwindle into insignificance. Moreover, the continuous elements in management may not persist because of their inherent relevance, but because of the very reluctance to change which makes companies miss the 10X forces and strategic inflection points in product technology.

In other words, it's a self-fulfilling prophecy; if you don't believe that there's a need for radical change in management, you don't change – thus proving your own point. The magazine's other interviewee, John Chambers of Cisco, clashed head on with Grove on this critical issue. In Chambers' view the Internet 'is about survival' and is 'essential to the future of any company'. An example is management accounting. He 'can now close my books in 24 hours. I've known for a month what my earnings are for this weekend. I know my expenses, my profitability, my gross margins, my components.'

The conservative response could be 'so what?' After all, the basic principles of management accountancy are the same now as they were 40 years ago, to cite Grove's career span. In fact, the new facility is by no means revolutionary only for management accounting; rather, it is revolutionary for management, period. It notably increases the scope for the Fusion Manager, enabling the company's ultimate authority to blend control (because of deeper and more timely information) with truly delegating power down the line.

Because Cisco's data is in real-time Web format, 'every one of my employees can make decisions that might have come all the way to the president . . . Quicker decision-making at lower levels will translate into higher profit margins.' Chambers reckoned that he and his chief financial officer would be saved from making 50 to 100 decisions a quarter. Thus it becomes easier for top management to concentrate on its job – managing the future – while others look after the present.

None of this prevented Cisco's comeuppance in 2001, when Chambers missed the coming slowdown in telecoms equipment, and when some of its practices (like financing customers to purchase equipment) were exposed as fundamentally unsound. But the mishandling of a machine doesn't condemn its design. By any criterion, the digital company represents a major step forward in the technology of management. This is the vital point that Grove missed: 10X forces and inflection points apply in the management of human beings, not only in that of technology.

That's true even though the humans do not change. Just as Grove said, individual brains don't and won't work any faster. But many brains working together are much more effective than a single brain working alone, no matter how powerful the lone mind. The Internet allows real-time collaboration across all frontiers, internal and external, with consequences that will only become fully apparent over time.

That last word – time – is another critical factor. If managers can get the quality information they need much faster, they have more time in which to analyse the data, to think constructively on the basis of their new (and old) knowledge, and to act. Speed of decision, and of subsequent action, were always critical in achieving effective management. But the trade-off between speed and safety has been reduced: fusion between the two can be an everyday reality.

Management is by no means the only area in which process technology is having a revolutionary impact. The technology of production is being transformed by the ability to disseminate information at high speed and to control product variations – making possible the customisation which brings individual treatment to the mass customer. That merges with the technology of service, where CRM (customer-relations management) will become essential for survival, if you believe Chambers:

> Customer priorities will change so rapidly and what [customers] will pay a premium for will commoditise so rapidly that if you don't have your finger on the pulse, you're going to be in trouble.

That reads ironically, coming from a CEO who was about to find his theories proved in such painful practice. But CRM is only one example of the revolution in the technology of service that, along with the revolutions in speed, production, product and global marketing, is confronting managers everywhere with a simple choice: between joining the revolution or being overrun by its consequences.

How can a static business compete with rivals whose productivity is rising as rapidly as Chambers predicts, with gains of 20% to 40% a year already being recorded? How can the rivals to Corning Glass stay in business unless they match its 95% reduction of procurement costs? The more companies see the power of process revolution, the more will enrol in the new technology, and the greater the pressure will mount on the laggards, as the threats become ever sharper.

In financial as well as competitive terms, the orders of magnitude are staggering. Companies – like Dell Computer – can actually find themselves enjoying negative working capital. That is, the customers pay Dell direct for their computers before the suppliers need to be paid. Because customers specify exactly what products they want, Dell also manufactures only what it sells: no write-offs, and no unsold stocks – which helps to produce an inventory turn of 60 times a year. That figure was only six times six years ago, which stresses another absolutely critical point: change is happening very fast.

This acceleration is ignored by conservative followers of Grove's line. Their folly is illustrated by his riveting account of the 1980s, when his company, almost destroyed by Japanese competition in memory chips, abandoned them and concentrated on microprocessors (page 45). It took several years for Intel to face the harsh facts, as 'meetings and more meetings, bickerings and arguments' resulted 'in nothing but conflicting proposals'. Even after the exit decision had been made, it took another year to sell the strategy internally and complete the switch – and a further year to return to profit.

Would an Intel be allowed so much time today? That is highly doubtful. But it wouldn't need so much time, either. With digitised management, everybody would have been in full, simultaneous possession of all the facts, including customer attitudes towards Intel's existing and possible future strategies. The debates would have taken place primarily over the intranet or e-mail, and the switch would have been implemented much faster, and with fatter, earlier returns, thanks to the rapid exchange and quick availability of the new plans and progress information.

This is not to denigrate Grove's conservatism. It remains absolutely true that management is inevitably rooted in unchanging human nature, and that a very sizeable percentage of every manager's time is spent in ways familiar to predecessors from decades back. But that percentage is shrinking as the new technology and allied thinking open new windows for the organisation and those who serve it. Grove was a truly great manager in his day. But a new day has dawned – and only new ideas and thinking will win that day.

Fusion Management, blending the new with the lasting values of the old, is no panacea. Indeed, one of its fundamental tenets is that there are no panaceas, and never will be. But for every set of people, in every management group, there is always a choice of better, more effective and more successful methods. They will change, as will the people – not fundamentally, but in the ways they tackle their tasks, blending basic human strengths with constant adaptation to ever-changing times. That's the ultimate in fusion, and it will rule the future.

PART VI: SHATTERING THE SHIBBOLETHS

How to break free from the old constraints and build a new and lasting company that will live and learn

reversing life-cycles

Corporate decline and fall are only inevitable if Five Fatal Flaws are allowed to flourish

The notion of a corporate life-cycle seems perfectly rational. If everything else, from nation states to small enterprises, passes through a sequence of rise, maturity, success and decline, why not major businesses? In fact, the mortality rate of large Anglo-Saxon companies is high, much greater than that of Continental or Japanese corporations. That, however, is because of differing social and legal conditions, rather than any managerial superiority on the Continent or in the East.

In *The Naked Manager*, published in 1972, I reported research which showed, in apparent paradox, that companies which made continuity their goal were the least likely to survive: companies which, instead, concentrated on either growth or profits, lasted far better. But the ideal company fuses the two aims. The Fusion Manager seeks profitable growth and does so by combining desirable continuity with progressive radicalism. Just as pursuing growth without profits, and *vice versa*, damages continuity, so does failure to fuse past, present and future.

So the overriding issue is why corporate death occurs at all, and what, if anything, can be done to prevent that fate – and even to achieve a rebirth. Is that a reasonable hope? The pre-eminently rational Warren Buffett wrote and, more important, invested as if he believed in everlasting corporate triumph, regarding some of his stock-market investments as permanent, even calling them 'The Inevitables'. The title included two dearest loves in Coca-Cola and Gillette. Buffett claimed that, 'no sensible observer . . . questions that Coca-Cola and Gillette will dominate their fields worldwide for an investment lifetime. Indeed, the dominance will probably strengthen.'

No doubt, the managements of both companies fully shared Buffett's sentiments. But the harsh fact is that both companies faltered badly as the Old Millennium ended. The death from lung cancer of Robert Goizueta coincided eerily with the abrupt end of the unique success (30.1% p.a. return to investors from 1988–98) over which he had presided at Coke. At Gillette, too, the leadership changed – and again the rich period of profitable growth (29.5% p.a.) came to an end. From 1998 to well into the New Millennium, investors had little to relish in either company. By 2002, the 10-year annual growth rate for Coke had slumped to 10.3% and for Gillette, to 10.6%.

It is tempting to associate these setbacks, not with the lifecycle of corporations, but with that of individuals. Managers, too, may pass through a personal sequence of rise, maturity, success and decline – even those with real talent. At Coke, however, the evidence suggests strongly that Doug Ivester, the handpicked successor to Goizueta, had nothing of the latter's genius (see page 154). Although Buffett (a Coke director as well as a huge investor) stood loyally by Ivester for a while, the latter showed himself to be a numbers-obsessed manager – and the direction of giant corporations should put people far ahead of digits.

Al Zeien, the Gillette boss during its palmy period, exemplified this truth by heeding his 'human-resources' people and personally conducting 300 appraisals a year. That gave him unrivalled knowledge, not just of key people, but of what was really happening in the businesses. That understanding of reality is the key issue, and by the same token wishful thinking is the danger point. Buffett wrote as follows about The Inevitables:

> Nor is our talk of inevitability meant to play down the vital work that these companies must continue to carry out, in such areas as manufacturing, distribution, packaging and product innovation.

What goes wrong is that the company unknowingly suffers relative declines in efficiency in such areas (relative either to its own previous standards or the competition's). Reaction is either too little and/or too late. There are five explanations.

1 Denial. Because of its high opinion of itself, management cannot accept criticism of its operations.
2 Systemic failure. The organisation is geared to continuity, not to systematic, radical improvement and reform.
3 Bureaucracy. The layers of command and control slow down reactions.
4 Complacency. A rich cash flow cushions any sense of urgency.
5 Conservatism. Dissenting voices are ignored or suppressed by senior managers who are sure that they know better.

The Five Fatal Flaws interplay and interrelate to produce incompetence and inertia. These had beset Coke before Goizueta took charge. He was able to demonstrate that the great company was earning less than its cost of capital. By totally changing the way in which the businesses and managers were assessed, and by other strategies, like radically reforming key relationships with the Coke bottlers, Goizueta engineered a spectacular improvement in performance.

That is another aspect of the corporate life-cycle. If downturns in performance do occur, a striking once-for-all recovery is within the reach of top management, even if performance merely returns to previous levels. This is far easier than surging ahead to new peaks. The first-stage rocket gives the new man's reign a huge and lasting boost. The next incumbent, however, coming in on the crest of the rise, has an impossible act to follow. The once-for-all benefits have been won, and there's no encore readily to hand.

This unpromising situation, of course, is not the fault of the successor. The operating problems at Marks & Spencer, previously considered Britain's best-managed company of any kind and a retailer second-to-none worldwide, were building long before Sir Richard Greenbury finally handed over. His misfortune was that the board, unable to endorse the heir-apparent, put off the decision and delayed Greenbury's departure. By then the damage done by the Fatal Flaws had clearly and painfully emerged.

Greenbury, like Goizueta at Coke, began his reign by forcing through powerful reforms that produced marked gains in growth and profits. But success in a chief executive is a two-edged sword. It can easily introduce or reinforce the Fatal Flaws. Not only can he become less responsive to criticism: he gets less of it, anyway. Exactly the same process of dominance and deference may happen when decisions are taken as management becomes less collective and more dictatorial.

The damaging M&S results of the early 2000s (the worst sales declines in its history) have been blamed on failure to keep up with fashion on the clothing side. It's true that the goods, and the stores themselves, had come to look out-of-date, dowdy. This coincided with, and reinforced, a deadlier perception among customers. They perceived that, from offering high quality at moderate prices, the chain had shifted to providing only moderate quality at high prices. In other words, the crucial lever in customer behaviour – value for money – had been devalued.

Such seismic shifts in perception do not take place overnight. External tracking studies had long shown an unprecedented drop in customers' regard for the chain, which had previously run far ahead of all other retailers on every single count. Declines in esteem of this nature invariably precede falls in sales, but usually with a long enough lead-time to forestall the trouble – if the business is geared to action and takes it.

Enter the malign effect of the Five Fatals. At M&S, crucially, internal studies had confirmed the deteriorating external picture. The inside analysis pointed to exactly the same decline in quality that was also appearing in customer anecdotes. The reports stimulated action, of a sort: a study group was set to work. Yet the location of the problem was stunningly obvious without study – the source could only be the supplier relationship.

One of the supreme claims to fame at M&S was its path-finding for what's now known as 'the virtual company'. Self-styled famously as 'a manufacturer without factories', M&S

itself designed the clothing products, bought the fabric, pre-scribed the quality and the manufacturing methods, ordained the price and set the deliveries. Food and other offerings were procured in the same highly controlled manner. The relation-ship, though, was old-fashioned by today's standards, in which the supplier is a genuine partner who takes initiatives to improve the product and raise efficiency, and then shares in the achieved economies.

The ageing M&S system had become too slow, cumbersome and inefficient for fast-moving modern markets. Many months were taken over processes that newer retail challengers com-pleted in a few weeks or days. When the system also failed to stop quality from suffering, that struck to the very heart of the business. As venture capitalist John Moulton recalled in June 2001:

> I first knew M&S was going into problems when I stuck my finger through the side of my underpants when I was putting them on. I thought, hang on, that hasn't happened before.

The system should have prevented such mishaps. Failing that, the system should have prevented them from recurring. The specific troubles reported by the press and suffered by the cus-tomers were symptoms of systemic decline, not its causes. The systemic causes are usually insidious and slow-working, while the symptoms are obvious and immediate.

But any expert in Total Quality Management will tell you that treating the symptoms without removing the causes is a dead end (often literally). Like most retail chains, M&S had developed a highly centralised, over-prescriptive management system that stifled and wasted the talents of some brilliant recruits – with the result that the best became liable to move on. In the process, a success that once seemed as inevitable as that of Coke and Gillette proved evanescent.

Curiously, given the heavy weight he generally places on managerial excellence, Buffett paid it no attention in his dis-cussion of what makes The Inevitables inevitable. He mentioned but discounted market leadership, which 'alone provides no certainties: witness the shocks . . . at General Motors, IBM and Sears, all of which had enjoyed long periods of seeming invincibility'. Rather, he placed overwhelming weight on business economics:

> . . . some industries or lines of business exhibit characteristics that endow leaders with virtually insurmountable advantages, and . . . tend to establish Survival of the Fittest as almost a natural law.

Buffett added that most businesses do not share these wondrous characteristics. For once, though, the great man nodded. No natural law guarantees corporate success, or even 'almost' guarantees inevitability. The power of human beings to turn assured victory into defeat has been shown in every field from warfare to medicine. In fact, Buffett himself emphasised one way in which management can destroy inevitability – 'when it gets sidetracked' and neglects its 'wonderful base business' while purchasing other businesses 'that are so-so or worse'.

Loss of focus on its core definitely and permanently hurt one of Buffett's cautionary examples, Sears. But IBM's troubles flowed, in contrast, from excessive focus on its 'wonderful base business' in mainframe computers, which caused tragic neglect of the other marvellous opportunities burgeoning all around the company. As for GM, its purchases of other businesses – Hughes Aircraft and Electronic Data Services – were huge hits that offset some of the damage done by mismanagement of the automotive base.

Countering the corporate life-cycle therefore starts with one inevitable conclusion. The First Law is that there are no Inevitables. Any economic position, whether it's Coke's, or Gillette's, GM's or IBM's, is only as good as its exploitation. That applies to small companies as well as large: the only difference is that the large company has enormous reserves of financial wealth and other resources with which to defend itself against its own incompetence. M&S, after all, continued to make hundreds of millions in annual profit in a dreadful period.

The Second Law is that the organisation and its culture need continuous renewal – a cousin to the Japanese *kaizen*, or continuous improvement. So select the truly vital indicators of present and future performance. There will only be a few, but they must include external and internal perceptions. Set annual targets for these indicators: and act urgently if any indicator starts showing a downward trend.

Third, fuse *kaizen* with *kaikaku* – radical change. Re-examine the selected criteria annually to decide which are no longer relevant and which new ones are required. Also, conduct an exhaustive, continuous search for evidence of those Five Fatal Flaws:

- Denial
- Systemic failure
- Bureaucracy
- Complacency
- Conservatism.

Use a suggestion scheme approach and reward employees who identify examples of the Flaws and/or recommend radical ways of eliminating the defects. This methodology is similar to that of Total Quality Management, but without the intense discipline. It should produce quick pay-offs – and there will never be any shortage of faults.

Fourth, form squads of Young Turks to work on areas that are either self-selected or identified by senior management. At M&S, suitable cases for treatment abounded, ranging from revolutionising its awful window-dressing to cutting the appallingly long lead-times needed to get new clothing into the stores. Keep these multidisciplinary, cross-functional teams in permanent being, adding to and subtracting from membership as necessary, and watch their performance closely to identify the heretics, challengers and doers.

Fifth, review the chief executive's performance rigorously at regular intervals in relation to agreed targets, most of which should not be financial, and none of which should be operational – save one. That is the selection and management of operators who deliver required performance on the key indicators. The CEO's targets, moreover, should be publicised – not shrouded in secrecy like those which entitled the new M&S boss, Luc Vandevelde, to a substantial special bonus in a terrible year.

Sixth, develop a pool of rising managers who have proved their potential by the quality of their thinking and their practical achievement in a series of demanding roles. Their levels of heresy, challenge and 'making it happen' (very possibly as official Young Turks) should be crucial. They are your first line of replacements for the chief executive. If you name a date for the latter to step down (as you must), stick to it, whatever the circumstances – which didn't happen at M&S. Only if nobody in the pool measures up should you start looking outside: but do it well before need.

Finally, never leave this top appointment to the predecessor, or allow him to have a decisive say. Again, this golden principle was ignored at M&S, with the usual result of a failed appointment. You can get lucky. Roberto Goizueta became Coke's head on a choice made solely, not by his immediate predecessor, but by the Grand Old Man of former bosses, Robert Woodward. However it's done, getting Grand Young Men and Women to the top is the seventh step in making the corporate success cycle seem inevitable. But remember: it never is.

attract, motivate and retain

Companies can only recruit from the new generations who have all been reared as free-minded individuals

The Holy Trinity of managing people (aka human resources) is AMR: Attract, Motivate and Retain. In theory, the three are fused, indivisible. If your offer contains the right ingredients, you will attract top-class people who are self-motivated and will happily meet both their own objectives and the company's for ever more. In practice, working life is not so simple, and is daily getting more complex. You can Attract and Motivate marvellously well: but still not Retain.

The explanations are many and convincing. First, job-hopping, formerly a stigma, has become an asset. These days, employers value breadth of experience more than evidence of company loyalty. A whole army of headhunters has revolutionised attitudes. They have turned 'poaching' (long standard practice in the US, once anathema in the UK) into everybody's norm. As for the poached people, they are attracted by greater challenge, higher reward, and perhaps change itself.

Second, a new generation of career opportunities has developed in which those attractions – Challenge, Reward and Change – form a new Trinity. The most conspicuous examples were the hopeful companies in the delirious doomed dot.com boom. At its height, when the would-be entrepreneurs in a recent graduating class at Harvard Business School compiled their business plans, half opted for the World Wide Web in one form or another. Despite the bust of the boom, it remains true that, with the Web, barriers to entry have collapsed or weakened. New companies are still sprouting like weeds.

Many have ended and are ending up like that: as weeds. But

some will flower, and, anyway, others will spring up in the place of the departed. Previous Web experience, even in a failed dot.com, will still count for plenty. Enter the third factor affecting retention. Old-line companies in old-style businesses face rising pressure, not just from dot.coms, but from the general upsurge of entrepreneurial activity. This has made the old-liners, too, active recruiters in the e-world, but their Web-wise recruits are plainly more volatile than the organisation men and women of the past.

Pressure on established firms will not ease. Some are being threatened directly by the more successful newcomers. What happened to Barnes & Noble, ousted as the world's largest bookseller by Amazon, has been repeated in many markets less visible to the naked eye of outside viewers. Other old-liners see enormous opportunities (and threats) in the digital revolution's application to their existing businesses: witness Halifax, Abbey National and the clearing banks going on-line.

Halifax poached a whole team of executives for its greenfield venture. The fourth anti-retention factor is that poaching breeds poaching. The victims of exodus, whether they have lost one key executive or an entire troop, have to replace the losses. Inevitably, this weakens the old culture of loyalty from both sides. The footloose employees owe loyalty to themselves first, the company second. And the employers no longer feel that they owe the employee a life-long career.

Fifth, that life-long career may not exist, certainly not as the traditional climb up the sides of a pyramid to distinguished, gold-watched retirement at 65. Careers are becoming increasingly horizontal because companies are doing likewise. More and more activity is carried on through discrete projects, outside the traditional organisation. Some people are winning their advances, both financially and in achievement, as they move from one project to another. The last horizontal move may well be sideways and out, when the company turns to younger or differently qualified talent.

Retention, for all these reasons, has become less desirable from both sides of the table, the employer and the employed. But that's the generality. In specific cases, retention of a key executive can appear as vital as keeping a football team's top striker. It's no use pointing out that nobody's irreplaceable. If you've found a creative genius like Peter Wood, who sold his Direct Line insurance business to Royal Bank of Scotland, you will think him worth any price (his bonus and salaries totalled £30 million before he eventually left).

The price of retention has soared astronomically, again partly under the dot.com influence. When valuable executives saw their juniors in age reaping rapid fortunes in the tens (or hundreds) of millions, they naturally wanted some of the same, even if the fortunes were mostly paper. The evaporation of the paper gains hasn't affected the issue. Younger people's expectations have been elevated – not only by the dot.com rewards, but by those in ludicrously lavish areas like the City of London and Wall Street. People are no longer interested in the rewards of regulated salary scales.

But a mainline company simply cannot offer everybody stock options on the same lavish scale as start-ups. Moreover, anything that would match, or even near, the handsome rewards of its own chief executive would be anathema. For an interesting example of handsome is as handsome does, consider Jack Welch, a stock-option billionaire. He was awarded an extra $42 million, conditional on his meeting the corporate targets in what was supposed to be his final year at General Electric.

The idea of Welch, a far from extinct volcano, cooling off was laughable. But he wasn't about to extend similar goodies to people far down the management line. That faced Welch with a dilemma. He wisely insisted that every division should commission Web-wise executives to work out new ways of doing business that would exploit the internal and external opportunities offered by the Web. But Welch publicly refused to establish separate rewards for these and other managers who might create e-business successes.

He therefore faced a real threat: any e-stars might join the outward flood of the unretained. The outflow affected blue-chips everywhere. As McKinsey told the *Financial Times*, its own losses on both sides of the Atlantic were 'skewed towards New Economy companies'. One headhunter predict that 'you will see herds of people moving from one company to another. This is a gold rush, and if one gold mine is empty, they will rush to another one.' In fact, some famous mines briefly ran out of paper gold – including the discount broker, E*Trade – before stock options, made valueless by market collapses, were rewritten.

That won't necessarily deter people like James Benfield, no whiz-kid at 50, who left a senior marketing job at Marks & Spencer to chair Confetti, a website (still with us) dealing in weddings and special events; or the Bain consultant, who founded an Internet training company and claimed hopefully that 'market volatility is absolutely not making me regret my career move'. Every high-level mover, moreover, generates a rush of further recruitment. Thus a drug executive, who quit to run a 'business accelerator for Internet companies' planned to add 1000 people in 12 months.

Recruiters and would-be retainers have to bear in mind that the acceleration will continue, even if the dot.com share market were to die a total death (which it hasn't). The fact is that the stock-market bubble followed the upsurge in cyberspace, not the other way round. The Net offers a route to entrepreneurial success that anybody can travel, and many will. Big-time corporate employment will have to compete with the entrepreneurial alternative.

Money is not the answer – not when people will cheerfully trade salary cuts for large, performance-linked bonuses, stock options and unlimited opportunity. But great firms, like GE, can compete with a non-financial inducement: power. It was great fun running a Net start-up that was growing users exponentially while losing other people's money in large lumps. But it's also exciting (and much more secure) to run a business with profits in the multi-millions, famous brands, a large hoard of cash, and the resources to create new products and new markets at will.

You cannot enjoy that excitement, however, unless the big company makes itself a more attractive workplace. Above all, that means giving people greater autonomy in an environment where decisions are taken fast, bucks are not passed, and rank is not pulled. You could summarise this as a prime example of Fusion Management: transplanting the small company ethic into the big company world. It can be done: at their best, the electronic leaders like Intel, Cisco and Dell Computer, despite (or because of) high-speed growth rates, have achieved lightning reflexes without sacrificing essential control.

But people also want to be treated as people. Research carried out by the catering giant Sodexho shows that – as you might expect – the quality of life at work has a positive impact on the loyalty of staff and thus on the likelihood of retention. Health facilities, creches provision, etc., are highly valued. So are flexible working hours, the ability to work from home, and open lines of two-way communication. People want to know what's going on, and, equally, to contribute to decisions that affect them in the workplace.

Ignorance and impotence are deeply demotivating. The start-up usually has the advantage here, too, since smaller scale and the need to pull together make for sharing knowledge and decisions. But large corporations are increasingly being organised in special-purpose teams, the horizontal groupings mentioned above, which contain all the functions, disciplines and talents needed to achieve the objective – a new product, a new information system, a new plant, a departmental overhaul, or whatever.

A so-called 'hot group' can be every bit as open and stimulating as a dot.com start-up, and actually operates on much the same lines. Research done by Clayton M. Christensen, author of *The Innovator's Dilemma*, and Michael Overdorf, a colleague of Peter Senge, shows that to succeed with a major innovation, you must use high-powered, autonomous teams (see p. 106). They can stay inside the organisation only if the innovation is not disruptive to the main business. Where that is not so (like an e-venture), establish the innovators on their own site, free from the organisation.

If they succeed, the independent and independent-minded managers may start slavering for independent wealth. Hiving them off with a separate share quote (which Racal did with the future Vodafone Airtouch) can have stupendous financial effect – as when the latter's board voted chairman Sir Christopher

Gent a rightly controversial £10 million bonus, apparently for masterminding the merger with Mannesmann. So the only way to retain the brightest and best, in another paradox, may be to lose them. But if that's the best way to enrich the shareholders, who is going to complain?

If that argument is hard to swallow, consider the distressing case of Marconi. The remuneration committee was 'aware that the company's current approach to share option grants is not sufficiently competitive to that provided by its US competitors which currently dominate the industries where the company operates'. So Marconi proposed to revise its scheme, impertinently planning to reduce the option prices to below the sorry level to which management errors had contributed. This presumably meant more goodies for displaced CEO Lord Simpson.

His four-year take had already passed £14 million. Onward and upward is the top pay motto as company after company, with no visible reluctance, engages in this lucrative game of leapfrog. It hinges on two unlikely propositions; first, that Gent, Simpson *et al* will scarper to other employment unless paid more; second, that their best efforts are only forthcoming because they get best pay. The second proposition is insulting as well as absurd, since it implies that the recipient is a mercenary with no vision beyond his own pay-packet.

A third notion is that seeing their superiors being stuffed with gold will motivate their juniors to strive onwards and upwards. The sight is just as likely to demotivate, unless there is a clear linkage between exceptional rewards and exceptional performance. Dubious payments and doubtful propositions are symptoms of a demotivating corporate world in which behaviour is still determined and stultified by obsolete practices, old-fashioned hierarchies, and obsessional command-and-control.

An entirely new dynamic dominates the rampant high-tech contestants. If hot product launches, like personal computers, face a puny life-cycle of only six months, their successor, and the successor's successor, must already be in the works – complete for the first replacement, half-way there for the second. These companies don't plan three years ahead, but 18 months, tops: even as little as a mere three months.

The new imperatives also impose dazzling development cycles on innovation. In the world's Silicon Valleys, futuristic design and engineering methods are today's routine. The full powers of IT are essential tools of the technology – including that of management. Thus, synchronous, stimulating working by multidisciplinary, semi-autonomous teams becomes indispensable. Old-fangled sequential working, passing the parcel from design, to engineering, to production, to marketing, just takes too long and delivers too little.

High-speed efficiency is incompatible with the hierarchy, bureaucracy, due process, turf wars and top-down decision-making beloved by the corpocrats. High-tech high-fliers know none of these earthly non-delights, Yet the Valley's habits are new only in practice, not in theory. For at least two decades, not one management thinker has advocated the paraphernalia and practices of order-and-obey cultures.

The Valley's management fits, not only changing technology, but changing social patterns. Companies of all kinds can only recruit from new generations of humans who have been reared as free-minded individuals in a climate of questioning, dissent and expectations of greater, better, faster delivery. You cannot manage these people like their corporate ancestors. But herein lies corporate paradox. Most companies largely operate in the old unsuitable ways.

The grotesque disparity between remuneration at the very top and the rewards of even second-tier managers is richly (*le mot juste*) symbolic. In the corpocracies, money is power, and power is money. In Silicon Valley, for example, money is reward for achievement, not for rising to highest grimace on the totem pole. This monetary contrast symbolises a massive disconnect. The new generation, full of ideas and eager to act, is too often held down by superiors who use top-heavy powers of organisation, appointment, budgetary control and authority to block initiatives from below.

Most of these superiors would fervently deny that they and their cohorts squash the talent within. Those few who admit to the truth do nothing at all to cure the disease – another disconnect. The Internet dramatically exposes these flaws. The Web allows companies to achieve, with ease, speed and certainty, a new, high and highly potent degree of communication and information, internally and externally. It makes global presence automatic. It opens new channels of distribution, procurement and customer service to all, not just the established giants.

The Web thus creates all the necessary conditions for a revolution in management – save one. That is top management's decision to join the future, boldly and entirely. That alone will be a huge advance along the road to Attraction, Motivation and towards the most valuable force for Retention: work that people truly want to do – and do truly well.

CHAPTER THREE

the learning company

The learning company hinges on Fusion Management

All companies 'learn' all the time. That's to say, they acquire new knowledge, collectively and individually, by conscious and unconscious means. The 'learning company', however, learns by design rather than accident. As in all management, deliberate concentration on ends produces better means, and results in higher achievement – and this is yet another arena in which European companies have been playing catch-up with American rivals on many fronts.

The most notable example, of course, lies in the overspending wars in telecommunications and information technology. Here there's a prime concentration of learning companies: and here only Europe's mobile phone firms are market-leading, effective challengers to US domination. The larger Europeans have striven too manfully in the mega-merger arena; but few have the financial muscle that the Americans have brought to bear in deal after deal. And too few have the intellectual muscle to match a more insidious and serious threat than takeovers – the usurpation of intellectual leadership.

The advance of the learning company may well determine the final outcome of the corporate wars. The supremacy of Silicon Valley was not founded on abnormal wealth: nor, until recently, did it depend on mergers. Unsurpassed organic growth was predominantly created by applied brainpower. Some of this mental muscle was of the specialised variety that produced the technological breakthroughs in microprocessors, software, Internet hardware, etc. But the Valley's winners have also tackled the arts and crafts of 'knowledge management' and managing the 'learning company'.

The phrase is most often associated with MIT's Peter M. Senge, author of *The Fifth Discipline*. Senge has identified five 'learning disciplines' as the basis of 'learning organisation work'. They have been crucial to the headlong rise of the micro-electronic millionaires (and billionaires). The quintet are:

- Personal Mastery. People are expected to develop their personal capacity (their 'skills-set') to meet their own objectives, and thus those of the company, which in turn is organised to encourage that personal effort.
- Mental Models. Companies actively seek to establish the right 'mindset' to guide actions and decisions – for example, the 'can-do' mentality which believes that all tasks can be achieved.
- Shared Vision. All members of the organisation are committed to its aims and its ways of realising an over-arching vision like Bill Gates's original 'A PC on every desk and in every home, using Microsoft software'.
- Team Learning. Very bright people are hired, but teamed together, because group thinking is greater than the sum of its individual parts.
- Systems Thinking. These companies understand that actions and decision cannot be isolated, but have ramifications throughout the organisation – so all sections are brought into the act.

Get Senge's quintet rolling through a company, and its intellectual firepower must be greatly augmented. But you can only do that if enough intellectual capacity exists in the first place – and that is a matter, not only of recruitment, but training. If *Business Week* is right, that's where US companies are launching a major, behind-the-scenes drive for supremacy: 'Corporate America has concluded that investing in people is the way to stay ahead.' So executive education is 'suddenly every CEO's favourite strategic weapon'.

Does this amount to anything more than executive retention? True, giving managers education is a valuable perk, which may persuade them to stay longer: on the other hand, greater learning makes them more attractive to poachers. So the retention benefit is tenuous. But the magazine is plainly correct when it goes well beyond more mundane issues:

> Executives are also looking for help managing the speed of change . . . that trend has been exacerbated by the nagging fear of becoming obsolete in a world transformed by technology.

That transformation needs to dominate strategic thinking in companies of all shapes and sizes. Even small, owner-managed businesses have been transformed by new technology. Talking to hundreds of owner-managers over several months, however, I found little awareness of the digital threats and opportunities – with one particular exception. I was impressed by this proprietor's tale. He had called in an expert to update the software of his company, which distributes pharmaceuticals to independent pharmacies. The expert finished the job, but said he had thrown in something extra, for free: a website.

The company at first didn't know what to do with this new toy. But many of its customers proved to have PCs and Internet access. So the distributor started selling its wares over the Web, taking orders and handling the 'paperwork' electronically. The new approach had been so successful that the company was now wondering whether its costly salesforce could be dropped completely – or whether some personal contact was still necessary. Either way, the transformation of the business would be sustained.

Note that the change had not stemmed from the knowledge and insight of the management. The educated brainpower of an outsider had supplied the missing ingredient – by chance. But in these fast-moving times, you cannot rely on chance or outsiders. You have to develop the internal capacity required to meet the challenge of change. You start with yourself, naturally. How do you rate on Personal Mastery, Mental Models, Shared Vision, Team Learning and Systems Thinking? Start with the first:

- What is my current skills-set?
- Does it fully match the requirements of
  (a) my present job
  (b) the job I want next?
- Am I doing enough to update my existing skills?
- What must I do to enhance and augment those skills in the light of the first two questions above?

Unless you get yourself well-educated on all these Personal Mastery counts, and the other four Senge segments, you are in no position to lead and inspire others. This lesson is one that was rammed home hard by my investigation, at the peak of the enthusiasm for Total Quality Management, into 20 companies which all claimed to be pursuing TQM. The only real successes were those firms, like Honeywell UK and what is now STMicroelectronics, which had begun their TQM exercise at the top, in the boardroom, and carried it right the way through the organisation.

This meant spending time and money, not just for a few months, but for year after year after year, and involving everybody, from top to bottom of the business.

The lesson doesn't apply only to TQM.

No serious effort to drive change and develop strengths can succeed unless the money-and-time formula is applied relentlessly – and the Americans are certainly following the first part of this prescription. According to *Business Week*, the 'average US company' spent $10 million on internal and external executive development in 1998.

But the magazine did not define the average company, or say how much money went on updating top management itself. On the first point, to afford $10 million of educational overhead, the company has to be large. My guess is that top managers of such companies spend neither much time nor significant money on their own education. Whether they think there is nothing for them to learn, or that learning is ineffective, they are equally wrong. Some of them do visit executive classrooms, of course – but mostly just to bless the teaching with their fleeting presence.

As it happens, the classroom could be on the way out, or at

least down. Even the Harvard Business School's professors 'realise that they must go on-line to compete', reported *Business Week*. The business schools no longer have a monopoly on their game. They must fight for custom against 'consultants, Web-based learning companies, and freelance professors'. On-line gives powerful new options for do-it-yourself education, whether or not you use outsiders either as supplements or alternatives to in-house teaching.

More effectively, treat the whole company as a learning and teaching laboratory, experimenting with different methods of managing which have a direct impact on people, and to which they contribute. The company learns, and so do they. Here are some maverick examples, mostly culled from the *Harvard Business Review*:

- Ricardo Semler's Brazilian engineering business, Semco, has become world-famous because of its leader's innovations. He believes passionately in the 'amoeba approach', splitting factories that have 'become too large for their own good . . . into units small enough to ensure that the people who work in them would feel human again'. At one spun-off plant, productivity soared, inventories fell by 40% and defects dropped to under 1% as youngsters, known as 'The Kids', took over, 'innovated all over the place' – and learnt.
- At Romac Industries, Seattle, the pay of 300 hourly-paid workers is openly revealed. If they want a raise (any time, even a month after the last one), their names, current pay, new demand and photo are posted. Fellow-workers then vote secretly, using a 0–100 scale, on how much of the raise should be paid. That's after receiving foremen's recommendations, which the employees themselves request, but can ignore if they like. Is the process fair? The answer matters less than the education in economic realities.
- To inculcate perfect service, why not measure and reward people by the quality of their service? A Mid-West plumbing firm named De-Mar, one of Tom

229

Peters's small business heroes, awards 1000 points if a
Service Adviser (that's a plumber) is the subject of a
'good phone call' from a customer: a bad call loses 1000.
A good letter wins 2000 points, and a bad one loses the
same. If 'customer requests particular Adviser', that's
1000 points up. If the Adviser isn't wanted back at any
price, that's 2000 down. The month's three top points
earners get 50% extra sales commission.

- Don't fuss about paying your people in the top quartile.
Underpay them by 25% to 33% of the industry average.
Hold them responsible, too, for machine breakdowns and
quality failures – cut their bonuses accordingly. Five
minutes late, no bonus that day: half an hour late, and
back to the miserable basic pay for the whole week. The
company applying this Draconian regime, steel mini-mill
expert Nucor, became the fastest growing metals business
in the US. The secret ingredient in the formula is that
bonuses run at 80% to 200% of base pay, based on team
productivity and – here's the crucial twist – they are paid
every week.

- Artificially speed up reaction times. In General Electric's
three-day 'Work-Out' sessions, when teams of workers
present proposals (maybe 100-plus), the boss must decide
at once: either Yes, No, or I need more information –
even then, the decision can only be postponed for a
month. Four-fifths of the Work-Out proposals get
approved. High-flyer Akamai plans only 90 days ahead
(that's all) and ranks businesses *weekly*: Green = 'We did
it'; Yellow = 'Progress, not yet there'; Red = 'We didn't
do it'. When somebody starts getting a lot of reds, there's
no place to hide.

- US e-banker WingSpanBank.com accepts or rejects home
loan applications in 60 seconds. One sign-on connects
customers with all their accounts, on a '7 × 24' basis (i.e.,
open all hours). Non-tech aspects are just as important.
Employees must listen to customer calls for 90 minutes a
month: top executives must read a minimum of 20
customer e-mails daily. There isn't the usual all-embracing,

unresponsive customer service department: Wingspan has 'customer experience' units and 'customer advocacy teams'. Plus, customers advise on products and strategy as members of an 'iBoard of Directors'.

- How to find the highest price the traffic will bear? Scott McNealy, CEO of Sun Microsystems, may have the answer. Just don't fix prices at all. Let customers fix them through auctions, just as buyers do on eBay. Sun's already selling its computers, etc., over eBay and other auction sites; and, McNealy told the *Harvard Business Review*, is 'very pleased' with results. Eventually, Sun won't have any price lists – bereaving its poor sales reps. Not only are the reps taught to sell properly (at last), on attributes other than price, but they can't play 'liar-liar', pretending 'this is my best price' to prospects who counter with equally phoney top offers.

Such approaches are both experimental and educational, and you should be trying maverick ideas constantly. That fits a general clear need: to keep as much tailormade content as possible. Internal development is still the best starting point. It is cheaper and, even more importantly, it can be directly related (like the strong educational element in TQM) to the work of the individual, the unit and the company.

There's little point in education that doesn't relate in this potent manner. But there's far more to the story. The learning company hinges on the Fusion Manager. What's taught in the classrooms must be blended with what happens outside – in the executive suite, at the desks of lower managers, in the factories, in the showrooms. Otherwise, both learning and the company will fail.

The catch is that investment in learning is easier to finance and to sustain when a company is in comfort, and not in crisis. But comfortable companies and managers don't see the need to learn, and uncomfortable ones feel themselves under too much pressure. This two-way inertia is compounded by the apparent difficulty of teaching old dogs new tricks. Most companies face this puzzling problem. Go into the old telecoms monopolies, like Deutsche Telecom, AT&T and BT, and you will find hundreds of managers who still have the habits and ideas of monopolists. That makes them wholly unsuitable for an age of competition which will be dominated by the Internet.

However dynamic and far-sighted the men at the top, that must greatly hamper their efforts to compete against newcomers who are not encumbered by the lumber of the past. Refusing to learn is refusal to change. A true learning company hinges on Fusion Management and will not countenance this refusal. It teaches strategically all the way down the corporate scale. It seeks people everywhere who can understand the strategic needs, work out what these demand, and carry through their conclusions to successful implementation.

Starting on that journey is obviously the most important step. If you don't start a journey, you can't possibly arrive. But few managers at any level have the drive needed for this exercise in corporate and personal ambition. That general sluggishness gives a huge advantage to those who take the first fast step. You are competing against people who have actually chosen to be left at the starting line. That applies to virtually all the owner-managers I've met. It is a very poor choice in today's markets.

To succeed in these markets, you need education in the widest possible sense, embracing information systems and e-commerce, leadership, innovation and global business. What's taught should preferably be customised to suit your purposes, using for case studies the actual needs of your organisation – with a view to practical implementation of the study findings. Plenty of good outside help is available in all these key areas. But the most important contribution has to come from ambitious insiders. Make sure you are among them.

image, reputation and reality

Improve realities, and reputation, image (and the shares) will look after themselves

Recession is damaging for business reputations, as well as for business itself. It only takes a downturn in trade, or even a slowdown in growth, for yesterday's hero to become today's target of criticism and blame. Shortly into the Millenium, as noted earlier in this book, comeuppance came with a vengeance to John Chambers, chief executive of Cisco Systems. After being widely hailed as best in the West, a manager whose strategic strengths were supported by superb systems, he was let down by a failure that savaged the shares.

On his own admission, Cisco had badly missed the sharp decline in the world market for telecommunications equipment of all kinds. The special irony is that Chambers prided himself, and was praised by others, for the real-time, Internet-based systems that allowed him to keep constant track of sales, orders and margins. Either the system failed to throw up advance signs of the adverse trends, or the signs were ignored in the gung-ho climate of a sales-driven company that had been used to 50% annual growth rates.

It's a rare manager who not only sees that the party is over, but acts, well in advance, to deal with the consequences. It's an even rarer manager who can resist the seductive temptation to rejoice in his company's glories. If you have spent four years in producing a Digital Nervous System as universal and responsive as Cisco's, you are liable to boast about its merits – and to rest on those laurels. In fact, the glorification is ominous in itself.

Dell Computer fell into the same trap. There was Michael

Dell, for example, lauding his 'virtual' operations to the *Harvard Business Review*, oblivious of the fact that the personal computer market was heading for inevitable slowdown. His operational superiority (though it later proved its worth) couldn't save Dell from sales setbacks, and personnel cutbacks.

The issue is not how good you are now, still less how good you were, but how good you are *going* to be. To spell that out, no management achieves all-round perfection. Weaknesses exist in its strongest areas, and abound in the weaker ones. For example, Dell came out worst in one UK survey of sellers over the World Wide Web (where it is among the very largest) in exactly the area where you would have expected the company to excel: customer service.

Not only are inconvenient faults swept under the self-satisfied company's carpet, but good performance tends to deteriorate over time. That's partly because the disease of self-congratulation prevents objectivity. A powerful external pressure leads to this insidious and dangerous infection. The company's image and reputation are important business tools. They affect its marketing strength, its stock-market rating, its ability to attract the best recruits – and, of course, they feed the vanity of its top people.

It's all very well to say that you shouldn't believe your own publicity. But if you don't believe it, why should anybody else? The line between an effective public-relations policy and hubris is not easily drawn. When you actually do cross the border in the wrong direction, it's difficult to perceive that this has happened, and harder still to act on the perception.

That explains the ridiculous lengths of time that once-great companies can take over badly needed change. Eastman Kodak, Xerox and IBM all provide awful examples of companies that floundered for the best (or worst) part of a decade (and in the first two cases are still floundering). It was less the decisions that managements took than the decisions they avoided which led into the swamp.

The real-life experience of one private investor illustrates the strange power of indecision. He always knows when the stock market has reached its peak and a bear phase looms. How does he know? Because that's when he starts going through the portfolio, licking his chops at the huge gains which prove what a clever investor he has been. Experience has proved many times that this is the moment to sell. Yet he has never taken that logical and highly profitable action.

The correct decision is to liquidate the whole portfolio, taking the profits and waiting to reinvest at lower prices. Probably, the investor never will make the correct decision. By not acting on his dead-accurate information, he misses the crucial moment. So do nearly all companies that are riding high. They fail to analyse the root causes of their success and to act accordingly.

Whether it's a booming stock market in the case of the investor, or a booming telecoms equipment market for Cisco, the beneficiaries credit their own specific brilliance for what is, at least in major part, a general phenomenon. Far better to follow three Golden Rules. They fly in the face of apparent logic, but are truly made of precious metal:

1 The better everything is going, the harder you must strive to improve EVERYTHING.
2 Concentrate on the Weaknesses and Threats as well as the Strengths and Opportunities.
3 Build challenge and change into your personal and corporate way of life.

If you don't follow this golden formula, ridiculous and possibly serious results may well follow. Lack of self-awareness can be amazingly complete. I recall the remarkable case of one company which was hosting a seminar that was to consider some important questions:

- What is the business value of a company's share price?
- What must a company be aware of, and what must it do, to ensure that . . .
- the share price remains competitive . . .
- shareholders stay content . . .
- top management keeps their support – and its jobs?

These sensible enquiries had a bizarre side. The company concerned – Gamma Unlimited, let's say – had seen its shares fall by 60%, far worse than its leading domestic competitor; its largest shareholders were openly up in arms, and the two top job-holders were specifically under threat – within two months of the seminar, one had duly departed. In other words, Gamma's bosses apparently had no clear or satisfactory answers to critical questions that their very own seminar was addressing.

The top pair were, in fact, aware of the marketplace pressures, internal contradictions and external criticisms that threatened their positions. But their inability to act on this awareness meant that they might as well have been managing in the dark – certainly the share price would have fared no worse. A major factor in the strength of a share is that the management (as Gamma's was not) is perceived in the following light:

1 It knows what it is doing, and why, in the short, medium and long terms.
2 The three time-horizons add up to a cohesive, fused strategy that fits the technological, economic and commercial environments.
3 The strategy is fully understood within the company and is being effectively implemented.

It doesn't follow that achieving this perception will be followed by a leap in the shares – though analysts (and journalists) have often shown a credulous, knee-jerk tendency to react to every 'restructuring' (i.e., new round of lay-offs) as a potential strategic masterstroke. What is true, however, is that the opposite perception is invariably deadly – especially if the perception is accurate. In Gamma's case, poor perception and the facts of the case were one and the same:

1 The company had no clear strategy, but was continually reorganising in ways that impeded, rather than encouraged, strategic success.
2 In a high-tech industry undergoing fundamental and dynamic change, Gamma was lagging visibly behind in

the fastest-moving sectors and the newest technologies.

3 The company was plagued internally by overlapping services and operations, endemic indecision, and a top-heavy management structure.

These defects were no secret, either inside the company or outside. Likewise, many external and internal people recognised IBM's fateful obsession with mainframe computers in the 1980s, to the neglect of its vital businesses in PCs, software, services, etc. The parallel with IBM is close: Gamma also had a cash cow, a traditional, money-spinning quasi-monopoly whose care and nurture left everything else in its shadow – but whose long-term future (like that of the mainframe computer) was doomed by technological shift.

The greatest peril of the hubristic mindset is that management will miss such shifts. Both Andy Grove and Charles Handy have noted (see pages 39–40) that the critical point occurs before the moment of maximum prosperity. Miss the critical point, and you will be trying to restart or kick-start growth when the business has passed the peak. You have failed to obey the Golden Rules, and the company will pay the price – at best travail and hard-won triumph, at worst (and most common) decline and fall.

The solution for both Gamma and IBM was obvious to outsiders: break up the company into large, discrete businesses, with the particular aim of allowing the dynamic newcomers to grow independently, without interference or overshadowing from the old core business. For Gamma, this idea had been especially attractive. For a time, the stock market's infatuation with high technology meant that portions of the separated businesses could have been spun off at nonsensical, but richly rewarding valuations.

This proposition was debated often at the higher reaches of Gamma, and just as regularly rejected. When the issue finally became urgent, because the company needed to fund mountainous debts, the moment had passed. NASDAQ had plunged, and wondrous valuations were no longer available. Such failure to act in time is one of several giveaways which reveal that a company is in denial and slipping away down Handy's Sigmoid Curve, and past Grove's strategic inflection point:

1 Obviously beneficial, even crucial actions are aired but never resolved.
2 The top management remains in place and in total command long after the first deep cracks have appeared in the business.
3 Strategy and other paramount issues are referred to committees or study groups, often with very long deadlines.
4 The CEO is insulated from other managers and outsiders, often having a high-level 'personal assistant' for the purpose.
5 Specific criticisms, from inside or outside, are ignored or dismissed – but large general 'initiatives' are launched in response (to little or no good effect).

What, then, are the good signs? They are not totally reliable – in management, every idol is in danger of being fitted with feet of clay. This book contains many references to Jack Welch, the titanic CEO of General Electric. Welch's reputation, now badly damaged, was never sacrosanct. He presented himself with a tough final year in 2001, having delayed his retirement to mastermind the $42 billion Honeywell merger.

That was a double error. Postponing Welch's retirement was no compliment to his appointed and anointed successor, Jeff Immelt. And the antitrust implications of the deal had not been properly assessed – by mid-year it was in deep and fatal trouble with the European Commission. Instead of leaving on a triumphant note, Welch left in September 2001 as a disappointed man. But the facts of Fusion Management behind those many mentions of Welch are still excellent omens, like . . .

1 Setting up destroyyourbusiness.com (later changed to growyourbusiness.com) within established GE operations to challenge them like a hungry e-entrepreneur, *while* demanding superb results from the host businesses.

2 Leading from the front to give GE a strong sense of purpose or direction, *while* insisting that corporate renewal is essential to maintain a vital organisation.

3 Demanding that managers face reality and pass on bad news, taking full responsibility for running their own units, *while* looking four years ahead and ('probably more important') nine years on.

4 Practising hard-nosed management *while* insisting on shared corporate values, such as 'see change as opportunity, not threat'.

5 Insisting that managers deliver on their commitments, *while* removing 'Type IV' ones who deliver, but do not share or apply the values.

Other extremely effective Welch policies are less paradoxical. They included the demand that GE businesses be either first or second in their global markets – or get sold or closed: the use of GE's management training centre at Crotonville as the cornerstone of the company's progress; and the corporation-wide 'Six Sigma' drive, launched late in his career, to achieve the highest Total Quality ratings.

Note how well the Welch attributes and policies fit the three Golden Rules. The better everything is going, the harder you must strive to improve everything – by initiatives like the Six Sigma programme. You take weaknesses and threats so seriously that you act before they even appear (the idea behind the original 'destroyyourbusiness.com' initiative). Challenge and change are built into GE's values and into the way in which Welch ran it for 20 years.

His success is a textbook example of how to confront the issues which concerned Gamma when staging its seminar: share price, shareholder support, and top management security. Welch's regime drove up the share price to make GE the wealthiest company in the US (as he had aimed to do), while delighting the shareholders and making the top management the most admired (and secure) in the land.

Do shining image and high reputation ever fit reality? Probably, they never do. Certainly, Welch's grandiose arrangements for a rich retirement came as a rude shock to his fans. Remember that perceptions are reality, and that they can change abruptly – witness the falls from grace of IBM and Marks & Spencer. Their subsequent recoveries, however, show that genuine underlying strengths can always be cashed in. If you constantly seek to improve the realities, and do so, reputation, image (and the share price) will, by and large, look after themselves. And that's the way to do it.

CHAPTER FIVE

going for growth

Momentum is a vital element in the whole Fusion
Management blend

Why grow? This is a question that few ask, let alone answer. It's taken for granted in organisations that growth is good and non-growth is bad. The whole stock market industry, of analysts and journalists, fund managers and tipsters, is geared to the pursuit of growth in profits. Yet you can easily imagine a situation, growthless but not seriously declining, secure and seriously profitable, that is highly agreeable.

Suppose that you own a debt-free, private business – My Goldmine, Ltd – that earns an effortless, steady, inflation-proofed £1 million in after-tax profits, representing a much higher return on capital than any safe financial investment could provide. Other firms are expanding, true. But so what? You and those family members who work or share in the business draw handsome incomes from this lucrative cynosure. Why grow?

One answer is that earning £2 million a year is twice as agreeable as earning £1 million – other things, like the strain of running the business, being equal. In fact, effort will be required to double the earnings. There could also be unpalatable risks. These two obstacles – effort and risk – explain why so many privately owned businesses rest content with My Goldmine, Ltd. But there are no guarantees. These relatively tiny lodes can be easily destroyed by the avalanche of events, and thousands are, every year.

The fault in the My Goldmine argument is that it assumes a dichotomy that doesn't exist. Remember that a survey of printing companies which divided its subjects into companies that pursued either Continuity, or Profits, or Growth. The paradox was that the Continuity fans were far less likely to survive than those who sought either profits or growth. The best strategy is Fusion Management *par excellence*. You achieve Continuity by pursuing, not growth, but Profitable Growth.

For growth, read change. The conventional ways of defining and measuring growth mislead and misrepresent. These yardsticks are mostly financial: above all, expanded revenues and/or higher profits. You can understand such an emphasis in a public company. If its financial profile doesn't change, the share price (in theory) won't rise. Time was when investors bought shares for dividend income. That notion was superseded decades ago by the cult of the equity. Investors want capital gains. That's another financial definition of growth. It translates into an increase in 'shareholder value'.

The value of a share, however, is founded on the genuine value of the underlying business. Over the long term, this financial outcome ultimately derives from non-financial performance. My Goldmine has to answer some demanding questions:

- Does the company have a strong and improving customer franchise?
- Is the management able, up-to-date and up to the mark?
- Are operational efficiencies continuously rising?
- Is the company investing and planning well for the future?
- Is it stronger than the competition on every count that matters to customers?

This list could be longer. But all the questions revolve round another. Is the company geared to change? My Goldmine only makes a degree of sense in an unchanging environment. But even in less turbulent times than the 21st century, change is omnipresent. Societies change, technologies change, markets change, competition changes. My Goldmine's strategy, that of not changing at all, is not just ill-advised. It's impossible.

If others change and you don't, your relative position alters.

Inevitably and unknowingly, you change – or worse, you are changed by your competitors. A good illustration is price. If the competition lowers a price and you don't, you have changed (in fact, raised) the only price that counts: the relative price. The customers care only for the best value for money. If the competition *raises* a price, and you don't, you have cut your price. That may or may not be a great idea: but that's what you have done.

As for prices, so for every other component of the business model. If the technology changes, and you stay put, for obvious example, the results may well be catastrophic. In the past, large companies were able to dodge calamity by using monetary and marketing muscle. Even the largest firms no longer have that luxury. By missing technology after technology, Xerox Corp. converted itself from super-star to potential bankrupt.

Miss technological change, and you probably miss the target. But what about size? Surely that must have strategic value? Among financial-services executives surveyed on behalf of Unisys, a thumping 86.8% duly agreed that their companies had to grow. Yet 48.1% 'specifically disagreed that bigger is better'. Strategic planners were the parties pushing most strongly for growth and size. Chief executives apparently follow, sometimes reluctantly, in their wake. One way or another, though, size wins the mental argument.

CEO Lord Browne was only typical in deciding that giant BP was merely 'medium-sized' and that its future demanded vastness – hence the Amoco and Atlantic Richfield super-mergers. The mega-corporation has an inbuilt mega-drive towards bigger, but not necessarily better proportions. The contrast with businesses like My Goldmine couldn't be greater. They mostly have an in-built resistance to growth and scale.

Put the arguments for expansion to an audience of Gold-miners, owner-managers, and they will see the force of the logic which dictates that you cannot stand still in changing times. Acting on that progressive logic is another matter entirely, as I found when talking to a thousand or so proprietors up and down Britain, courtesy of the accountancy giant Ernst & Young. The numbers considering themselves to be progressive Visionaries (as opposed to stay-put Pragmatists or stuck-in-the-mud Conservatives) were very small.

The Pragmatists dominated – this is the Wait-and-See brigade, the people who prefer to let others try new things first and to act only when it is demonstrably necessary. Actually, the Pragmatists are mostly closet Conservatives: both types are averse to change, tend to deny its importance, and generally hope, even against hope, that they will be able to avoid action altogether. I was able to prove this discomforting assertion with a simple test – an exercise in How to Become a Visionary, which I tried on the Ernst & Young audiences. Here it is:

Get a sheet of paper, and write at the bottom a short, succinct description of where your business is now – using absolute and if necessary hurtful honesty. At the top of the paper, write down where you want the business to be in x years' time – the period is not important. Then write down the major steps that you think will be necessary to get from the bottom to the top of the paper. Congratulations: you're a Visionary.

Ever the optimist, I asked how many of the audience would go home and invent their futures. I expected a clear majority. I got a miserable collection of a few raised hands. Those people, no doubt admirable at business in many ways, hankered after My Goldmine. They dreamt of a company that would fly into the future on autopilot. In their minds, they understood that this would almost certainly not work. In their hearts, they shied away from the inexorable consequences of change.

The same phenomenon can be seen with even more clarity much higher in the corporate world – at the very top. Among the world's largest companies, only General Electric has consistently shown an appetite for change, not just through mergers and acquisitions, but through processes and people. The GE record to date shows that ardent pursuit of progressive change can pay off in spectacular rises in 'shareholder value'. Even here, though, the new CEO, Jeff Immelt, faces a daunting challenge in sustaining the growth rates of the past.

For the opposite end of the change spectrum, look at IBM, once renowned for its management, its technology, its products, its sales and marketing drive, and its innovation. The company abounded with plans and planners, but it was no longer driven by Visionaries in the 1980s. The Pragmatists were in command and control. Wait-and-see had worked brilliantly for them in the past. It was 14 years after Digital Equipment produced the first mini-computer that IBM entered the market. Eventually, its AS400 caught up and spun money by the billions.

When IBM crashed into the market four years after the Apple II launched the era of true personal computing, its PC swept past Apple and reinvented the industry. In laptops, IBM trailed five years behind Toshiba. But the world and the industry had changed – and IBM hadn't. Today time-lags have become irreversible. Confident that it would catch up, IBM never came near its leading laptop rivals. Far worse: market share in PCs collapsed because IBM's thinking was locked into the large mainframe computers that had made the company's fortunes and its awesome reputation. The unthinkable became reality. IBM went ex-growth.

Its fabulously rewarded CEO, Lou Gerstner, imported from American Express, achieved stardom for his feats in arresting the company's decline. But in 1989, IBM's sales were $63.4 billion and its profits $3.8 billion. In 1999, despite a fantastic boom in industry-wide computer hardware and software sales, IBM's sales were up 38% on ten years earlier – the kind of gain Cisco and Microsoft had been recording in a year, let alone a decade. True, IBM profits doubled in the decade: but the new super-stars in their prime did that in a couple of years.

The IBM share price also recovered handsomely from the doldrums. But the share price measures only one thing: the share price itself. The price is the net result of the balance between buyers and sellers of the stock. It has a relationship to underlying values, but that relationship is tenuous, volatile, unpredictable, unreliable, irrational, often downright silly. As a measure of corporate performance, the share price is meaningless. Yet this is the standard to which corporate chieftains committed themselves hook, line and sinker, back in the 1990s.

Their task, they declared nobly, was to grow the aforementioned 'shareholder value'. The message sped round the world. In Germany, Jürgen Schrempp was its foremost advocate (see page 127). Under that banner, as noted, his company, Daimler-Benz, destroyed 60% of shareholder value in a single year, thanks mainly to a horribly bungled acquisition of Chrysler. It may be that at some future point happy investors will applaud Schrempp's strategies as masterstrokes. More likely, the mistake will be buried by history.

Managers (and the stock-market analysts who feed their vanity) have been led up a deceptively attractive garden path. All equity investors seek value: they buy a share in the hope or expectation that at some time or other they will be able to realise that value by selling the share at a higher price. That chance clearly depends on how much they pay in the first place.

If the price is less than the underlying value of the business, well and good. You have a bargain. If future increases in value are already recognised ('discounted') in the share price, how is management going to oblige? All these issues have been patiently explained over the years by Warren Buffett. He has laid down some unarguable precepts.

1 Every business has an intrinsic, underlying value – technically, the worth of its future cash flows, discounted for the passing of the years.
2 Business value arises from the strength of the customer franchise and of the market that those customers represent.
3 Acquisitions can only grow business value if the buy is fairly priced – which is unlikely, because the buyer is normally forced to pay a premium.
4 Management's job is to increase the intrinsic value, which is real, and not the share price, which is evanescent.

Buffett makes an unassailable case for organic growth, ultimately the only kind worth having. Even mergers must pass the organic test. GE's blocked purchase of Honeywell would have been justified only if the results had included organic improvement in either Honeywell's or GE's performance, or both. The growth issue is as simple as Buffett suggests:

- What is the present worth of the business?
- What creates that worth?
- How good is management at protecting its current strengths?
- How good is management at creating new strengths to take advantage of change?

The basic exercise which I recommended to those thousand owner-managers also and always applies:

- Where precisely is the business now?
- Where do you want it to be 'then' – at a chosen date in the future?
- What must you do to move from now to then?

Even if 'you' are the entire owner of the company, others depend for their lives and livelihood on its business, and 'you' depend on them for their essential contributions to its value. Indeed, they – your people – are a major part of that value. How well are 'you' using that valuable asset and increasing its worth? Without the full contribution of others to the plan, it is far less likely to be either good or well executed.

Treat the company as everybody's My Goldmine, and that makes it far more likely to start growing genuine, organic nuggets for you (and them) as Fusion Management works its wonders. Momentum is a vital element in the mix, and the key reason why growth is an honourable and necessary pursuit. The wisdom of Edward Gibbon, writing about the decline and fall of the Roman Empire, still applies in the 21st century: 'All that is human must retrograde if it does not advance.'

That is the incontrovertible answer to the question at the start of this chapter: Why grow? Since the future is not known to man, nobody can specify what the coming decades hold for world business in general and individual managers and managements in particular. But looking back to 1980 in the 2000s is like returning to a world so different that many of its features seem archaic. The same, indeed, is true of the bizarre spectacle of the speculative bubble of the end-century. And the same will be true twenty years on.

The answer is not to deplore the difference, but to seek to exploit the good of the new while rejecting the bad of old and new alike. As a final paradox, the One Right Way is to understand that there is no one right way, nor ever will be. Managers who survive and thrive, along with their organisations, will be flexible, proactive pragmatists who grasp the key principle of Fusion Management – to dare to be different.

index

ABB 55
Accel Partners 104
acquisitions 36, 106, 127–34, 162–4, 170, 197
added value 37
Adriano, Dino 186
Airbus 110, 111, 116
Airtouch 129
Akamai 10, 11, 15, 16, 230
Akers, John 31
Allen, Herbert 154–5
Allis-Chalmers 170
Amazon 10, 15–16, 28, 51, 69, 90, 91, 103, 218
AOL; merger with Time Warner 15, 153
AOL Time Warhner 81
Apple 53, 119–20
Ariba 78
assumptions trap 195–6
Astra 129
@Home 69
AT&T 232
attract, motivate and retain (AMR) 217–24
auctions 51
Augean Stables Syndrome 110, 113, 116
Autobytel 51

Ballmer, Steve 22, 68, 73, 171
banks; and Internet 23–4, 194–5, 196, 218
Barnes & Noble 218
Barnevik, Percy 55
Beenz 51
Benfield, James 220
Berkshire Hathaway 98, 155, 169, 172
Best World, Worst World management technique 193–5
Bezos, Jeff 10
Bhide, Amar 79, 80
BMW; and Rover 127, 128–9, 130, 131–2, 148

boards 159–65; appointment of CEOs 160, 164–5; and stock markets 161–2
Boeing ix, 22, 27, 110–13, 114–15, 116, 193
Bonfield, Sir Peter 149
bonus payments 35
boo.com 13
Boston Consulting Group 97
Boston Matrix 97
BP 243
Brabeck, Peter 26–7, 29–31, 32
branding 89–90
British steel (now Corus) ix
Browne, Lord 243
BT 148–9, 232
BTR ix
Buffet, Warren 98, 174, 246; and acquisitions 36, 101, 162, 163–4, 170; on CEOs 154–5; on Inevitables 209–10, 213–14; style 172–3, 175; stock portfolio 169–70
bureaucracy; as Fatal Flaw 211
Business Masterminds 98
business model 146–7, 149–50
business plans 13, 49
Business Process; Reeingineering 52
business schools 229
Business Strategy Review 56
Business Week xii, xiii, xv, 17–18, 26, 66, 122, 171, 199, 200, 201, 228
'Business X-Ray' 6–7, 9
buyer aggregation 51
Byrne, John A. 122, 200

call centres 61–2
Callaghan, James 50
Campbell Soup 160, 164, 185
Canion, Rod 148
Canon 98
car industry 52, 59
Carvell, Tim 14, 87
centres of excellence 20

CEOs 165, 181, 215–16; all-powerful 151–8; appointment by boards 160, 164–5; dismissal of 159; hired from outside 165; reasons for cult of riding high 154; responsible for key systemic actions 159–60; and Seven Critical Questions 151–3, 155; six habits of highly ineffective 181–2; toppling of 8
Cerent 6
Chambers, John 13, 122, 123, 202, 203, 204, 233
change 201–2, 242, 244; disadvantages of radical 26–7
Charan, Ram 181, 182
Christensen, Clayton M. 104–5, 107, 143, 145, 221; *The Innovator's Dilemma* 103, 221
Chrysler xii, 127, 246
Churchill, Sir Winston xiv–xv, 47
Cisco Systems ix, 6, 12–13, 58, 69, 72, 122, 203, 221, 233
Clark, Jim 12, 13
Cleese, John 62
Club Med ix
CNET 69
Coca-Cola 154, 155–6, 160–1, 163, 185, 209–10, 211
Cohen, Sir Jack 187
Colvin, Geoffrey 181, 182
Compaq 7–8, 73, 121, 146–7, 148
competition; dealing with 117–23
complacency; as Fatal Flaw 211
Condit, Phil 114, 115
Confetti 220
Conrades, George 10–11, 16
Conservatism; as Fatal Flaw 211
'contextual marketing' 91
continuity; combining with progressive radicalism 209
contractors; and outsourcing 55
core competencies concept 143, 145
Corning Glass 204
Covey, Stephen R. 99; *The Seven Habits of Highly Effective People* 161
Customer Relationship Management (CRM) 61, 204
customer value 36–7; building of added value and enhancing of intrinsic value 37–41
customers; addressing complaints 63; automating of contact between buyer and seller 62; captivating the 60–7; employee satisfaction and satisfaction of 62, 115; and entrepreneurial manager 74; and Gates' digital

nervous system 19, 20; growing importance of 88; and the Internet 61, 66; perception gap between managers and strategic response to 63–4; and zero-based strateg 66–7

Daft, David 163, 164
Daimler-Benz 127, 246
Davidow, William H. and Malone, Michael, S.; *The Virtual Corporation* 53
Davis, Sir Peter 187
De-Mar 229–30
decentralisation 20
delegation 114–15
Dell Computer 46, 51, 57–8, 69, 121, 221, 233–4; and Compaq 73, 121; customer-service plan 66; enjoyment of negative working capital 204–5; opening of Premier Page website 71; and virtual integration 54
Dell, Michael 46, 54, 233–4
Deming, W. Edwards 61, 115
denial; as Fatal Flaw 211
destroyyourbusiness.com 8, 81–2, 238, 239
Deutsche Telecom 232
differentiation 144
Digital Equipment 73, 148, 188, 202
Digital Nervous System 17–25, 233
Digitas 91
disintegrated management 112
disruptive technologies 143, 145
diversification 40
Dorling Kindersley 193–4
dot.coms 10–15, 36, 82, 162, 217–18, 219; attraction to by experienced managers as well as youngsters 11–13; branding strategy 90; collapse of start-ups 11, 76; and competition 118; drawing together of traditional management and 14–15; explosion of and achievement 10; failure of and reasons 81, 87, 89
Double Click 69
downsizing operations xi
Drake Beam Morin 165
Drucker, Peter 6, 9, 99, 100, 114; *Innovation and Entrepreneurship* 68

e-CEOs 69, 70
e-companies; and 5F management 15–16; *see also* dot.coms
e-mail 23, 92, 93
Eastman Kodak 234

eBay 13, 51, 82, 231
economic downturns 136
Economic Value Added (EVA) 36
Edvinsson, Leif 24
eFrenzy 78–9
Eisenmann, Tom 82
electronic banking *see* banks
EMI 193
emotional intellligence 143, 148
Enderle, Ron 74
Enron ix, xvi, 29, 49, 87, 135
Ericsson ix, 57, 133
Ernst & Young 243
eToys 117, 118, 123
evolution; fusing with revolution 26–33
excite 51

Factor Direct 80–1
Federal Express 72
Fiat ix
financial incentives; and managers 173;
    see also remuneration
Financial Times 21, 130
Fingleton, Eamonn 181; *In Praise of Hard
    Industries* 177
Five Fatal Flaws 211–16
5F management 15–16
focus 144
Ford, henry 52
Ford Motor xi–xii, xiv, xv–xvi, 57, 71,
    184–5
forecasting 29
Fortune xiii, 14, 27, 32, 48, 64, 69, 70, 89,
    90, 112, 113, 115, 154, 156, 181, 199
4S company 72–3
France 194
'free' websites 89
Fuji 156
fusion management; definition 110;
    described x–xi; dominant
    characteristics of 149; factors for
    implementation 153–4
future; achieving balance between past,
    present and 46; protecting of 45–51

Gamma Unlimited 236–7
Gates, Bill 13, 58, 68, 73, 98, 101, 119,
    169, 170–1; and anti-trust case 171;
    Business@the Speed of Thought 18, 22;
    Digital Nervous System 17–25; and
    the Internet 17–18;
    management 171–2
General Electric (GE) ix, 14, 48, 58,
    158; abortive takeover of
    Honeywell 138, 246–7; accounting
    systems 107; appetite for change 244;

destroyyourbusiness.com initiative 8,
    81–2, 238, 239; financial
    results 138–9; Six Sigma drive 239;
    Work-Out sessions 230; *see also*
    Welch, Jack
General Motors ix, xi, 92, 184
Gent, Sir Christopher 221–2
Germany 176, 180, 194
Gerstner, Lou xiv, 153, 245
GetConnected 78, 79
Ghosh, Shikhar 58–9
Gibbon, Edweard 247
Gillette 160, 185, 209–10
globalism 20
GM 157, 214
Goizueta, Roberto C. 160–1, 210, 211,
    216
Goleman, Daniel 143
Gould, Inc. 35
Graham, Ben 98
Green, Sir Owen ix
Greenbury, Sir Richard 211–12
Grove, Andrew S.; 47, 50, 63, 80, 92,
    187, 201, 205, 237; *High Output
    Management* 98; *Only the Paranoid
    Survive* 45, 99, 202
growth; pursuit of 241–8
growth, annual 29–30, 32; 15%
    goals 27–8; survey of companies 32

Halifax 218
Hamel, Gary 47, 48, 143, 145
Handy, Charles 48, 99, 139, 237; *The
    Empty Raincoat* 39–40; *Gods of
    management* 38
Harvard Business Review 10, 26, 58, 73,
    90, 91, 105, 144, 145, 147, 150
Harvard Business School 78, 217
Harvey-Jones, Sir John 187
Hasselkus, Walter 130
headhunting 217
Heller's Law 86–7
Hewlett-Packard ix, 73
Hoff, Ted 49
Honda 132
Honeywell 138, 228, 238, 246–7
human resources policy 60

Iacocca, Lee *Incocca* 99
IBM xiii, xiv, 31, 52, 144, 202, 214,
    234, 237; and Apple 119–20; decline
    and reasons for 28, 32, 107, 138,
    244–5
ICI 129, 132, 187
ideas; open to new 48–9
IDEO 53

image, company's 234–40
Imai, Masaki; *Kaitzen* 30
Immelt, Jeff 238, 244
individuality 149
information technology; and
    outsourcing 55–6
innovation 102–9; and 'Business X-
    Ray' 6–7; creating organisation space
    where capabilities can be
    developed 106; translating ideas into
    action 102; turning action into
    profit 103
insourcing 52
insurance companies; and annual
    growth 30
Intel 12, 45–6, 47, 48, 49, 63, 138, 205,
    221
intellectual capital 24
internal development 231
Internet 4–6, 59, 121–2, 194, 223–4;
    advantages and opportunities 76–7;
    and banking 23–4, 194–5, 196, 218;
    buying over 64–5; creating the e-
    corporation 87–94; and customer-
    orientated culture 61, 66;
    disadvantages and arguments for 'do
    nothings' 5; e-strategy 92–3; features
    of successful start-ups and start-up
    pioneers 79–80; and Gates' digital
    nervous system 17–25; growth of and
    increase in users 70, 192; and
    journalists 199–200; offering of route
    to entrepreneurial success 220;
    opportunities seized by
    entrepreneurial e-companies 71–2;
    reactions to and choices 4–5;
    reinforcing of trends transforming
    organisations 20; service failure 61;
    small internal start-ups 198; start-
    ups 11, 14; successful start--
    ups 78–9; and transformation of
    business 77–8; *see also* dot.coms
intrinsic value (IV) 36, 37
Intuit 69
IT BECAME FASTEST acronym ix, x
Ivester, Doug 154, 155, 156, 161, 210

Japan 176, 180, 183
job-hopping 217
John Lewis 31
Johnson & Johnson 57
Jones, Daniel 179, 180
journalists; and Internet 199–200

kaikaku 31, 215
kaizen 215

Kaku, Ryazaburo 98
Kami, Michael J. 6
Kay, Alan 45, 195
Keep It Simple, Stupid (KISS) 140
Kenny, David 91
Keough, Don 155–6
knowledge management (KM) 23, 24
Kodak 156–7
Kondratieff, Wassily 136

Lawlor III, Edward E. 122
leadership 146, 147
learning company 225–33
learning disciplines 226, 227–8
Leighton, Allan 10
life-cycles, reversing 209–16
Linux 138
Loomis, Carol 27–8, 29, 32
Lucent Technologies ix, 34, 160, 164, 185

McDonnell Douglas 115
McIvor, Ronan 56
McKinsey 219
Maclaurin, Lord 186, 188, 191
Maclean, Sir Alexander 140
McNealy, Scott 231
Majaro, Simon 141
mall site 50, 51
management accountancy 202–3
Management by Budget (MBB) 198
managers; differences between
    entrepreneurs and 74; differences
    between old model and new 70–1; as
    entrepreneurs 68–9; features of 'old
    model' 70; and financial
    incentives 173; going back to basics
    for fusion 10–16; and ideas 95; as
    innovators and masterful
    managers 68–75; issue of evolution
    and revolution 26–33; living in the
    past 45; management of 169–75; and
    time management 113–14; and
    transformation 143–50
Managing for the Future (Mff) 198
Mannesman 107, 129, 222
Marconi ix, 36, 222
Marks & Spencer (M&S) ix, 22, 64, 185,
    189, 190, 211, 212–13, 214, 216
Marshall, John F. 91
Martinez, Al 191
Marx, Elizabeth; *Breaking through Culture
    Shock* 130
Mattel 160, 185
Maytag 160, 164, 185
Mercata 51
Mercedez-Benz xii

index

Mercer Management Consulting 90
Merck 27
mergers 107–8, 127–34, 162, 197 see
  also acquisitions
Microsoft xiii, xiv, 137, 138, 170–1,
  173–4; anti-trust trial 21, 171;
  defects 20–1; dissatisfaction of
  customers 73–4; and Internet 15,
  119; and rise of Netscape 119; see also
  Gates, Bill
middle managers 157
Millennium Dome 193, 194
Mintzberg, henry 153, 156
mobile phones xi, 225
momentum 241–8
Monsanto 35–6, 145
Morita, Akio 183
Morrison, David 90
Motorola ix, 133
Moulton, John 213
Murdoch, Rupert 76

Naked Manager, The (Heller) 209
Nassser, Jac xi–xii, xv
Nestlé 26, 29–30, 30–1
Netscape 12, 13, 21, 90, 119
New Business 79
NextCard 72
Nocera, Joseph 14, 87
Nokia 132–3
Nucor 230
Nypro 37, 57

oil price crisis (1973) 133
organisations; trends transforming
  19–20
outsourcing 20, 52–9; benefits 54; and
  contractors 55; disadvantages 56, 57;
  ineptitude of execution of 54–5; and
  information technology 55–6; issues
  to be tackled 56–8; results of
  companies 54
Overdorf, Michael 105, 221

PA Consulting Group 54, 57
Pagonis, General Gus 73
Palo Alto Research Centre (PARC) 102
Papadimitriou, Angeles 220
Pareto's Law 141
past; achieving balance with present and
  future 43; managers living in the 45
pay regime 49
Paypal 197
Penrice, Daniel 79
Pepsico 163
Perris, Jack 220

personal mastery 226, 228
Peters, Tom 37, 57, 99, 100–1, 103, 229
Pfeiffer, Eckhard 7–8, 148
Philip Morris 27
Piechestrieder, Berndt 130
Pierer, heinrich von 157
Pitney-Bowes 72
PLAUT consultancy 61
Polaroid ix
Porter, Michael 143, 144–5, 150
power complexes, curing 151–8
Pragmatists 244, 245
Prahalad, C. K. 143
pre-merger 107–8
private investors 234–5
process analysis 105, 106, 107
Procter & Gamble (P&G) 157–8, 160,
  161, 164, 185
productivity 20
Putnam, Robert; Bowling Alone 148

Quaker oats 163
quality 152

Racal 107, 108, 129, 221
radical change imperative 146
Railtrack 55
recession 233
Red Herring 142
relationships 147–8
remuneration 220, 221–2, 223
reorganisation 74–5; as governing
  principle of management 73
reputation 234–40
resource ananlysis 105, 107
restructuring charges 29
retention; and education 226–7; reasons
  for difficulty in employee 217–19
Revenues, Costs, Quality (RCQ)
  formula 140–1
RJR Nabisco xii
Romac Industries 29
Rosen, Ben 8
Rosenbluth, hal, The Customer Comes
  Second xii
Rover; and BMW 127, 128–9, 130,
  131–2, 148
Rubbermaid 160, 164, 185

Sainsbury's 64, 185, 189, 190
Salsbury, peter 186
Schacht, Henry 34, 35
Schrempp, Jürgen 127, 246
Sears Roebuck 191, 214
Semco 229
Semler, Ricardo 229

Senge, Peter M. xi, 221; *The Fifth Discipline* 226
Seven Satisfiers 79
shareholder value 34–5, 36, 245–6
Siemens ix
Sigmoid Curve 39–40, 139, 238
Silicon Valley 15, 53, 223, 225
Silver, Michael de kare 144–5
Simpson, Lord 222
Sinclair, Sir Clive 56
Six Forces theory 143
Six Sigma programme 239
size 243
skunk-works ethos 103, 108
Sloan, Alfred M. 99
slowdowns; exploiting of 135–42
Smithkline Beecham 132
Sodexho 221
Soviet Union 122
speed 203–4
Stewart, Thomas A.; *Intellectual Capital* 24; STMicroelectronics 228; stock markets 34–5, 153, 161; Stonecipher, Harry 114; *Straight from the CEO* 7; strategic plans; and strategic actions 47
strategy; revolutionising the 184–91
subdividing; of business 49
subsidiary managements 131
Sun Microsystems 53, 72, 231
Supertanker Myth 157
supplier relationships 57–8
Suppliermarket.com 78
Sweden 192
SWOT analysis 133–4
systematic failure; as Fatal Flaw 211

takeovers; problems with 127–34; reasons for 127–8
targets; setting unreasonable 48
teams/teamwork 113, 115–16, 154
telcos 195
Telequip 56
Ten Commandments; of a business 46–7, 50
Tesco 64, 186, 188–9, 191
time management 113–14
Time Warner; merger with AOL 15, 153
Total Productive Maintenance (TPM) 178–83
Total Productive management (TPM2) 176–83
Total Quality Management (TQM) 30, 42, 213, 215, 228

Toys 'R' Us 17, 18, 120–1, 123
training 226–7
transformation; of theories 143–50
turnarounds 185–8

Unisys 202
United Distillers and Vintners (UDV) 178, 182
United States 176, 180–1
Useem, Jerry 89, 90

Vandevelde, Luc 216
Vallance, Sir ian 148–9
value 35, 37–8, 106; enforcing of through three Rs 38–9
value mapping 141
venture capitalists 48, 49
virtuality 20, 52–3
Vodafone 107–8, 129, 221
VW xii

Wagoner, G. Richard 157
Wal-Mart 103–4, 107, 117, 186, 191
Wall Street Journal 121, 157, 174
Walton, sam 186
Waterman, Robert 99
Web *see* Internet
web currency 51
'web lifestyle' 18, 19
'web workstyle' 18, 19
Weinstock, Lord ix
Welch, Jack xv, 98, 138, 139, 161, 219, 238–9; on categories of managers 38; delaying of retirement 238; ideas and policies 96–7, 158, 238–9; and Internet 8, 14–15; Jack 96; strengths 239–40
WingSpanBank.com 230–1
Wise, Richard 90
Wood, Peter 219
Woodward, Robert 216
workplace; making more attractive 220–1
Wyatt, Watson 165

Zerox ix, 31, 102, 103, 160, 161, 164, 185, 234, 243

Yahoo! 69

Zeien, Al 210
Zeneca 129, 131
zero-based strategy 66–7